# 504 Essential Words for SSAT & ISEE (Upper)

With Roots/Synonyms/Antonyms/Usage and more...

By

J. Jonathan

# Copyright Notice

# Table of Contents

# How to increase your vocabulary quickly

Vocabulary is becoming increasingly important for the SSAT/ISEE Upper, and it helps to devote sufficient time to it, as it takes a long time to build an effective vocabulary.

This book contains 504 Essential words that appear frequently in the SSAT/ISEE Upper, and uses some of the following techniques to help you remember these words faster and better!

### - Word Roots;

Since many English words are derived from Greek & Latin **roots**, it makes sense to be aware of these.

### - Prefixes/Suffixes;

Pay attention to the **tone** of the words, whether soft or hard, harsh or mind, negative or positive. This could help you guess when needed.

Prefixes/Suffixes can often help you with identifying the meaning of a word, when in doubt.

### - Usage of the Word;

Perhaps the **Best way to increase your vocabulary** is to read, read and read. There is absolutely no substitute for that!

Reading helps you learn new words from the context in which they are used, thereby making it easy to remember the new words and more importantly, how and when they are used.

This book provides you with multiple examples of how a word is used in different contexts.

### - Synonyms/Antonyms

Being familiar with related words, increases the number and variety of your **mental associations**.
This helps you retain the meaning of the word more easily.

### - Related Words

In order to 'deeply' understand the meaning of a word, it is helpful to study related words at the same time.

e.g. The word **plenty** connotes "sufficient for what is needed" while **abundance** means "more than what is needed".

*and*

**ameliorate** is to "make better" while **alleviate** is to "make less severe".

### - Pronunciations

Each word has a pronunciation key that helps you say the word out correctly, thereby aiding retention.

### - Practice makes perfect!

Finally, this book has <u>over one thousand exercises</u> to make sure that you remember the meanings of the newly learnt words *'forever'*!

Many ingenious methods, scientifically correct, have been devised to aid the recall of particular facts. These methods are based wholly on the principle that that is most easily recalled which is associated in our minds with the most <u>complex and elaborate groupings</u> of related ideas.

All of the above methods are designed to create a word network in your mind, thereby helping you develop a lasting understanding of the word in the SSAT/ISEE Upper relevant context.

# WORD SET 1

**abject**: [AB-jekt] Adjective.
Existing to the highest amount, extreme. (Used to describe something bad.)
Lacking dignity or pride, despicable. (Used to describe a person/behavior.)

- Some people in the developing country live in **abject** poverty.
- The accused criminal sat alone, an **abject** figure.

*Synonym:* hopeless, contemptible, worthless, pathetic, low, wretched
*Antonym:* noble, proud, worthy

Further Information
- Originated from the Middle English word *abiect* meaning "outcast."
- **Abject** is often used to describe certain nouns, including fear, failure, condition and apology.
- Other commonly used word forms include **abjectness** (n.) and **abjectly** (adv.).

**abjure**: [ab-JOOR] Verb.
To relinquish or give up.

- She **abjured** her inheritance and asked that it be donated to her favorite charity.
- The new dictator forced the citizens to **abjure** their political beliefs.

*Synonym:* recant, withdraw, retract, renounce, deny, forswear
*Antonym:* allow, emphasize, adhere

Further Information
- Originated from the Latin word *abjurare* meaning "away" (*ab*) and "swear" (*jurare*).
- Not to be confused with **abrogate** which means "to abolish."
- Other commonly used word forms include **abjuration** (n.) and **abjuring** (v.).
- **Abjure** is often used as a legal term meaning "to formally renounce."

**abnegation**: [ab-neh-GAY-shun] Noun.
The act of rejecting or renouncing something; self-denial.

- Her **abnegation** of sweets happened because she is on a strict diet.
- The father's **abnegation** of responsibility for his daughter's behavior shocked the principal.

*Synonym:* denial, refusal, abandonment, abstinence, disavowal, temperance
*Antonym:* approval, allowance, acquiescence

Further Information
- Originated from the Latin root *negare-* meaning "to deny."
- **Abnegation** was one of the five factions in the novel *Divergent*.
- The word **abnegation** began appearing in 14th century English writing, meaning "denial."

**abrogate**: [AB-ruh-gayt] Verb.
To formally abolish or repeal.

- Outdated laws should be **abrogated**.
- The King **abrogated** slavery across his kingdom.

*Synonym:* annul, invalidate, revoke, cancel, nullify, repeal
*Antonym:* sanction, permit, approve

Further Information
- Originated from the Latin word *abrogare* meaning "to annul or repeal."
- Not to be confused with **abdicate** which means "to renounce one's throne or duty."
- Other commonly used word forms include **abrogation** (n.) and **abrogator** (n.).


**abstemious**: [ab-STEE-mee-uhs] Adjective.
Moderate or sparing, especially in eating and drinking.

- She was **abstemious** with her meals as she was trying to lose weight.
- His religion requires him to be **abstemious** and avoid eating meat.

*Synonym:* frugal, restrained, temperate, ascetic, austere, moderate
*Antonym:* greedy, gluttonous, hungry

Further Information
- Originated from the Latin root *temetum* meaning "strong drink" and *ab* meaning "from."
- Not to be confused with **abstinent** meaning "refraining from excess indulgence."
- Other commonly used word forms include **abstemiously** (adv.) and **abstemiousness** (n.).


**accost**: [uh-KAWST] Verb.
To approach and address someone in an aggressive manner.

- The person who **accosted** me stole my purse.
- The celebrity was **accosted** by fans and photographers when she left her home.

*Synonym:* annoy, confront, bother, propose, address, solicit
*Antonym:* help, avoid, evade, dodge

Further Information
- Originated from the Old French word *accoster* meaning "to go alongside of."
- The modern meaning of **accost** was not commonly used until the 17th century.
- Other commonly used word forms include the verbs **accosted** and **accosting**.

**Achilles**: [uh-KIL-eez] Noun/Adjective.
In Greek mythology, a great warrior and Trojan War leader. (n.)
May also be used to describe a weakness (such as in **Achilles'** heel). (adj.)

- According to Greek mythology, **Achilles** killed Hector in the Trojan War. (n.)
- The country's **Achilles'** heel is its lack of a robust military. (adj.)

*Synonym:* weakness
*Antonym:* strength

Further Information
- Originated from the Greek *Achilles* referring to the character in Greek mythology.
- The term **Achilles'** heel or tendon derived from the Greek warrior's only vulnerable spot.
- **Achilles** should always be capitalized as it refers to a proper name.


**acumen**: [AH-kyoo-men] Noun.
Having the keenness of mind to make good judgements and quick decisions.

- His business **acumen** made him very successful as a Wall Street trader.
- Candidates must have political **acumen** to win an election.

*Synonym:* shrewdness, expertise, discernment, perception, intelligence, discrimination
*Antonym:* ignorance, ineptness, insanity

Further Information
- Originated from the Latin word *acuere* meaning "to sharpen."
- The first known usage of **acumen** in 1500s English meant "displaying a sharpness of wit."
- Related word forms include the adjective **acuminous**.


**adulterate**: [uh-DUL-tuh-reyt] Verb.
To corrupt or make impure.

- Their water supply had been **adulterated** with chemicals.
- The man complained that his cola had been **adulterated** with water.

*Synonym:* pollute, contaminate, dilute, debase, corrupt, pervert
*Antonym:* clean, purify, clarify

Further Information
- Originated from the Latin word *adulterare* meaning "to pollute."
- An archaic meaning of **adulterate** is as an adjective, meaning "false."
- Related word forms include the nouns **adulteration** and **adulterator**.

**adumbrate**: [AH-dum-brayt] Verb.
To foreshadow in a vague way; to indicate faintly.

- The book summary is designed to **adumbrate** the plot of the novel.
- The dim light **adumbrated** the woman, creating a ghostly outline of her.

*Synonym:* suggest, foretell, outline, sketch, intimate, foreshadow
*Antonym:* illuminate, bare, light

Further Information
- Originated from the Latin word *adumbrates* meaning "to shade."
- **Adumbrate** is commonly used in political and academic writing, not every day writing.
- Related word forms include the verbs **adumbrated** and **adumbrating**.

**aggrandize**: [uh-GRAN-deyz] Verb.
To make greater or enhance the reputation, power or wealth of someone or something.

- The ruler tried to **aggrandize** his position without thinking of the good of his people.
- He donates to charities only to **aggrandize** himself in the perception of others.

*Synonym:* increase, heighten, magnify, acclaim, extend, augment
*Antonym:* disgrace, dishonor, belittle

Further Information
- Originated from the French word *agrandiss* meaning "to magnify or increase."
- Other commonly used word forms include the nouns **aggrandizer** and **aggrandizement**.
- Often used in the term "self-**aggrandizing**" to describe an egotistical person.

**alacrity**: [uh-LAK-ruh-tee] Noun.
Promptness, cheerful readiness.

- She took the exam with **alacrity** because she had studied hard for it.
- His **alacrity** to learn French grew after visiting the French countryside.

*Synonym:* willingness, eagerness, promptitude, readiness, preparedness, forwardness
*Antonym:* apathy, indifference, reluctance

Further Information
- Originated from the Latin word *alacer* meaning "brisk."
- **Allegro** is a related musical term meaning "at a brisk and lively tempo."
- "I have not that **alacrity** of spirit," wrote William Shakespeare in King Richard III.

# REVIEW EXERCISE 1

*Match the word with its synonym.*

| | | | | |
|---|---|---|---|---|
| ___ | 1. | abject | a. | eagerness |
| ___ | 2. | abjure | b. | outline |
| ___ | 3. | abnegation | c. | weakness |
| ___ | 4. | abrogate | d. | frugal |
| ___ | 5. | abstemious | e. | denial |
| ___ | 6. | accost | f. | hopeless |
| ___ | 7. | Achilles | g. | pollute |
| ___ | 8. | acumen | h. | expertise |
| ___ | 9. | adumbrate | i. | renounce |
| ___ | 10. | aggrandize | j. | invalidate |
| ___ | 11. | alacrity | k. | confront |
| ___ | 12. | adulterate | l. | magnify |

*Fill in the blanks with the most appropriate word from list above.* (*Word form may need changing.*)

1. His diet was _____ and he avoided rich meals.

2. Please don't _____ my cola by mixing it with your diet cola.

3. The _____ tendon connects the leg muscles to the calf and foot.

4. Rick's self- _____ remarks were not well-received at the conference.

5. The candlelight _____ the shadows on the wall.

6. She was an _____ woman following the death of her son.

7. His teaching _____ predicted his success in the classroom.

8. The stalker _____ the woman and was taken away by the police.

9. She _____ her faith and left the church.

10. The government tried to _____ the protester's right to free speech.

11. As he approached the pet store, the pet lover beamed with _____.

12. His _____ of responsibility for the crime resulted in a harsh sentence.

# WORD SET 2

**alias**: [AY-lee-us] Noun/Adverb.
An assumed or additional identity. (n.)
Otherwise known as. (adv.)

- The celebrity uses an **alias** when he checks into a hotel in order to remain anonymous. (n.)
- Stephen King, **alias** Richard Bachman, is the author of many popular novels. (adv.)

*Synonym*: pseudonym, moniker, otherwise, nickname, sobriquet
*Antonym: none*

Further Information
- Originated from the Latin word *alius* meaning "other."
- **Alias** is often interchangeable with **a.k.a**. which stands for "also known as."
- Other words that mean **alias** include "nom de plume" (or "pen name") and "nom de guerre" (lit. "war name," but meaning a name under which one fights, writes, or acts.)


**alleviate**: [uh-LEE-vee-ayt] Verb.
To make less severe, to make more bearable.

- The aspirin should **alleviate** your back pain.
- The creation of new jobs at the factory **alleviated** the city's job shortage.

*Synonym:* relieve, allay, lessen, ease, soothe, assuage
*Antonym:* increase, aggravate, intensify

Further Information
- Originated from the Latin roots *ad* meaning "to" and *levare* meaning "raise."
- Other commonly used word forms include the nouns **alleviation** and **alleviator**.
- Note that **alleviate** does not mean "to remove," but rather, "to make more tolerable."


**allude**: [uh-LOOD] Verb.
To indirectly hint at, to suggest.

- The candidate **alluded** to his healthcare reform plan during his speech.
- The prosecutor may not **allude** to the defendant's prior crimes during an opening statement.

*Synonym:* imply, insinuate, refer, hint, suggest, intimate
*Antonym:* publicize, advertise

Further Information
- Originated from the Latin roots *ad* meaning "toward" and *ludere* meaning "to play."
- Not to be confused with **elude** which means "to escape."
- In modern English usage, **allude** has also been used to mean "to refer to directly."

**altruistic**: [al-troo-IS-tik] Adjective.
Showing an unselfish concern for others' welfare.

- The **altruistic** youth decided to join the Peace Corps after college graduation.
- His **altruism** has caused some people to take advantage of his selflessness.

*Synonym:* selfless, unselfish, charitable, philanthropic, benevolent, kindhearted
*Antonym:* stingy, selfish, uncharitable

Further Information

- Originated from the French word *autrui* meaning "other people."
- Other commonly used word forms include **altruism** (n.) and **altruistically** (adv.).
- **Altruistic** is also used in zoology to describe the behavior of an animal that is not beneficial or may even be harmful to itself, but benefits others of its species.


**ameliorate**: [uh-MEEL-yuh-rayt] Verb.
To make better or to improve.

- Scratching the mosquito bite will not **ameliorate** its itching.
- The famine was **ameliorated** through donations from other countries.

*Synonym:* improve, lighten, mitigate, better, amend, correct
*Antonym:* intensify, worsen, aggravate


Further Information

- Originated from the French word *meilleur* meaning "better."
- Note that **ameliorate** means "to make better" while **alleviate** means "to make more bearable."
- In medicine, **ameliorate** is used to describe improvement in a patient's condition, while **alleviate** is used to describe relieving pain.


**amorphous**: [uh-MOR-fes] Adjective.
Lacking a clearly defined form, character or shape.
Having no focus or structure (when describing an organization or group).

- The **amorphous** painting provided no clues as to its meaning.
- Without a proper mission statement, your group is **amorphous** and lacks true purpose.

*Synonym:* vague, nebulous, shapeless, formless, indistinct, indefinite
*Antonym:* definite, distinct, shaped


Further Information

- Originated from the Greek roots  *a*  meaning "without" and *morphe* meaning "form."
- **Amorphous** is also used in mineralogy to describe a mineral with no crystalline structure.
- Other commonly used word forms include **amorphousness** (n.) and **amorphously** (adv.).

**anachronistic**: [uh-nak-ruh-NIS-tik] Adjective.
Belonging to another chronological period, usually an earlier one.

- The lone typewriter in a room full of computers seemed **anachronistic**.
- The presence of a laptop in the film about World War I was a definite **anachronism**.

*Synonym:* obsolete, antiquated, outmoded, dated, incongruous, outdated
*Antonym:* current, modern, contemporary

Further Information
- Originated from the Greek words *ana* meaning "backward" and *chronos* meaning "time."
- **Anachronistic** may also be interchanged with the word anachronic.
- Other commonly used word forms include **anachronism** (n.) and **anachronous** (adj.).
- The word **parachronism** means "chronological errors of dates being set later."

**anathema**: [uh-NAH-the-muh] Noun.
A thing or person that is intensely disliked.
A formal denouncement or curse by a religious leader or authority.

- The tornado was an **anathema** that destroyed the entire town.
- The witch placed an **anathema** on the citizens of the town, wishing them eternal bad luck.

*Synonym:* pariah, abomination, condemnation, excommunication, hate, curse
*Antonym:* love, blessing, benediction

Further Information
- Originated from the Greek word *anathema* meaning "thing dedicated."
- **Anathema** was once used to describe "something dedicated to divine use."
- **Anathemas** is the plural of **anathema**.

**annex**: [AH-neks] Verb/Noun.
To add as an extra part. (v.)
An addition to a building or a document. (n.)

- They hold their gatherings in the church's **annex**. (n.)
- The city **annexed** the land to the west of the town to increase its size. (v.)

*Synonym:* addendum, adjoin, append, affix, attach, join
*Antonym:* base, detach, separate

Further Information
- Originated from the Anglo-French word *annexe* meaning "to attach."
- Other commonly used word forms include **annexation** (n.) and **annexational** (adj.).
- **Annex** once meant "a right or privilege being attached to a person as a condition."
- In British English, the noun is sometimes spelt as **annexe.**

**antediluvian**: [an-te-de-LOO-vee-en] Adjective.
Old fashioned, dating from the past; referring to the time before the Biblical flood.

- Her **antediluvian** ideas about the role of women caused arguments among her peers.
- The country's **antediluvian** monetary system caused an economic crash.

*Synonym:* primitive, antique, ancient, old, archaic, prehistoric
*Antonym:* current, modern, new

Further Information
- Originated from the Latin roots *ante* meaning "before" and *diluvium* meaning "flood."
- **Antediluvian** and **anachronistic** both mean "out of date." However, **antediluvian** often refers to attitudes or ideas, whereas **anachronistic** more commonly refers to things.
- The word **antediluvian** is rarely used in modern English.


**antithesis**: [an-TITH-uh-ses] Noun.
Something or someone that is the direct opposite of something/someone else.

- The evil character she plays in the film is the **antithesis** of the generous person she really is.
- Juliet's death at the end of the play was the **antithesis** of what I expected to happen.

*Synonym:* contrast, opposite, antipode, reverse, converse, contradiction
*Antonym:* same, copy

Further Information
- Originated from the Greek roots *anti* meaning "against" and *tithenal* meaning "to place."
- The plural of **antithesis** is **antitheses**.
- Writers and politicians often use **antithesis** to contrast two ideas.


**apocryphal**: [uh-PAH-kreh-ful] Adjective.
Something of doubtful authenticity.

- The **apocryphal** ghost stories were entertaining even though they were likely not true.
- The **apocryphal** scientific theory was disproved after years of scientific research.

*Synonym:* spurious, questionable, unsubstantiated, fictitious, false, untrue
*Antonym:* true, authentic, doubtless

Further Information
- Originated from the Medieval Latin words *scripta apocrypha* meaning "uncanonical writings."
- The plural of **apocryphal** is **apocrypha**.
- When **Apocrypha** is capitalized it refers to writings that are not part of accepted Scripture.

# REVIEW EXERCISE 2

*Match the word with its synonym.*

| | | | |
|---|---|---|---|
| ___ | 1. alleviate | a. | primitive |
| ___ | 2. allude | b. | questionable |
| ___ | 3. altruistic | c. | adjoin |
| ___ | 4. ameliorate | d. | vague |
| ___ | 5. amorphous | e. | selfless |
| ___ | 6. anachronistic | f. | pseudonym |
| ___ | 7. anathema | g. | opposite |
| ___ | 8. annex | h. | abomination |
| ___ | 9. antediluvian | i. | improve |
| ___ | 10. antithesis | j. | refer |
| ___ | 11. apocryphal | k. | relieve |
| ___ | 12. alias | l. | obsolete |

*Fill in the blanks with the most appropriate word from list above.* (*Word form may need changing.*)

1.  The detective used an _____ when he went undercover.

2.  This medicine should help to _____ your pain.

3.  My frivolous dress was an attempt to _____the dark mood of the funeral.

4.  The _____ story of Santa Claus still delights many children worldwide.

5.  He _____ to the reasons for his crime but did not explain them.

6.  The clothing of the villagers seems quite _____ in today's modern world.

7.  Slavery is the _____ of freedom.

8.  Is his helping a result of his _____ or just to make himself look good?

9.  Taking a gift to new neighbors is an _____ practice rarely observed today.

10. The _____, poorly defined rules are hard for the group to follow.

11. The _____ increased the size of the school and accommodated more students.

12. His heinous crimes made him an _____ to the civilized world.

# WORD SET 3

**approbation**: [ah-pruh-BAY-shun] Noun.
Formal approval, commendation or praise.

- Her well-written report earned her professor's **approbation**.
- You must receive **approbation** from your doctor before increasing the medication's dosage.

*Synonym*: praise, approval, endorsement, sanction, esteem, admiration
*Antonym*: disapproval, opposition, contempt

Further Information
- Originated from the Latin word *approbare* meaning "to approve."
- The first usage of **approbation** in 14th century English referred to "proof."
- Other commonly used word forms include **approbatory** (adj.) and **approbative** (adj.).

**arcane**: [ahr-KAYN] Adjective.
Something few people know or understand; secret or mysterious.

- I picked up some **arcane** knowledge about dragon folklore while talking to my brother.
- I was fascinated by the **arcane** rituals described in the religious text.

*Synonym:* obscure, esoteric, impenetrable, secret, dark, mysterious
*Antonym:* commonplace, normal, known

Further Information
- Originated from the Latin words *arcanus* meaning "secret or hidden" and *arcere* meaning "to shut up or keep."
- Don't confuse **arcane** with **archaic,** which describes something that is antiquated or from an earlier period.
- **Arcane** is sometimes used as a boy's name.

**archetypal**: [ahr-ki-TEYP-ul] Adjective.
Relating to an original model or archetype.

- The **archetypal** hero and the **archetypal** villain were both represented in this novel.
- My grandmother is the **archetypal** matriarch, presiding over her family with love and wisdom.

*Synonym:* quintessential, stereotypical, representative, model, exemplary, classic
*Antonym:* atypical, unique, irregular

Further Information
- Originated from the Latin word *archetypum* meaning "an original" and the Greek word *archetypon* meaning "a model or pattern."
- Not to be confused with **prototype,** which refers to an experimental model.
- Other forms include **archetype** (n.), **archetypical** (adj.) and **archetypic** (adj.).

**ardent**: [AHR-dent] Adjective.
Having or expressing great feeling, passion, or intense devotion.
Vehement, fierce or burning.

- The bride and groom looked at each other with **ardent** eyes, obviously very much in love.
- His **ardent** devotion to politics kept him from missing a single debate during the campaign.

*Synonym:* fervid, eager, impassioned, avid, intense, passionate
*Antonym:* apathetic, calm, cool, dispassionate, indifferent
<u>Further Information</u>
- Originated from the Latin word *ardere* meaning "to burn."
- Used in the form of **ardant** in Old French, meaning "burning" or "hot."
- Some related forms include **ardently** (adv.) and **ardency** (n.).


**artifact**: [AHR-tuh-fakt] Noun.
An object made by humans, or remains of an object from an earlier period.
A mass-produced object that reflects a specific society or culture.

- The museum displayed several rare **artifacts** found in ancient Chinese tombs.
- There were 1970s **artifacts** in my grandma's trunk - plastic beads and bell-bottom pants.

*Synonym:* remains, remnant, fragment, relic, antique, ruin
*Antonym: None*
<u>Further Information</u>
- Originated from the Latin *arte factum* meaning "made with skill."
- Related to other words associated with handicrafts, including "art" and "craft."
- In medicine, **artifact** means "a substance/structure produced by an external agent." In science, **artifact** means "a product introduced in an investigation by artificial means."


**artifice**: [AHR-tuh-fis] Noun.
Using cunning or stratagem to create false appearances or trickery.

- Her **artifice** was easy to spot, despite her sweet words and bright smile.
- The entire room was built on **artifice:** the plastic plants, recorded sound effects and projected stars.

*Synonym:* deception, duplicity, subterfuge, deceit, art, cunning, contrivance
*Antonym:* honesty, candor, artlessness, frankness, sincerity
<u>Further Information</u>
- Originated from the Latin word *artificium* meaning "craftmanship, art or craftiness."
- In the 17th century, **artifice** meant "a device or trick."
- Related to **artificial** (adj.), meaning "synthetic" or not real.

**ascetic**: [uh-SEE-tik] Noun/Adjective.
One who lives a simple life, free from pleasure or material comforts. (n)
Relating to the belief that people can attain deep spirituality through self-denial. (adj)

- The **ascetic** lived in a small, unadorned hut where he could meditate on spiritual matters. (n.)
- The woman had an **ascetic** experience during her walking tour in South America. (adj.)

*Synonym:* austere, self-denying, abstinent, spartan, celibate, abstemious
*Antonym:* self-indulgent, hedonistic, epicurean
Further Information
- Comes from the Greek word *asketicos* meaning "subject to rigorous exercise" or "hardworking."
- Other forms include **ascetical** (adj.) and **asceticism** (n.).
- Don't confuse **ascetic** with **acetic** (which means pertaining to vinegar or acetic acid) or **aesthetic** (which refers to a concern with beauty).
- In early Christian times, an **ascetic** referred to a monk or hermit.

**aspersion**: [uh-SPUR-shuhn] Noun.
A derogatory or damaging comment or criticism; slander.

- I felt enraged when she cast **aspersions** on me, as none of her statements were true.
- The former employee's public **aspersion** of our company could cause us some trouble.

*Synonym:* censure, reproach, defamation, slander, slur, libel
*Antonym:* adulation, approval, commendation, compliment, praise
Further Information
- Originated from the Latin word *aspersion* meaning "a sprinkling."
- A rare definition of **aspersion** is "sprinkling," as with water in baptism.
- Don't confuse **aspersion** with **dispersion,** (which refers to separating or scattering of light or variables) or **aspiration** (which means ambition of achieving something).

**assiduous**: [uh-SIJ-oo-uhs] Adjective.
Constant, diligent and unremitting in an effort or at a task.

- He was an **assiduous** student, and his hard work paid off with perfect scores on his tests.
- The gymnast was **assiduous** in practicing her routine.

*Synonym:* persevering, industrious, tireless, persistent, diligent, sedulous
*Antonym:* lazy, inconstant, negligent, indifferent
Further Information
- Originated from the Latin word *assiduus* meaning "to sit near, beside, dwell close to."
- Some other word forms include **assiduously** (adv.) and **assiduousness** (n.).
- Not to be confused with **insidious**, which means "treacherous or beguiling."

**attenuate**: [uh-TEN-yoo-ayt] Verb.
To weaken in force or reduce in intensity.
To make thin or slender.

- We can boost our team's confidence by **attenuating** our previous failures.
- The humane society's goal is to **attenuate** the number of animals without safe homes.

*Synonym:* reduce, constrict, debilitate, vitiate, thin, weaken
*Antonym:* amplify, aid, assist, help

<u>Further Information</u>
- Originated from the Latin word *attenuatus* meaning "to thin or reduce."
- **Attenuate** is less commonly used as an adjective meaning reduced, weakened, diminished or diluted.
- Other forms of **attenuate** include **overattenuate** (v.) and **subattenuate** (adj.).


**austerity**: [aw-STER-i-tee] Noun.
Strict economy or severity of life or manner.

- The stranger's **austerity** made him difficult to approach.
- Her **austerity** had come from many years of war and poverty.

*Synonym:* harshness, strictness, prudence, rigor, severity, sternness
*Antonym:* extravagance, leniency, informality

<u>Further Information</u>
- Originated from the Old French *austerite* meaning "harshness" or "cruelty."
- The word can be plural, as in **austerities**, as in: They were not prepared for the **austerities** of life.


**avaricious**: [av-uh-RISH-uhs] Adjective.
Greedy; strongly desiring material wealth.

- The woman was **avaricious;** she cared more for money than for her family or friends.
- The **avaricious** miller had one objective: for his daughter to marry the king.

*Synonym:* covetous, selfish, greedy, materialistic, grasping, rapacious
*Antonym:* generous, altruistic, charitable, unselfish

<u>Further Information</u>
- Originated from the Old French word *avaricios* meaning "greedy" or "covetous."
- Can be used as a noun: **avarice** meaning an insatiable greed.
- Avaricious is related to **acquisitive** (adj.), meaning "eager to acquire knowledge or material things," and **avid** (adj.), meaning "enthusiastic."

# REVIEW EXERCISE 3

*Match the word with its synonym.*

| | | | | |
|---|---|---|---|---|
| ___ | 1. | approbation | a. | quintessential |
| ___ | 2. | arcane | b. | harshness |
| ___ | 3. | archetypal | c. | endorsement |
| ___ | 4. | ardent | d. | duplicity |
| ___ | 5. | artifact | e. | remains |
| ___ | 6. | artifice | f. | reduce |
| ___ | 7. | ascetic | g. | obscure |
| ___ | 8. | aspersion | h. | greedy |
| ___ | 9. | assiduous | i. | persistent |
| ___ | 10. | attenuate | j. | defamation |
| ___ | 11. | austerity | k. | self-denying |
| ___ | 12. | avaricious | l. | impassioned |

*Fill in the blanks with the most appropriate word from list above.* *(Word form may need changing.)*

1. Mike is an _____ businessman with much money but few friends.

2. There is never any _____ with her; she is completely genuine.

3. My English teacher pointed out some _____characters in the novel.

4. I have no interest in _____ facts, I just want to know the basics.

5. An _____ life on my own in the mountains appeals to me.

6. I'd like to discover an _____ on an archaeological dig.

7. We need to _____ the damage done by our recent press interview.

8. He showed _____ devotion to his mother throughout her illness.

9. Her _____gave her a reputation for being stern, strict and economical.

10. His _____of me was severe and made me cry.

11. With the boss's_____, I will move forward with the new campaign.

12. My _____ study habits allowed me to graduate a year early.

# WORD SET 4

**balk**: [bawk] Verb/Noun.
To become an obstacle to something, to hinder from proceeding. (v.)
A defeat, hinderance or disappointment. (n.)

- Although she wouldn't tell me what she wanted to do, she **balked** at my every idea. (v.)
- The storm was an unexpected **balk** that set us back at least two weeks. (n.)

*Synonym:* obstruct, check, impede, prevent, frustrate, hinder
*Antonym:* help, aid, accept

Further Information
- Originated from the Old English word *bolca* meaning "plank."
- Other forms of the word include **balker** (n.) and **balkingly** (adv.).
- The verb **balk** is often used with "at," such as in the phrase "to balk at."

**bedlam**: [BED-luhm] Noun.
A state of confusion or chaos.

- I came home to **bedlam:** the children were running wild with no babysitter in sight.
- The camping trip gave us time away from the **bedlam** of our large city.

*Synonym:* disorder, chaos, tumult, commotion, turmoil, pandemonium
*Antonym:* order, harmony, calm

Further Information
- An archaic definition of **bedlam** is madhouse or insane asylum.
- The word **bedlam** comes from London's Hospital of St. Mary of Bethlehem, an insane asylum.

**beguile**: [bih-GEYL] Verb.
To trick, mislead, or cheat.
To divert or charm.

- The seemingly helpful and friendly man **beguiled** us all, turning out to be a thief.
- I was supposed to study tonight, but Jason **beguiled** me into seeing a movie instead.

*Synonym:* cheat, deceive, entertain, amuse, charm, fascinate
*Antonym: none*

Further Information
- Originated from the Middle English word *bigilen,* made up of "be" and "guile."
- **Beguile** is less commonly used to mean "to pass time in a pleasant way."
- The verb **beguile** is used with an object (i.e., to beguile someone or something).
- Other forms include **beguiler** (n.) and **beguilement** (n.).

**benevolent:** [buh-NEV-uh-luhnt] Adjective.
Showing kindness, goodwill or charity.
Set up for benefits as opposed to profit.

- The **benevolent** woman donated her rare book collection to our public library.
- Our community's **benevolent** society collects money for children's charities.

*Synonym:* generous, charitable, caring, kind, compassionate, philanthropic
*Antonym:* hateful, cruel, miserly, mean

Further Information
- **Benevolent** comes from Latin: *bene* meaning "well" and *velle* meaning "to wish."
- The word **benevolent** was used in Late Middle English.
- Some related forms include **benevolently** (adv.) and **benevolence** (n.).


**besmirch:** [bih-SMURCH] Verb.
To tarnish or soil; to remove honor from.

- My former best friend now spends her time trying to **besmirch** my reputation.
- I don't want to **besmirch** your opinion of James, but I am not impressed with him.

*Synonym:* stain, soil, dishonor, sully, smear, blacken
*Antonym:* honor, praise, clean

Further Information
- The origin of **besmirch** is unknown. It appeared in English in the late 1500s.
- **Besmirch** is a transitive verb, often followed by a person's name.
- The word **besmirched** appears as "besmyrcht" in Shakespeare's *Henry V.*


**bigot:** [BIG-uht] Noun.
Someone showing extreme intolerance or prejudice to those of differing beliefs or race.

- We cannot allow a **bigot** to make employees at our company feel unaccepted or unsafe.
- Although Steve was a **bigot** when he was younger, he has since learned to be more open minded.

*Synonym:* extremist, racist, zealot, fanatic, dogmatist, sectarian
*Antonym:* moderate, humanitarian, tolerator

Further Information
- **Bigot** may come from Old French, where it was a derogatory term for Normans used by the French.
- Another possible origin of **bigot** is the Old English *bi God* meaning "by God."
- Some related forms include **bigoted** (adj.) and **bigotry** (n.).

**blandishment**: [BLAN-dish-muhnt] Noun.
A speech or action intended to coax, flatter or entice.

- Our **blandishments** worked; Ben is coming to the party.
- He accused me of **blandishment,** but my words were quite sincere.

*Synonym:* flattery, wheedling, cajolery, ingratiation, adulation, sycophancy
*Antonym:* criticism, insult

Further Information
- **Blandishment** is most often used in its plural form, **blandishments.**
- The word **blandishment** originated between 1585-95 meaning "flattering speech."
- **Blandishment** comes from the Latin word *blandiri,* which means "to soothe or flatter."


**bogus**: [BOH-guhs] Adjective.
Counterfeit, not genuine; a sham.

- I dismissed his **bogus** story and asked again to hear what had really happened.
- She is very knowledgeable about foreign money and wouldn't be fooled by a **bogus** coin.

*Synonym:* fraudulent, fake, phony, pseudo, counterfeit, sham
*Antonym:* authentic, genuine, actual, real

Further Information
- **Bogus** is an American word, originally referring to "a device for making false money."
- **Bogus** might be related to "bogy," meaning "something that frightens or haunts."
- Since the 1980s, **bogus** has been used as slang for both "lame" and "not to be trusted."


**boor**: [bor] Noun.
A rude person without manners.

- I would never invite him to dinner; he is a **boor.**
- A true **boor,** he rarely shopped, bathed, or entered the city.

*Synonym*: barbarian, oaf, brute, peasant, lout, churl
*Antonym*: gentleman, charmer

Further Information
- Originated from the Germanic prefix *bu-* meaning "to dwell, cultivate or build."
- Do not confuse **boor** with **boar** (referring to male swine) or **bore** (to overwhelm with dullness).
- Other word forms include **boorish** (adj.), **boorishly** (adv.) and **boorishness** (n.).

**brittle**: [BRIT-el] Adjective/Noun.
Hard and rigid, not able to be stretched or drawn out; easily damaged. (adj.)
Lacking in sensitivity, warmth, or compassion. (adj.)
Candy made with melted sugar and often nuts. (n.)

- I tried to use the old hockey stick, but it was **brittle** and broke when it struck the ball. (adj.)
- The new teacher seemed **brittle,** and I hesitated to approach her. (adj.)
- My grandmother's peanut **brittle** is the best I've ever tasted. (n.)

*Synonym:* breakable, stiff, edgy, curt, fragile, delicate
*Antonym:* flexible, durable, relaxed
Further Information
- Originated from the Middle English *brit-* (fragment) and *el* (suffix).
- **Brittle** has different connotations including **fragile** or **frail.**
- Some related forms include **brittleness** (n.) and **unbrittle** (adj.).

**bulwark**: [BUHL-werk] Noun.
A wall or protection built for defense against danger.
Someone giving strong support during a trial or struggle.

- We felt secure knowing our **bulwark** was in place and that our camp was protected.
- He was a **bulwark** to me when I lost my mom to cancer.

*Synonym:* support, fortress, buttress, dike, rampart, wall
*Antonym:* none
Further Information
- Likely originated from the Middle Dutch *bol-* (trunk of a tree) and *werk* (work).
- **Bulwark** can also be used as a verb meaning to secure with a fortification.
- **Bulwarks** refer to "a solid wall that protects the main deck of a boat."

**burgeon**: [BUR-juhn] Verb.
To develop or flourish; to grow quickly.
To begin to bud.

- These baby chicks will **burgeon** before your eyes over the next few days.
- The **burgeoning** trees on our street will soon be covered with flowers.

*Synonym:* sprout, bloom, prosper, grow, develop, flourish
*Antonym:* diminish, decline, decrease, shrivel
Further Information
- Originates from the Latin *burra* meaning "shaggy cloth."
- The word *borjoner* appears in Old French meaning "to bud or sprout."
- Commonly used as an adjective: **burgeoning.**

# REVIEW EXERCISE 4

**Match the word with its synonym.**

| | | | |
|---|---|---|---|
| ___ 1. | balk | a. | fake |
| ___ 2. | bedlam | b. | stiff |
| ___ 3. | beguile | c. | bloom |
| ___ 4. | benevolent | d. | deceive |
| ___ 5. | besmirch | e. | impede |
| ___ 6. | bigot | f. | flattery |
| ___ 7. | blandishment | g. | disorder |
| ___ 8. | bogus | h. | dishonor |
| ___ 9. | boor | i. | fortress |
| ___ 10. | brittle | j. | philanthropic |
| ___ 11. | bulwark | k. | brute |
| ___ 12. | burgeon | l. | racist |

**Fill in the blanks with the most appropriate word from list above (Word form may need changing.)**

1. She has lived a  _____ life, always giving to those in need.

2. If the _____ holds our city will be safe from flooding.

3. After a morning of _____the client was convinced to invest in our company.

4. I won't allow him to _____ my sister; I will warn her about his deceitful plan.

5. The daycare center was in complete _____when I arrived.

6. Please don't _____ your peers; reputations are difficult to rebuild.

7. She spotted the _____ coin immediately.

8. He might _____ at our efforts, but we can proceed without his help.

9. These plants will _____ in early spring.

10. My dad insists on good manners; I could not take that _____ home.

11. A _____ would never tolerate the multicultural atmosphere of our school.

12. The elastic had become _____, losing its stretch.

# WORD SET 5

**buttress**: [BUH-tris] Noun/Verb.
An external prop or support used to steady a structure. (n.)
To support or give encouragement. (v.)

- The soldiers used the rock as a **buttress** to prop up the crumbling walls of the fortress. (n.)
- More facts will help you **buttress** your arguments for the debate. (v.)

*Synonym:* support, prop, bolster, reinforce, brace, strengthen
*Antonym:* weaken, debunk

Further Information

- Originated from the Old French word *bouterez* meaning "thrusting (arch)."
- Other forms of the word include **buttressless** (adj.) and **buttresslike** (adj.).
- Related terms include **flying buttress** (n.) and **buttress root** (n.).

**cache**: [kash] Noun/Verb.
A hiding place. (n.)
To conceal, to hide. (v.)

- A large **cache** of arms was discovered by the police. (n.)
- She **cached** her jewelry in the hotel safe. (v.)

*Synonym:* store, hoard, reserve, stockpile, stash, stock
*Antonym:* discover, disclose

Further Information

- Originated from the French word *cacher* meaning "to hide."
- A **cache** is also a computer component that stores data so that future requests are served faster.
- Related terms include **cachet** (n.) and **reserve cache** (n.).

**cacophony**: [kuh-KOF-uh-nee] Noun.
Harsh discordance of sound.

- His grandmother could not hear him over the **cacophony** of voices in the room.
- After the **cacophony** of the party, the room felt very quiet after everyone left.

*Synonym:* discord, noise, disharmony, racket, dissonance, commotion
*Antonym:* harmony, euphony, quiet

Further Information

- Originated from the Greek words *kakos* and *phone* meaning "bad sound."
- Other forms of the word include **cacophonous** (adj.) and **cacophonic** (adj.).
- The opposite of **cacophony** is **euphony**, which means "having harmonious, pleasant effects."

**cajole:** [kuh-JOHL] Verb.
To persuade by flattery or promises.

- The council member tried to **cajole** the others into voting with him against the law.
- It is always better to **cajole** someone rather than to threaten them.

*Synonym:* coax, wheedle, persuade, inveigle, flatter, entice
*Antonym:* nag, harass, pester

Further Information
- Originated from the Middle French word *cageoler* meaning "to chatter like a jay in a cage."
- Related word forms include **cajolement** (n.) and **cajolingly** (adj.).
- Another synonym for **cajole** is **soft-soap**, which refers to "insincere talk for personal gain."

**callow:** [KAL-oh] Adjective/Noun.
Inexperienced or immature. (adj.)
A worker ant that is recently hatched. (n.)

- The **callow** youth was just 18 when he arrived in Tokyo. (adj.)
- The recently hatched ant is referred to as a **callow** worker. (n.)

*Synonym:* naive, green, fresh, inexperienced, young, immature
*Antonym:* multi-skilled, sophisticated, experienced

Further Information
- Originated from the Old English word *calu* meaning "bare or bald."
- In the 17th century **callow** was used to describe "young birds without feathers not ready to fly."
- Related word forms include **callowness** (n.).

**calumny:** [KAL-uhm-nee] Noun.
A false, malicious statement to injure reputation.

- Although she was subjected to vicious **calumny**, she never protested nor sued over it.
- He rejected her observations about the teacher's personal life as **calumny**.

*Synonym:* slander, aspersion, obloquy, scandal, defamation, vilification
*Antonym:* dignification

Further Information
- Originated from the Old French word *calomnie* meaning "false accusation or slander."
- Related word forms include **calumnious** (adj.) and **calumniously** (adv.).
- **Calumny** appears in William Shakespeare's Hamlet: "Be thou chaste as ice, as pure as snow, thou shalt not escape **calumny**."

**candor**: [KAN-der] Noun.
The quality or state of being sincere, open and frank in expression or speech.

- In a moment of **candor**, she revealed that she was an orphan.
- Maintaining a friendship requires **candor** and commitment.

*Synonym:* honesty, sincerity, frankness, candidness, truth, openness
*Antonym:* deceit, fabrication, artifice
Further Information
- Comes from the Latin word *candere* meaning "to shine or glow."
- An archaic meaning of the word **candor** is "kindliness."
- Related words derived from *candere* include **incandescent**, **candid** and **candle**.

**cant**: [kant] Noun/Verb.
Insincere expression of enthusiasm for goodness. (n.)
Special words or phrases used by a group. (n.)
A sloping or slanting surface, or a tilt. (n.)
To engage in hypocritical talk, to beg. (v.)

- The **cant** of the boat led the passengers to believe that it was about to sink. (n.)
- She could not understand the religious **cant** when she visited her friend's church. (n.)
- He has a real contempt for **cant** and hypocrisy. (n.)
- The group kept **canting** about honest work for honest pay, but never did any work. (v.)

*Synonym:* jargon, slang, patois, tilt, slope, slant
*Antonym:* standard
Further Information
- Originated from the Old French word *chanter* meaning "to sing, to chant."
- The medical definition of **cant** is "a slanting or oblique surface."
- In England the word **cant** is dialectical and means "lusty" or "lively."

**capitulate**: [kuh-PICH-uh-leyt] Verb.
To surrender unconditionally, to give up resistance.

- If you do not **capitulate**, we will take your army by force.
- The mother refused to **capitulate** to her toddler's tantrum.

*Synonym:* surrender, yield, concede, submit, succumb, acquiesce
*Antonym:* conquer, withstand, defend
Further Information
- Originated from the Latin word *capitulare* meaning "to draw up in heads or chapters."
- An archaic meaning of the word **capitulate** is "to negotiate."
- Related word forms include **capitulation**.

**capricious**: [kuh-PRISH-uhs] Adjective.
Indicating a sudden unpredictable change, erratic, fanciful.

- The leader of the small country was accused of being undemocratic and **capricious**.
- Employees should be protected from **capricious**, unfair actions of their employers.

*Synonym:* fickle, erratic, changeable, whimsical, unpredictable, volatile
*Antonym:* steady, constant, stable
Further Information
- Originated from the Italian word *capriccio* meaning "to shudder suddenly with fear."
- The word **capriccio** is used today to mean "whimsy" or "fancy."
- Related word forms include **caprice** (n.), **capriciously** (adv.) and **capriciousness** (n.).

**carp**: [kahrp] Verb/Noun.
To complain or find fault in an annoying way. (v.)
A petty complaint. (n.)
A freshwater fish. (n.)

- She continued to **carp** about the missed airline reservation even after it was refunded. (v.)
- He fished for **carp** in the small stream. (n.)
- Her many **carps** about the airline reservation were becoming tiresome. (n.)

*Synonym:* cavil, criticize, complain, quibble, nag, knock
*Antonym:* praise, compliment
Further Information
- Originated from the Icelandic *karpa* meaning "to dispute" or to "wrangle."
- The noun **carp,** meaning "a complaint," did not come into English usage until the 20<sup>th</sup> century.
- **Carpogonium** is derived from **carp** and means "the cellular organ found in red algae."

**castigate**: [KAS-ti-geyt] Verb.
To punish in order to correct, to reprimand severely, to criticize.

- The principal **castigated** the student for being late to class every day this week.
- She **castigated** herself for believing his story once again.

*Synonym:* chastise, punish, scold, reprimand, rebuke, correct
*Antonym:* celebrate, laud, exalt
Further Information
- Originated from the Latin word *castigus* meaning "to correct" or "to set right."
- Related words include **castigation** (n.) and **castigator.** (n.)
- A related word derived from *castigus* is **chasten**, which means "to discipline" or "to subdue."

# REVIEW EXERCISE 5

*Match the word with its synonym.*

| ___ | 1. | buttress | a. | punish |
|---|---|---|---|---|
| ___ | 2. | cache | b. | fickle |
| ___ | 3. | cacophony | c. | hoard |
| ___ | 4. | cajole | d. | naive |
| ___ | 5. | callow | e. | jargon |
| ___ | 6. | calumny | f. | surrender |
| ___ | 7. | candor | g. | coax |
| ___ | 8. | cant | h. | complain |
| ___ | 9. | capitulate | i. | discord |
| ___ | 10. | capricious | j. | slander |
| ___ | 11. | carp | k. | support |
| ___ | 12. | castigate | l. | honesty |

*Fill in the blanks with the most appropriate word from list above.* (Word form may need changing.)

1.  The _____ of hidden jewels was buried under the house.

2.  Politicians spoke in the party _____ at the convention.

3.  I feel like I should _____ myself for believing his lies.

4.  If the army does not _____, the soldiers will be killed.

5.  She was _____ and flighty for most of her life.

6.  His presence was a _____ against the possibility of outside violence.

7.  The _____ of instruments on the street drowned out their conversation.

8.  No one listened to the opinions of the _____ youth.

9.  He tried to _____ me into agreeing with him although I knew he was wrong.

10. She continued to _____ about his many shortcomings.

11. It is often best to answer _____ with silence.

12. His reputation for _____ and integrity got him elected to office.

# WORD SET 6

**catalyst**: [KAT-uh-list] Noun.
In chemistry, a substance that causes or accelerates a chemical reaction.
Something/someone that causes activity or precipitates a change.

- Chlorine acts as a **catalyst** in the experiment, speeding up the chemical reaction.
- The **catalyst** for change came from outside of the group.

*Synonym:* incentive, agitator, accelerator, impetus, stimulus, impulse
*Antonym:* block, prevention, obstruction

Further Information
- From the English word *catalysis* meaning "increased rate of chemical reaction."
- In the 1940s, **catalyst** began meaning "something that quickly causes change or action."
- The financial definition of **catalyst** is "news or information that changes a pricing trend."


**celerity**: [suh-LER-uh-tee] Noun.
Speed or swiftness.

- The subway has the advantage of **celerity** over the bus.
- When their leader tells them to move, the soldiers act with **celerity**.

*Synonym:* speed, rapidity, alacrity, quickness, swiftness, haste
*Antonym:* sluggishness, slowness, deliberateness

Further Information
- Originated from the Latin root *celer* meaning "swift."
- Benjamin Franklin used the word **celerity** as a synonym for "velocity."
- William Shakespeare used **celerity** in Henry V: "In motion of no less **celerity**."


**chagrin**: [shuh-GRIN] Noun/verb.
A feeling of frustration caused by humiliation or disappointment. (n.)
To cause frustration by humiliating or disappointing. (v.)

- Much to my **chagrin**, I lost the election. (n.)
- He was **chagrined** when the boy poured soup on his head. (v.)

*Synonym:* shame, disappointment, mortification, humiliation, embarrassment, vexation
*Antonym:* delight, pleasure, satisfaction

Further Information
- Originated from the French word *chagrin* meaning "grief or sorrow."
- **Chagrin** also meant "rough skin" or "rough leather" in French.
- The American word **shagreen** derived from **chagrin** and means "untanned leather."

**chauvinism**: [SHOH-vun-niz-uhm] Noun.
Aggressive, biased, blind patriotism, devotion or enthusiasm.
The disparagement of a group based upon a belief that one group is inferior to the other.

- The tourists in the foreign country felt the **chauvinism** expressed against them by the natives.
- Male **chauvinism** was once rampant in government, but now many women hold elected offices.

*Synonym:* jingoism, apartheid, nationalism, xenophobia, racism, discrimination
*Antonym:* open-mindedness, fairness
Further Information
- Originated from the French *chauvinisme* meaning "idealistic devotion to Napoleon."
- Related word forms include **chauvinistically** (adv.), **chauvinistic** (adj.) and **chauvinist** (n. or adj.).
- **Chauvinism** was named after the excessively patriotic French soldier Nicholas Chauvin.

**chimerical**: [kih-MER-i-kuhl] Adjective.
Absurd, imaginary, indulging in unrealistic fantasies.

- His claim that he saw a UFO in the night sky was dismissed as **chimerical** nonsense.
- The inventor's plans to create a solar weapon were chastised as **chimerical** thinking.

*Synonym:* imaginary, visionary, unreal, fanciful, illusory, fantastic
*Antonym:* genuine, real, factual
Further Information
- Originated from the Greek *chimera*, meaning "she-goat."
- In Greek mythology, the **Chimera** was a fire-breathing monster with a goat's body.
- Related words include **chimera** (n.) and **chimerically** (adj).

**circumlocution**: [sur-kuhm-loh-KYOO-shuhn] Noun.
An indirect, roundabout way of speaking or expressing an idea.

- "The husband of your mother's sister," is a **circumlocution** for "your uncle."
- His speech was filled with **circumlocution** and lost our attention halfway through.

*Synonym:* wordiness, redundancy, periphrasis, verbiage, verbosity
*Antonym:* conciseness, bluntness
Further Information
- Originated from the Latin *circum* meaning "around" and *locution* meaning "to talk."
- Related words include **circumlocutory** (adj.) and **circumlocutional** (adj.).
- Charles Dickens created a fictional **Circumlocution** Office in political satire, a government office that prevented information from getting out to the public.

**circumvent**: [sur-kuhm-VENT] Verb.
To go around, to bypass, to avoid.

- In order to **circumvent** the traffic accident, we took the side roads.
- Try to **circumvent** the problem instead of hiding from it.

*Synonym:* evade, avoid, elude, sidestep, dodge, bypass
*Antonym:* confront, allow, aid

Further Information
- The word **circumvent** originates from the Latin *circumventus*, meaning "to get around."
- Related word forms include **circumventable** (adj.) and **circumvention** (n.).
- The earliest meaning of **circumvent** was to entrap or surround, such as an enemy.


**cogent**: [KOH-jent] Adjective.
Believable or convincing due to clear presentation, relevant, pertinent.

- He pointed out some **cogent** reasons to abandon our plan.
- The judge said he needed **cogent** evidence before he would overturn the decision.

*Synonym:* convincing, persuasive, compelling, valid, forceful, powerful
*Antonym:* weak, impotent, feeble

Further Information
- Originated from the Latin *cogere* meaning "to drive together or collect."
- Related words include **cogency** (n.).
- **Cogent** literally refers to "the driving intellectual force behind an argument."


**cognizant**: [KOG-nuh-zuhnt] Adjective.
Being aware of or having legal jurisdiction.

- The lawyer is **cognizant** of the fact that we tried to pay our debts.
- You should always be **cognizant** of what is going on around you.

*Synonym:* knowledgeable, aware, conscious, informed, knowing
*Antonym:* unaware, ignorant, oblivious

Further Information
- Originated from the Latin *cognoscere* meaning "to get to know."
- Other word forms include **cognizance** (n.) and **cognition** (n.).
- **Cognizant** usually refers to "having first-hand, certain or special knowledge about a fact or situation."

**comely**: [KUHM-lee] Adjective.
Pleasing in appearance, fair, attractive, seemly, becoming.

- Although she was not **comely**, she had a spark to her personality that attracted men.
- The **comely** village, aptly named **Comely**, attracts many tourists each year.

*Synonym:* handsome, attractive, fair, lovely, gorgeous, beautiful
*Antonym:* ugly, unattractive, homely

Further Information
- Originated from the Middle English *comly* meaning "glorious."
- **Comely** usually describes people in modern usage but at one time referred to things such as clothing.
- A related word form is **comeliness** (n.).


**commodious**: [kuh-MOH-dee-uhs] Adjective.
Spacious and convenient, roomy, ample or adequate for a specific purpose.

- This apartment is not **commodious** enough for our large family.
- Her new home was both stylish and **commodious**.

*Synonym:* spacious, roomy, comfortable, large, capacious, big
*Antonym:* confined, cramped, small

Further Information
- Originated from Latin *commodosus* meaning "fertile or useful."
- An archaic meaning of **commodious** is "handy or serviceable."
- Related word forms include **commodiously** (adv.) and **commodiousness** (n.).


**compunction:** [kuhm-PUHNGK-shuhn] Noun.
A feeling of uneasiness or anxiety about the rightness of an action.

- She had no **compunction** about reading her teenage daughter's diary.
- I felt some **compunction** at keeping my father waiting after school.

*Synonym:* regret, shame, remorse, contrition, repentance, qualm
*Antonym:* defiance, meanness, apathy

Further Information
- Originates from the Latin *com-* and *pungere* meaning "to prick hard" or "to sting."
- Related word forms include **compunctious** (adj).
- Other words derived from these Latin roots include **puncture** and **point**.

# REVIEW EXERCISE 6

**Match the word with its synonym.**

| | | | |
|---|---|---|---|
| ___ | 1. | catalyst | a. humiliation |
| ___ | 2. | celerity | b. discrimination |
| ___ | 3. | chagrin | c. imaginary |
| ___ | 4. | chauvinism | d. speed |
| ___ | 5. | chimerical | e. regret |
| ___ | 6. | circumlocution | f. impetus |
| ___ | 7. | circumvent | g. roomy |
| ___ | 8. | cogent | h. attractive |
| ___ | 9. | cognizant | i. aware |
| ___ | 10. | comely | j. evade |
| ___ | 11. | commodious | k. wordiness |
| ___ | 12. | compunction | l. convincing |

**Fill in the blanks with the most appropriate word from list above.** *(Word form may need changing.)*

1. She left the office with _____ after she was fired.

2. National _____ was high after the country engaged in the war.

3. His plans to build a steamboat were dismissed as _____ nonsense.

4. We tried to _____ the problem by brainstorming for novel solutions.

5. The new law was a _____ for change in the society.

6. He is a master at _____ but still holds his audience's attention.

7. The jury was convinced by the attorney's _____ arguments.

8. Our new house is _____ and accommodates our huge family.

9. He had no _____ about taking the day off to lie around the house.

10. He was _____ of the truth yet continued to lie.

11. The _____ woman won the beauty pageant.

12. Much to my _____, I lost the competition.

# WORD SET 7

**concoction**: [kon-KOK-shuhn] Noun.
A preparation or mixture of combined ingredients.

- The vile **concoction** of seaweed, garlic and mustard was supposed to make her healthy.
- The **concoction** of vegetables in that specific dish is a mystery.

*Synonym:* mixture, brew, blend, combination, compound, intermixture
*Antonym:* separate, dismantlement, decomposition

Further Information
- Originated from the Latin word *concoctus* meaning "cooked together."
- The original meaning of **concoct** in the 1500s was "to digest."
- Other commonly used word forms include **concoct** (v.), **concocter** (n.) and **concoctive** (adj.).

**concomitant**: [kon-KOM-i-tuhnt] Adjective.
Existing or occurring with something else.

- When the country's trading grew, it saw a **concomitant** increase in domestic wealth.
- Should loss of memory be considered a natural **concomitant** part of the aging process?

*Synonym:* attendant, accompanying, concurrent, coincident, contemporaneous, incidental
*Antonym:* unrelated, chance, accidental

Further Information
- Originated from the Latin word *concomitari* meaning "to accompany."
- Other commonly used word forms include **concomitantly** (adv.) and **concomitance** (n.)
- **Concomitance** is a medical term describing "a condition in which both eyes move as a unit."

**condone**: [kuhn-DOHN] Verb.
To treat something bad as forgivable or harmless.

- The president would not **condone** the use of violence in handling the protestors.
- The priest did not **condone** the man's sins.

*Synonym:* forgive, overlook, pardon, excuse, allow, approve
*Antonym:* forbid, punish, censure

Further Information
- Originated from the Latin *condonare* meaning "to absolve" or "to grant pardon."
- In British law, **condone** means "to imply forgiveness" (such as **condoning** a violation of a marriage vow).
- Related words include **condonable** (adj.), **condoner** (n.) and **uncondoned** (adj.).

**conduit**: [KON-doo-it] Noun.
A channel or passageway through which something travels.

- The tunnel was used as a **conduit** for drugs traveling into the country.
- The committee acts as a **conduit** for ideas to flow through from the employees to the executives.

*Synonym:* channel, aqueduct, canal, course, flume, passageway
*Antonym: none*

Further Information
- Originated from the Anglo-French word *cunduit* meaning "pipe" or "passage."
- An archaic meaning for **conduit** is "fountain."
- Types of electrical **conduits** include rigid steel conduit (RSC) and electrical metallic tubing (EMT).

**conflagration**: [kon-fluh-GRAY-shuhn] Noun.
A large, disastrous, destructive fire.
A conflict or war.

- The **conflagration** of the 1920s destroyed most of the buildings in that part of the town.
- As the **conflagration** grew, the National Guard was called in to assist the police.

*Synonym:* inferno, blaze, flame, fire, conflict, hostility
*Antonym: none*

Further Information
- Originated from the Latin *conflagrans* meaning "to burn up."
- Other commonly used word forms include **conflagrant** (adj.), **conflagrative** (adj.).

**congruity**: [kuhn-GROO-i-tee] Noun.
A point of agreement; the state of being in harmony.

- The candidates' approach to the health care problem shows a definite **congruity**.
- The **congruity** of the puzzle pieces was evident to the boy putting the puzzle together.

*Synonym:* harmony, agreement, conformity, congruence, consistency, accord
*Antonym:* incongruity, conflict, disagreement

Further Information
- Originated from the Latin word *congruere* meaning "to come together."
- The verb **congrue** is rarely used anymore but once meant "to agree."
- Other commonly used word forms include **congruent** (adj.) and **congruous** (adj.).

**conjecture:** [kuhn-JEK-cher] Noun.
An opinion or theory formed without sufficient proof.

- There was much **conjecture** in the press about what type of dress she would wear to the gala.
- Your opinion is **conjecture** and not based upon facts.

*Synonym:* guess, suppose, surmise, speculate, hypothesize, imagine
*Antonym:* fact, proof, truth

Further Information
- Originated from the Latin *conicere* meaning "to throw together."
- Other word forms include **conjecturer** (n.).
- An obsolete meaning for **conjecture** from 14th century English is "interpretation of signs or omens."

**connive:** [kuh-NEYV] Verb.
To cooperate secretly; to pretend ignorance of.

- Buying the cheap clothing made from child labor is **conniving** at that country's poverty.
- The student and her friend **connived** to cheat on the examination.

*Synonym:* conspire, scheme, plot, collude, machinate, contrive
*Antonym:* preclude, combat

Further Information
- Originated from the Latin word *connivere* meaning "to close the eyes."
- The original meaning of **connive** was "to wink at," echoing the Latin meaning.
- Related word forms include the noun **conniver** and the adjective **conniving**.

**connoisseur:** [kon-uh-SUR] Noun.
A discerning judge of the best in the field; a person who is competent to pass judgment in the field.

- Only a **connoisseur** can tell the difference between the two wines.
- The art **connoisseur** likes to appreciate the paintings at smaller art museums on weekends.

*Synonym:* specialist, expert, maven, master, authority, cognoscente
*Antonym:* amateur, beginner, novice

Further Information
- Originated from the Old French word *conoiseor,* meaning "knower."
- Also comes from the Latin word *cognoscere* meaning "to learn or to know."
- Related word forms include the noun **connoisseurship**.

**consternation**: [kon-ster-NAY-shuhn] Noun.
A sudden amazement or dismay that results in confusion.

- Her **consternation** was evident after the announcement of the election's winner.
- To his **consternation**, when he arrived at the airport he found that he'd forgotten his luggage.

*Synonym:* dismay, fear, dread, alarm, horror, fright
*Antonym:* calmness, peacefulness, composure

Further Information
- Originated from the Latin word *consternare* meaning "to throw into confusion."
- Possibly derived from the Latin *sternere* root meaning "to strike or throw down."
- Other words with the *sternere* root include **stratus**, **stratum** and **prostrate.**

**constituent**: [kuhn-STICH-oo-uhnt] Adjective/Noun.
Making up a thing, a component. (adj.)
An element that makes up a thing. (n.)
A person who authorizes another to act on his/her behalf. (n.)

- The **constituent** parts of the sentence include nouns, verbs and adverbs. (adj.)
- The senator's **constituents** begged him to help push the legislation through Congress. (n.)
- The community college is a **constituent** of the larger university system. (n.)

*Synonym:* element, part, component, factor, ingredient, feature
*Antonym:* whole

Further Information
- Originated from the Latin word *constituere* meaning "to set up."
- Other word forms include **constituency** (n.), **constituently** (adv.) and **constitutional** (adj.).
- **Constituent** is commonly used to denote "a citizen who is represented by a government official for whom he/she votes."

**construe**: [kuhn-STROO] Verb.
To give the meaning of; to deduce by interpretation.

- The law may be **construed** by different judges in different ways.
- Please don't **construe** my observations of your appearance as criticisms.

*Synonym:* interpret, explain, expound, translate, define, explicate
*Antonym:* misunderstand, confuse, misconstrue

Further Information
- Originated from the Latin word *construere* meaning "to put together."
- **Construe** can also be used to mean "translate."
- Other words forms include **construer** (n.), **misconstrue** (v.) and **unconstrued** (adj.).

# REVIEW EXERCISE 7

*Match the word with its synonym.*

___ 1. concoction       a. component
___ 2. concomitant      b. guess
___ 3. condone        c. interpret
___ 4. conduit         d. channel
___ 5. conflagration     e. expert
___ 6. congruity        f. forgive
___ 7. conjecture       g. accompanying
___ 8. connive         h. conspire
___ 9. connoisseur      i. dismay
___ 10. consternation    j. conflict
___ 11. constituent      k. mixture
___ 12. construe        l. harmony

*Fill in the blanks with the most appropriate word from list above.* *(Word form may need changing.)*

1. I cannot _____ your bullying of the younger child.

2. The underground _____ was used by prisoners to escape the prison.

3. The man's grandchildren _____ to surprise him on his 80th birthday.

4. The popular teacher's resignation was greeted with _____ by the students.

5. Tsunamis are often _____ with earthquakes.

6. She sipped the _____ cautiously, not knowing what it contained.

7. We _____ the acts of the rogue nation as a hostile attack.

8. Ever since the _____ began we expected a quick surrender.

9. Caffeine is a _____ of coffee and cola.

10. There was a lot of _____ about its contents before the reading of her will.

11. Because he was a _____ of chili, he was chosen as a judge for the contest.

12. The _____ of the group led to them easily making decisions.

# WORD SET 8

**consummate**: [KON-se-met] Verb, Adjective.
To bring to completion, to achieve. (v.)
Complete, utter or perfect. (adj.)

- Her dream was **consummated** with the publication of her first book. (v.)
- He was a **consummate** master of chess and beat all his opponents. (adj.)

*Synonym:* perfect, complete, supreme, superior, absolute, achieve
*Antonym:* imperfect, incomplete, neglect

Further Information
- Originated from the Latin word *consummare* meaning "to sum up or finish."
- Other commonly used word forms include **consummately** (adv.) and **consummation** (n.).
- **Consummate** is also used as a verb to mean "to make a marriage complete by having sex."


**contravene**: [kon-truh-VEEN] Verb.
To be in violation of, to be inconsistent with.

- The soldier **contravened** a direct order from his sergeant and was therefore court-martialed.
- The reproduction of that article **contravenes** copyright laws.

*Synonym:* contradict, oppose, infringe, defy, transgress, violate
*Antonym:* collaborate, endorse, help

Further Information
- Originated from the Latin word *contraveniere* meaning "to transgress."
- Other commonly used word forms include **contravener** (n.) and **contravention** (n.).
- **Contravene** is often used as a legal term; as in the **contravention** of copyright law.


**contrite**: [kuhn-TREYT] Adjective.
Full of remorse or guilt; caused by or showing sincere regret.

- She was so **contrite** that she wrote me a letter of apology.
- Being **contrite** will not save you from arrest if you're caught stealing.

*Synonym:* repentant, remorseful, apologetic, penitent, regretful, sorry
*Antonym:* shameless, unrepentant, unapologetic

Further Information
- Originated from the Latin *contritus* meaning "worn out."
- Related words include **contritely** (adv.) and **contriteness** (n.).
- In Christianity, **contrite** means "being regretful of past sin and resolved to avoid future sin."

**conundrum**: [keh-NUN-drum] Noun.
A riddle or seemingly unanswerable, difficult problem, a dilemma.

- The country's economic situation was a **conundrum** with no easily defined solution.
- The man is a true **conundrum** – a person with serious character flaws but inner strengths.

*Synonym:* enigma, riddle, mystery, puzzle, problem, dilemma
*Antonym:* clarification, answer, key

Further Information
- The origin of the word **conundrum** is unknown, possibly coined as a parody of Latin by Oxford University students in the 1600s.
- Previous spellings of **conundrum** include **quandundrum, conucrum** and **conimbrum.**
- The plural of **conundrum** is **conundrums.**

**copious**: [KOH-pee-us] Adjective.
Large in number or quantity.

- She sat in the back row and took **copious** notes during the lecture.
- The **copious** harvest yielded us an abundant crop of corn.

*Synonym:* abundant, plentiful, ample, profuse, bountiful, generous
*Antonym:* lacking, scarce, meager

Further Information
- Originated from the Latin *copia* meaning "abundance."
- Other commonly used word forms include **copiously** (adv.) and **copiousness** (n.).
- Do not confuse **copious** with **copiosity**, which means "redundancy or circumlocution."

**corpulence**: [KOR-pye-lents] Noun.
The state of having a large, bulky body.

- **Corpulence** has been shown to be related to heart disease and high cholesterol.
- She dropped 20 percent of her **corpulence** while on the diet.

*Synonym:* stoutness, overweight, obesity, plumpness, portliness, rotundity
*Antonym:* slenderness

Further Information
- Originated from the Latin word *corpulentus* meaning "body."
- Other commonly used word forms include **corpulent** (adj.) and **corpulency** (n.).
- Common terms describing **corpulence** include beer-belly, spare tire, and bay window.

**coterie**: [KO-teh-ree] Noun.
A small group with common interests who often associate with one other.

- The king's loyal **coterie** of intellectuals advised him daily.
- The four book-loving women formed a **coterie**.

*Synonym:* clique, set, circle, group, party, gang
*Antonym: none*

Further Information
- Originated from the Old French *cotier* meaning "association of tenants or cottagers."
- Another less-used meaning of **coterie** is "a group of prairie dogs who live in a communal burrow."
- The plural of **coterie** is **coteries**.

**countenance**: [KOUN-ten-uhns] Noun/Verb.
The appearance, especially the face. (n.)
To support, encourage, tolerate or endure. (v.)

- The school's administration will not **countenance** cheating. (v.)
- Her pleasant **countenance** made her seem approachable. (n.)

*Synonym:* sanction, support, permit, appearance, form, face
*Antonym:* disallow, forbid, disapprove

Further Information
- Originated from the Old French word *contenir* meaning "to behave."
- An obsolete meaning of **countenance** is "demeanor or bearing."
- Related word forms include **countenances** (n.), **countenancing** (v.) and **countenancer** (n.).

**coup**: [KOO] Noun.
A brilliant and sudden triumph or successful act.
The sudden overthrow of a government by a small group of persons (short for coup d'etat).

- He pulled off a **coup** when he booked an interview with the reclusive musician.
- The military **coup** resulted in a son deposing his father as leader of the country.

*Synonym:* revolution, feat, accomplishment, exploit, triumph
*Antonym:* failure

Further Information
- Originated from the Latin word *colaphus* meaning "blow with the fist."
- **Coup** is short for **coup d'etat**, a French term, which literally means "blow of state."
- Among the Plains Indians of North America, a **coup** means "a brave, reckless act conducted in battle by a single warrior without the warrior sustaining injury himself."

**crescendo**: [kri-SHEN-doh] Noun/Adjective/Adverb/Verb.
A slow, steady increase in loudness, force or intensity. (n.)
The peak of a gradual increase. (n.)
Gradually increasing in force, loudness or volume. (adj. or adv.)
To increase in force or loudness. (v.)

- The applause rose to a **crescendo** as the group took another curtain call. (n.)
- The orchestra worked up with a **crescendo** to the musical piece's climax. (adv.)
- The cheers in the crowd began to **crescendo** as the candidate stepped to the podium. (v.)
- The band's drummer played a short **crescendo** drum roll. (adj.)

*Synonym:* crest, apex, climax, elevation, culmination, apogee
*Antonym:* decrescendo, base, diminuendo
Further Information
- Originated from the Italian word *crescere* meaning "to increase."
- The plural of **crescendo** is **crescendoes** or **crescendi.**
- Other words derived from *crescere* include **increase** and **decrease**.

**culpable**: [KUHL-puh-buhl] Adjective.
Deserving of blame.

- The leader's decision to do nothing after the natural disaster makes him **culpable** for the thousands of deaths that ensued.
- Both parties were held to be **culpable** for the country's economic problems.

*Synonym:* liable, sinful, blameworthy, reprehensible, responsible, censurable
*Antonym:* innocent, blameless, faultless
Further Information
- Originated from the Latin word *culpare* meaning "to blame."
- Other word forms include **culpability** (n.) and **culpably** (adv.).
- **Culpable** was once a synonym for guilty or criminal, but that usage is now considered to be archaic.

**cupidity**: [kyoo-PID-uh-tee] Noun.
Excessive, strong desire, especially for money.

- His **cupidity** led him to attempt to rob the bank.
- **Cupidity** can make people steal things that do not belong to them.

*Synonym:* greed, desire, covetousness, avarice, lust, craving
*Antonym:* generosity
Further Information
- Originated from the Latin word *cupere* meaning "to desire."
- In 15th century English **cupidity** meant "lust," referring to the Roman god of love, Cupid.

# REVIEW EXERCISE 8

*Match the word with its Synonyms.*

| | | | | | |
|---|---|---|---|---|---|
| ___ | 1. | consummate | a. | liable |
| ___ | 2. | contravene | b. | feat |
| ___ | 3. | contrite | c. | obesity |
| ___ | 4. | conundrum | d. | enigma |
| ___ | 5. | copious | e. | contradict |
| ___ | 6. | corpulence | f. | greed |
| ___ | 7. | coterie | g. | complete |
| ___ | 8. | countenance | h. | clique |
| ___ | 9. | coup | i. | repentant |
| ___ | 10. | crescendo | j. | abundant |
| ___ | 11. | culpable | k. | face |
| ___ | 12. | cupidity | l. | climax |

*Fill in the blanks with the most appropriate word from list above.* (*Word form may need changing.*)

1. The theory was supported by _____ evidence.

2. His _____ for wealth led him to work excessive hours.

3. You were suspended from school because your actions _____ school policy.

4. She was a _____ professional and accepted the loss with grace.

5. Her _____ of friends were always surrounding her in public.

6. As the music reached a_____ the audience went wild with applause.

7. Trying to solve this _____ is giving me a headache.

8. She was _____ the morning after the argument with her husband.

9. Getting the signature of her favorite musician was a real _____ for her.

10. His _____ showed no wrinkles or sagging skin despite his advanced age.

11. Her _____ prevented her from fitting into the airplane seat.

12. He is _____ for the accident because he drove while drunk.

# WORD SET 9

**decadence**: [DEK-uh-dens] Noun.
A period, process, or condition of decline or deterioration.

- The increase in teenage crime is not necessarily indicative of the **decadence** of that generation.
- Some people describe the 1980s as the decade of **decadence**.

*Synonym:* decline, decay, degeneration, downfall, stagnation, failure
*Antonym:* morality, decency, rehabilitation

Further Information
- Originated from the Latin word *decadentia* meaning "a declining or decaying."
- **Decadence** is also used to describe a literary movement of late 19th century England and France characterized by the search for new sensations, artifice and aestheticism.
- Other word forms include **decadency** (n.) and **decadent** (adj.).

**decrepit**: [di-KREP-it] Adjective.
Worn out, weakened, or impaired by illness, old age or hard use.

- The workers are demolishing the **decrepit** building.
- The **decrepit** elderly man had trouble walking from the house to the car.

*Synonym:* weak, rickety, feeble, infirm, dilapidated, frail
*Antonym:* healthy, strong, robust

Further Information
- Originated from the Latin word *decrepitus* meaning "worn out, feeble."
- Other word forms include **decrepitly** (adv.) and **decrepitude** (n.).
- **Decrepit** usually describes "a person or thing that is old, worn out and broken down."

**defunct**: [di-FUNGKT] Adjective.
Having ceased to live or to exist, no longer in use.

- He bought the **defunct** car model because he knew where he could still obtain parts for it.
- Latin has been called a **defunct** language.

*Synonym:* extinct, dead, deceased, gone, fallen, perished
*Antonym:* existing, alive, operative

Further Information
- Originated from the Latin *defunctus* meaning "dead."
- Related words include **defunctive** (adj.) and **defunctness** (n.).
- It is believed that William Shakespeare was the first writer to use the word **defunct,** in *Henry V.*

**deleterious**: [del-uh-TEER-ee-us] Adjective.
Having a harmful effect.

- Alcohol can be **deleterious** if one overindulges in it.
- The oil spill has **deleterious** effects for the environment.

*Synonym:* harmful, injurious, detrimental, damaging, pernicious, destructive
*Antonym:* beneficial, helpful, advantageous

Further Information
- Originated from the Greek word *deleterious* meaning "injurious."
- Other word forms include **deleteriously** (adv.) and **deleteriousness** (n.).
- **Delete** meaning "to remove" is a related term to **deleterious.**

**delirious**: [duh-LEER-ee-us] Adjective.
Marked by wild excitement, ecstasy or emotion.
Not able to speak or think clearly due to confusion or illness.

- She was **delirious** from the fever, saying things that made no sense.
- **Delirious** with happiness, the bride could not recite her vows because of her joyful crying.

*Synonym:* crazy, wild, mad, frantic, hysterical, excited
*Antonym:* sane, normal, relaxed

Further Information
- Originated from the Latin *delirare* meaning "to be deranged."
- Other word forms include **delirium** (n.), **deliriously** (adv.) and **deliriousness** (n.).
- **Delirium**, from which **delirious** is derived, is a psychological condition of severe mental confusion.

**deluge**: [DELL-yooj] Noun/Verb.
A heavy downpour, a great flood. (n.)
To overrun with water; to overwhelm with a large amount. (v.)

- He received a **deluge** of awards at his school's awards assembly, as he earned straight A's. (n.)
- After the rain **deluged** our property for days, our house became flooded. (v.)

*Synonym:* flood, inundate, overflow, torrent, swamp, submerge
*Antonym:* drought, drizzle, trickle

Further Information
- Originated from the Latin word *diluere* meaning "to wash away."
- **Deluge** also refers to the Biblical flood during the time of Noah.
- Other word forms include **deluges** (n. or v.), **deluged** (v.) and **deluging** (v.).

**demagogue**: [DEM-uh-gog] Noun.
A leader who appeals to the public's emotions and prejudices and makes false promises to obtain power.

- The **demagogue** persuaded the people to rebel against their existing government.
- He was a **demagogue** who used social media to influence the opinions of voters.

*Synonym:* agitator, rebel, troublemaker, instigator, inciter, revolutionary
*Antonym:* appeaser, intermediary, accommodator

Further Information
- Originated from the Greek *demagogos* meaning "popular leader."
- **Demagogue** is also less commonly used as a verb meaning "to speak about an issue in the manner of a demagogue."
- **Demagogue** is also less commonly spelled **demagog**.


**demur**: [dee-MUR] Verb/Noun.
To object or voice opposition. (v.)
The act/process of hesitating or objecting. (n.)

- She wanted to stand up and **demur** at the meeting but didn't want to speak out against popular opinion. (v.)
- Citizens should lodge their **demurs** and protest laws they feel are unconstitutional. (n.)

*Synonym:* object, protest, disagree, hesitate, oppose, challenge
*Antonym:* agree, accept, acquiesce

Further Information
- Originated from the Latin word *demorari* meaning "to delay."
- An archaic meaning of **demur** is "to delay."
- In law, **demurrer** means "an objection."


**denigrate**: [DEN-uh-grayt] Verb.
To attack the reputation and character of something or someone.

- The talk show host tried to **denigrate** the reputation of her guest by bring up past misdeeds.
- If you **denigrate** someone publicly, you should expect to have your reputation attacked in turn.

*Synonym:* disparage, deprecate, belittle, defame, decry, smear
*Antonym:* praise, compliment, commend

Further Information
- Originated from the Latin word *denigrare* meaning "to blacken or defame."
- Other word forms include **denigration** (n.) and **denigrator** (n.).
- An archaic use of **denigrate** was "to make black" as in, "Factory smoke denigrated the sky."

**deride**: [di-REYD] Verb.
To laugh at, speak of, or write about contemptuously or dismissively.

- The newspaper's music critic **derided** the band's new song as sounding like children's music.
- Bullies **deride** others to feel superior to them.

*Synonym:* ridicule, mock, taunt, jeer, scoff, scorn
*Antonym:* commend, compliment, praise

Further Information
- Originated from the Latin word *deridere* meaning "to laugh at."
- *Ridere*, the root of *deridere*, is also found in the words **risible** and **ridiculous**, both relating to laughter.
- Other word forms include **derider** (n.), **derision** (n.) and **deridingly** (adv.).

**desultory**: [DES-ul-tor-ee] Adjective.
Disconnected, moving or jumping from one thing to another randomly or sporadically without plan or purpose.

- The teacher's **desultory** lecture seemed to have no focus and made no sense.
- When he didn't get the raise he wanted, he decided to perform his work **desultorily**.

*Synonym:* aimless, random, erratic, irregular, fitful, haphazard
*Antonym:* methodical, thoughtful, supportive

Further Information
- Originated from the Latin word *desultorius* meaning "leaping."
- The Latin word *desultorius* referred to a circus performer who leapt from one horse to another.
- Other word forms include **desultorily** (adv.) and **desultoriness** (n.).

**dexterity**: [deks-TER-uh-tee] Noun.
Grace and skill in physical movement; mental skill or cleverness.

- He caught the ball with much **dexterity**.
- Both manual and mental **dexterity** was needed to excel at the video game.

*Synonym:* skill, adroitness, ability, expertise, proficiency, knack
*Antonym:* clumsiness, inability

Further Information
- Originated from the Latin word *dexter* meaning "on the right side."
- In physiology, **dexterity** means 'the characteristic of being right-handed."
- Related word forms include **dexterous** (adj.), **dexterously** (adv.) and **dexterousness** (n.).

# REVIEW EXERCISE 9

*Match the word with its synonym.*

| | | | | | |
|---|---|---|---|---|---|
| ___ | 1. | decadence | a. | random |
| ___ | 2. | decrepit | b. | object |
| ___ | 3. | defunct | c. | flood |
| ___ | 4. | deleterious | d. | harmful |
| ___ | 5. | delirious | e. | weak |
| ___ | 6. | deluge | f. | skill |
| ___ | 7. | demagogue | g. | decline |
| ___ | 8. | demur | h. | extinct |
| ___ | 9. | denigrate | i. | wild |
| ___ | 10. | deride | j. | ridicule |
| ___ | 11. | desultory | k. | disparage |
| ___ | 12. | dexterity | l. | agitator |

*Fill in the blanks with the most appropriate word from list above.* (*Word form may need changing.*)

1. The playground equipment is so _____ our mother won't let us play there.

2. Hitler has been described by many as a _____.

3. If anyone _____ this marriage, speak now or forever hold your peace.

4. His _____ attempts at conversation on diverse topics made no sense.

5. Do you have the _____ necessary to juggle oranges?

6. The teacher_____ the student in front of the class, making her feel small.

7. Smoking cigarettes is_____ to your health.

8. The gold fixtures in the celebrity's kitchen were a sign of sheer_____.

9. My friend was _____ with grief at her father's funeral.

10. She got the promotion by _____ her coworkers in front of her boss.

11. It seemed that the soaking _____, lasting almost a month, would not end.

12. The _____ building sat sadly in the middle of the city, unused.

# WORD SET 10

**diaphanous**: [di-AF-uh-nus] Adjective.
Thin or airy enough to be translucent; easily damaged, delicate.

- Her gold gown was made of a **diaphanous** material and made her look like a ray of light.
- It was easy to see through the **diaphanous** drapes into their house.

*Synonym:* transparent, filmy, sheer, ethereal, delicate, gossamer
*Antonym:* thick, opaque, solid

Further Information
- Originated from the Greek word *diaphainein* meaning "to show through."
- Other words with the Greek root *phaina* include **epiphany** and **theophany**.
- Related word forms include **diaphanously** (adv.), **diaphaneity** (n.) and **diaphanousness** (n.).


**diatribe**: [DI-uh-treyb] Noun.
A bitter, abusive piece of writing or speech; ironic criticism.

- His **diatribe** at the town meeting brought shame and embarrassment to his family.
- The candidate's **diatribe** against his opponent caused anger between the political parties.

*Synonym:* harangue, tirade, invective, denunciation, fulmination, vituperation
*Antonym:* honor, praise, exaltation

Further Information
- Originated from the Greek words *diatribe* meaning "pastime, discourse" and *diatribein* meaning "to waste time or wear away."
- The word **diatribe** is therefore related to "serious study" and "the wasting of time."
- An archaic meaning of **diatribe** is "a prolonged lecture or discourse."


**didactic**: [di-DAK-tik] Adjective.
Intended or designed to teach or moralize.

- Sometimes my parents' advice seems **didactic,** but I know they are just trying to help me.
- The **didactic** presentation was designed to teach students about the dangers of smoking.

*Synonym:* educational, instructive, preachy, moralistic, academic, pedantic
*Antonym:* uninformative, uninstructive, ignorant

Further Information
- Originated from the Greek *didaktikos* meaning "apt at teaching."
- **Didactic** is often used to describe in a disapproving way "a fixed, overeager, moralistic approach to teaching."
- Related words include **didactical** (adj.), **didactically** (adv) and **didacticism** (n.).

**dilettante**: [DIL-eh-tant] Noun/Adjective.
A person who dabbles in a field of knowledge or an art. (n.)
Amateurish or superficial. (adj.)

- He is a **dilettante** who likes to practice his instrument as little as possible. (n.)
- Her friends applauded her **dilettante** performance, but the critics panned it. (adj.)

*Synonym:* dabbler, amateur, nonprofessional, trifler, novice
*Antonym:* professional, expert

Further Information
- Originated from the Italian word *dilettare* meaning "to delight."
- An archaic meaning of **dilettante** is "a lover of the fine arts."
- Other word forms include **dilettantish** (adj.) and **dilettantism** (n.).

**disparate**: [DIS-pehr-et] Adjective.
Fundamentally different or distinct; made up of different elements.

- The student received a D on his report because he tried to combine **disparate** elements into the same essay.
- Their **disparate** opinions made it impossible for them to come to an agreement.

*Synonym:* incongruous, different, distinct, divergent, diverse
*Antonym:* similar, analogous, alike

Further Information
- Originated from the Latin *disparare* meaning "to separate."
- Other word forms include **disparately** (adv.), **disparity** (n.) and **disparateness** (n.).
- **Disparate** is not to be confused with the word **desperate** which means "having no hope."

**domicile**: [DOM-uh-sil] Noun/Verb.
A residence or home. (n.)
To establish oneself in a residence or provide housing. (v.)

- The police went to the child's **domicile** when he was reported missing.
- The maid is cleaning my mother's **domicile** while she is recovering from illness.

*Synonym:* home, abode, residence, house, dwelling, habitation
*Antonym:* none

Further Information
- Originated from the Latin word *domicilium* meaning "house."
- **Domicile** may also be spelled **domicil.**
- In legal terms, **domicile** means "a permanent legal residence."
- Related word forms include **domiciled** (v.), **domiciles** (n. or v.) and **domiciling** (v.).

**dour**: [dower] Adjective.
Stern, harsh, unyielding, gloomy or obstinate.

- Because of her attitude and appearance, the **dour** old lady was known as a witch in the village.
- The **dour** man refused to laugh at any of the comedian's jokes.

*Synonym:* grim, glum, morose, sullen, harsh, stern
*Antonym:* cheerful, bright, happy

Further Information
- Originated from the Latin *durus* meaning "hard."
- Other related word forms include **dourly** (adv.) and **dourness** (n.).
- **Dour** once rhymed with "tour" but for the last century has rhymed with "sour."


**drudgery**: [DRUHJ-uh-ree] Noun.
Menial, tedious or unpleasant work.

- After a year of **drudgery** and low wages, I decided to look for another job.
- The heiress believed only her servants should perform the **drudgery** involved in keeping house.

*Synonym:* travail, chore, grind, labor, slavery, toil
*Antonym:* relaxation, fun, recreation

Further Information
- Originated from the Middle English word *druggen* meaning "to do menial or monotonous work."
- Other word forms include **drudgeries** (n.), **drudge** (v.) and **drudger** (n.).
- **Drudgery** is associated with "tiresome, boring work one does begrudgingly."


**duplicity**: [doo-PLIS-uh-tee] Noun.
Deliberate contradictory deceptiveness in thought, speech or behavior.

- The con man used **duplicity** to trick his victims.
- The accountant used financial **duplicity** to embezzle money from his clients.

*Synonym:* deception, deceit, hypocrisy, guile, trickery, chicanery
*Antonym:* honesty, candor, forthrightness

Further Information
- Originated from the Latin word *duplicitas* meaning "doubleness."
- In law, **duplicity** means "the technically incorrect usage of two different items in one legal action."
- Related word forms include **duplicities** (n.) and **duplicitous** (adj.).

**duress**: [duh-RES] Noun/Verb.
Compulsion through violence or threat. (n.)
Constraint caused by misfortune. (n.)
To pressure someone. (v.)

- The man's confession was given under **duress**, so the judge overturned his sentence. (n.)
- Under the **duress** of the moment, the act of him walking into the room was unnoticed. (n.)
- The nation was **duressed** into giving up territory. (v.)

*Synonym:* coercion, constraint, pressure, compulsion, restraint, confinement
*Antonym:* autonomy, freedom
Further Information
- Originated from the Latin root *durus* meaning "hard."
- Other words derived from *durus* include **durable**, **obdurate**, **endure**, **during** and **dour**.
- In law, **duress** means "a fraud achieved through an act of compulsion or threat," or "a criminal defense for an act that was committed under threat of bodily harm."

**ebullient**: [i-BOOL-yent] Adjective.
Enthusiastic and lively; agitated.

- The **ebullient** song made me so joyful that I had to stand up in church and sing along.
- He feels **ebullient** after drinking his morning coffee.

*Synonym:* exuberant, vivacious, effervescent, enthusiastic, lively, animated
*Antonym:* disinterested, apathetic, unenthusiastic
Further Information
- Originated from the Latin word *ebullire* meaning "to bubble out."
- The earliest meaning of **ebullient** was "to boil or bubble over."
- Other word forms include **ebulliently** (adv.) and **ebullience** (n.).

**eclectic**: [ih-KLEK-tik] Adjective/Noun.
Made up of elements from a variety of sources, styles or systems. (adj.)
A person who follows an approach or method made up of varying elements. (n.)

- The restaurant's menu was **eclectic** and included foods from many different cultures.
- The library contains an **eclectic** mix of books.

*Synonym:* varied, assorted, indiscriminate, heterogeneous, mixed
*Antonym:* specific, particular, narrow
Further Information
- Originated from the Greek word *eklektos* meaning "selected."
- An archaic meaning of **eclectic** was used to describe "philosophers who selected doctrines from many and varied schools of thought."
- A related word form is **eclectically** (adv.).

# REVIEW EXERCISE 10

**Match the word with its synonym.**

| | | | | | |
|---|---|---|---|---|---|
| ___ | 1. | diaphanous | a. | compulsion |
| ___ | 2. | diatribe | b. | home |
| ___ | 3. | didactic | c. | incongruous |
| ___ | 4. | dilettante | d. | deception |
| ___ | 5. | disparate | e. | assorted |
| ___ | 6. | domicile | f. | instructive |
| ___ | 7. | dour | g. | tirade |
| ___ | 8. | drudgery | h. | transparent |
| ___ | 9. | duplicity | i. | chore |
| ___ | 10. | duress | j. | amateur |
| ___ | 11. | ebullient | k. | grim |
| ___ | 12. | eclectic | l. | exuberant |

**Fill in the blanks with the most appropriate word from list above.** *(Word form may need changing.)*

1. Her_____ against the teacher got her sent to the principal's office.

2. His _____ disposition during the interview made me afraid to smile.

3. She used _____ to get the old man to include her in his will.

4. Her_____ attitude makes her a favorite among her coworkers.

5. The driveway leads to his _____ at the top of a steep hill.

6. Her home is filled with _____ works of art from her travels around the world.

7. Their _____ backgrounds made it difficult for them to relate.

8. She was under_____ when she asked her friend to steal money.

9. The bride's veil was _____ so her husband could see her face.

10. She will always remain a _____ unless she practices her art often.

11. The job at the fast food restaurant seemed to the teen to be pure _____.

12. The fiction books were both entertaining and _____ simultaneously.

# WORD SET 11

**edict**: [EE-dikt] Noun.
A proclamation or decree issued by an authority and backed by law.

- The **edict** made it against school policy for students to use cell phones while in school.
- The soldiers obeyed the **edict** from their commanding officer.

*Synonym:* order, decree, command, ordinance, pronouncement, mandate
*Antonym:* request, appeal

Further Information
- Originated from the Latin word *edictere* meaning "to declare."
- Other words derived from *edictere* include **dictator** and **dictate**.
- Related word forms include **edictical** (adj.) and **edictically** (adv.).


**edifice**: [ED-uh-fis] Noun.
A building, especially a large, imposing structure.

- Staring up at the gigantic **edifice** made me feel quite small.
- One of the famous **edifices** that people like to visit in New York is the Empire State Building.

*Synonym:* structure, building, skyscraper
*Antonym:* none

Further Information
- Originated from the Latin word *aedificare* meaning "to build."
- Related words include **edificial** (adj.).
- **Edifice** can also mean "a complex system of beliefs."


**effigy**: [EF-uh-gee] Noun.
A representation or image, especially of a person.

- The citizens happily burned the **effigy** of their dictator after learning he was dead.
- The protestors carried an **effigy** of the mayor which they intended to deface later.

*Synonym:* image, picture, representation, icon, likeliness, statue
*Antonym:* none

Further Information
- Originated from the Latin word *effingere* meaning "to form, mold, fashion or portray."
- Related words include **effigial** (adj.).
- The burning of **effigies** was originally done by judicial authorities to symbolically punish criminals who had escaped. Later burning an **effigy** of someone was an expression against a hateful person.

**egalitarian**: [ee-ga-luh-TAR-ee-un] Adjective.
Characterized by a belief in equal political, social, economic and civil rights for all people.

- This is an **egalitarian** country with equal rights for all citizens.
- The **egalitarian** belief that men and women are equals was not always written into law.

*Synonym:* equal, equalitarian, moralist, democratic, equitable, impartial
*Antonym:* elitist, snobbish

Further Information
- Originated from the French word *egalite* meaning "equality."
- Other word forms include **egalitarianism** (n).
- The government resulting from the French Revolution was called an "**egalitarian** despotism."

**egregious**: [uh-GREE-jes] Adjective.
Conspicuously bad, flagrant.

- His cheating on the exam was considered an **egregious**, unforgiveable mistake.
- Their **egregious** habit of talking loudly in church was frowned upon by the minister.

*Synonym:* outrageous, glaring, flagrant, gross, atrocious, monstrous
*Antonym:* little, slight

Further Information
- Originated from the Latin *egregius* meaning "outstanding."
- Other word forms include **egregiously** (adv.) and **egregiousness** (n.).
- An archaic meaning of **egregious** is "distinguished or eminent."

**elegy**: [EL-uh-gee] Noun.
A song or poem expressing sorrow, especially for one who is dead.

- The songwriter wrote an **elegy** for the princess who had just died.
- She sang an **elegy** to her dead goldfish at the small memorial service she held for it.

*Synonym:* lament, dirge, requiem, ode, sonnet, ballad
*Antonym:* celebration

Further Information
- Originated from the Greek word *elegeia* meaning "mournful song."
- Not to be confused with **eulogy**, which refers to a praiseful speech about a dead person.
- Related word forms include **elegiac** (adj.).

**elicit**: [uh-LIS-it] Verb.
To call forth or draws out.

- The policeman hoped to **elicit** a confession from the man who was accused of stealing.
- The photos of the crime **elicited** cries from the courtroom attendees.

*Synonym:* evoke, extract, arouse, draw, provoke
*Antonym:* repress, conceal, hide

Further Information
- Originated from the Latin *elicere* meaning "to allure."
- Other related word forms include **elicitation** (n.) and **elicitor** (n.).
- **Elicit** should not be confused with **illicit,** which means "unlawful."

**elucidate**: [uh-LOO-se-dayt] Verb.
To explain or make clear.

- The interpreter **elucidated** the instructions for the non-English speaking persons in attendance.
- After my grandmother's death, her diaries helped to **elucidate** her life for those left behind.

*Synonym:* clarify, explain, explicate, expound, illuminate, illustrate
*Antonym:* confuse, obfuscate, puzzle

Further Information
- Originated from the Latin word *elucidare* meaning "to make light or clear."
- Words derived from the Latin *elucidare* include **lucid**, **lucidity**, and **translucent**.
- Other related word forms include **elucidation** (n.), **elucidator** (n.), and **elucidating** (v.).
- Not to be confused with **enunciate** which means "to pronounce clearly."

**emaciated**: [uh-MAY-shee-ayt-ed] Adjective.
The state or condition of being very thin. (adj.)

- Some of the sick animals refused to eat and became **emaciated**.
- The prisoners of war appeared **emaciated** from their long captivity.

*Synonym:* gaunt, lean, haggard, thin, skinny, scrawny
*Antonym:* chubby, obese, overweight

Further Information
- Originated from the Latin word *maciare* meaning "to make thin."
- Related words include **emaciation** (n.).
- **Emaciated** implies more than just thinness; rather, "malnourishment often resulting from illness."

**embezzlement**: [em-BEZ-el-ment] Noun.
The state or condition of having taken money or property one has been entrusted with for one's own personal use.

- The teller received 20 years in prison for **embezzlement** of the bank's funds.
- The accountant was easily able to **embezzle** money from his clients without their knowledge.

*Synonym:* stealing, misappropriation, robbery, theft, larceny, piracy
*Antonym:* reimbursement, compensation

Further Information

- Originated from the Anglo-French word *embesiller* meaning "to make away."
- Other related words include **embezzle** (v.), **embezzler** (n.) and **embezzling** (v.).
- Not to be confused with the British word **bezzle** which means "to waste or plunder" or "to eat or drink to excess."

**emollient**: [ih-MOL-yent] Adjective/Noun.
Softening and soothing, especially to the skin; making less harsh. (adj.)
Something that softens or soothes the skin; something that has a softening effect. (n.)

- Her kind words were an **emollient** to me after my boss's tirade against me this afternoon.
- The dermatologist recommended an **emollient** to soften her rough, dry skin.

*Synonym:* cream, ointment, salve, lotion, balm
*Antonym:* hardener

Further Information

- Originated from the Latin word *emollire* meaning "to soften."
- Other word forms include **emollience** (n.).
- **Emollient** is also less commonly spelled **emolient**.

**empirical**: [em-PEER-uh-kel] Adjective.
Originating in or based upon experience.

- The scientist's data was based on **empirical** evidence collected from many studies.
- She wanted **empirical** truth that he was lying to her before she would leave him.

*Synonym:* realistic, practical, observed, confirmable, provable, demonstrable
*Antonym:* theoretical, hypothetical, conjectural

Further Information

- Originated from the Greek word *empeirikos* meaning "based on observation of medical treatment."
- Related word forms are **empirically** (adv.) and **empiric** (n.).
- In ancient Greece, an **empiric** was a member of a sect of doctors who practiced medicine based solely on experience.

# REVIEW EXERCISE 11

*Match the word with its synonym.*

___ 1.   edict                 a.   stealing
___ 2.   edifice               b.   equal
___ 3.   effigy                c.   explain
___ 4.   egalitarian           d.   outrageous
___ 5.   egregious             e.   structure
___ 6.   elegy                 f.   provable
___ 7.   elicit                g.   requiem
___ 8.   elucidate             h.   gaunt
___ 9.   emaciated             i.   decree
___ 10.  embezzlement          j.   image
___ 11.  emollient             k.   evoke
___ 12.  empirical             l.   cream

*Fill in the blanks with the most appropriate word from list above.* *(Word form may need changing.)*

1.   The dictator laughed at the opposition's _____ ideas about economic status.

2.   The comedian hoped his jokes would _____ laughter from the audience.

3.   Science is based on _____ observations.

4.   The _____ properties of the lip balm helped to ease my chapped lips.

5.   The accountant was accused of _____ of his wealthy clients.

6.   The locket has an _____ of my mother inside it as a remembrance.

7.   Those fluent in sign language can use their hands to _____ their thoughts.

8.   My friend composed an _____ to sing at her mother's funeral.

9.   This state has an _____ forbidding texting while driving.

10.  He was _____ after spending five days in the desert without food or water.

11.  The man was sentenced to life in prison for his _____ acts of terrorism.

12.  The _____ where the royal couple was married receives millions of tourists each year.

# WORD SET 12

**emulate**: [EM-yoo-layt] Verb.
To try to equal or match, especially through imitation.

- She **emulated** the recipes and cooking techniques of her mother, hoping to become a good cook like her.
- The contestant on the singing competition **emulated** his favorite singer.

*Synonym:* imitate, mimic, copy, ape, echo, mirror
*Antonym:* neglect, ignore, spurn

Further Information

- Originated from the Latin word *aemulari* meaning "competing with."
- In computers, **emulate** refers to "imitating the function of another system through hardware or software modifications, allowing the imitating system to achieve the same results as the imitated system."
- Related word forms include **emulation** (n.), **emulative** (adj.) and **emulator** (n.).


**encumbrance**: [en-KUM-brens] Noun.
Something that is a burden, a hindrance or an impediment.

- Her debt was an **encumbrance** preventing her from obtaining a mortgage.
- My broken leg is an **encumbrance** to my social life, and I can't easily go anywhere because of it.

*Synonym:* hindrance, impediment, obstruction, burden, handicap, obstacle
*Antonym:* privilege, advantage, benefit

Further Information

- Originated from the Old French word *encombrance* meaning "obstruction, calamity, trouble."
- Related words include **encumber** (v.).
- In law, **encumbrance** refers to "a claim on property, such as a lien or mortgage."


**enervate**: [EN-er-vayt] Noun.
To weaken or destroy the strength of something or someone.

- The wolf chased the buffalo, hoping to **enervate** it enough to be able to kill it.
- The medication **enervated** her ability to concentrate at school.

*Synonym:* weaken, debilitate, sap, exhaust, fatigue, tire
*Antonym:* invigorate, energize, empower

Further Information

- Originated from the Latin *nervus* meaning "sinew."
- Related words include **enervation** (n.), **enervative** (adj.) and **enervator** (n.).
- As a medical term, **enervate** means "to remove a nerve or part of a nerve."

**enhance**: [en-HANS] Verb.
To improve or make better, especially in attractiveness, value or effectiveness.

- The saleswoman told him the blue suit would **enhance** his eyes.
- You can **enhance** your vocabulary by reading and discovering new words.

*Synonym:* improve, upgrade, heighten, raise, increase, magnify
*Antonym:* decrease, diminish, reduce

Further Information
- Originated from the Old French word *enhaucier* meaning "to raise."
- Another word derived from this Old French word is **haughty**.
- Related word forms include **enhancement** (n.), **enhancer** (n.) and **enhancive** (adj.).

**enigma**: [uh-NIG-muh] Noun.
A person, situation or thing that is ambiguous, mysterious or puzzling.

- The motive for the crime was an **enigma**.
- The doctor found his patient's abnormal behavior to be an **enigma**.

*Synonym:* riddle, mystery, conundrum, puzzle, secret, problem
*Antonym:* clarity, clearness

Further Information
- Originated from the Greek word *ainissesthai* meaning "to speak in riddles."
- The plural form of enigma is **enigmas** or **enigmata**.
- Related word forms include **enigmatic** (adj.), **enigmatical** (adj.) and **enigmatically** (adv.).

**ennui**: [ahn-WEE] Noun.
Dissatisfaction and listlessness resulting from lack of interest, boredom.

- He escaped the **ennui** of sitting around his mansion by going outside to play tennis.
- If you feel a sense of **ennui** working at your present job, you should change careers.

*Synonym:* boredom, tedium, fatigue, tiredness, apathy, dissatisfaction
*Antonym:* excitement, energy, liveliness

Further Information
- Originated from the Old French word *ennuyer* meaning "to annoy or bore."
- **Ennui** is also related to the Latin root *odio* meaning "to hate."
- **Ennui** often refers to "a feeling of boredom that results from living a life of luxury."

**entourage**: [AHN-tuh-razh] Noun.
A (usually important person's) group of attendants or associates; a person's environment or surroundings.

- The President is always accompanied by an **entourage** whenever he leaves the White House.
- The rock star had a devoted **entourage** of fans who followed him everywhere he went.

*Synonym:* retinue, train, suite, cortege, followers, milieu
*Antonym: none*
Further Information
- Originated from the Old French word *entour* meaning "surroundings."
- In topology, **entourage** means "a binary relation in a uniform space that generalizes the idea of two points being no farther apart than a given fixed distance."
- **Entourage** is sometimes used as slang for "one's social group of friends."

**enunciate**: [ih-NUN-see-āt] Verb.
To articulate or pronounce.

- The inebriated man could not **enunciate** his address so that the taxi driver could understand it.
- On the first day of class, the language teacher **enunciated** the rules of her classroom.

*Synonym:* pronounce, utter, articulate, voice, declare, announce
*Antonym:* mumble, mispronounce, muffle
Further Information
- Originated from the Latin word *enuntiare* meaning "to announce."
- Other related word forms include **enunciable** (adj.), **enunciation** (n.), and **enunciative** (adj.).
- **Enunciate** is often used when speaking about pronouncing in foreign languages, as in "be sure to properly **enunciate** when ordering in a French restaurant."
- Not to be confused with **elucidate** which means "to explain."

**ephemeral**: [ih-FEM-er-el] Adjective/Noun.
Lasting for a short time. (adj.)
Something that lives for a short time. (n.)

- Due to his **ephemeral** memory, he is always forgetting his car keys. (adj.)
- The **ephemeral** plant only blooms once before it dies. (n.)

*Synonym:* transitory, temporary, brief, passing, transient, momentary
*Antonym:* permanent, eternal, lasting
Further Information
- Originated from the Greek word *ephemeros* meaning "lasting only a day."
- Related words include **ephemerally** (adv.), **ephemerality** (n.) and **ephemeralness** (n.).
- **Ephemeral** is often used in biology or botany to describe "plants or living organisms that are short-lived."

**epitome**: [ih-PIT-uh-mee] Noun.
A perfect example; a brief summary of a written work.

- The runway model was the **epitome** of style and fashion.
- The emergency room doctor kept his cool in a crisis and was the **epitome** of professionalism.

*Synonym:* embodiment, example, ideal, summary, digest, synopsis
*Antonym:* expansion

Further Information
- Originated from the Greek word *epitemnein* meaning "to cut short."
- Related words include **epitomize** (v.), **epitomic** (adj.) and **epitomical** (adj.).
- While **epitome** used to mean "a summary," now it is more commonly used to mean "a clear, good example of something or someone."

**erudite**: [ER-eh-dīt] Adjective.
Having or demonstrating great learning or knowledge.

- The **erudite** librarian was able to answer almost every question posed to her by visitors.
- With my poor grade point average, I felt out of place among all the **erudite** scholars in the room.

*Synonym:* scholarly, learned, educated, knowledgeable, well-read, literate
*Antonym:* ignorant, uneducated, dumb

Further Information
- Originated from the Latin word *eruditus* meaning "to instruct."
- Other word forms include **erudition** (n.), **eruditeness** (n.) and **eruditely** (adv.).
- **Erudite** can also be pronounced ER-yuh-dīt.

**eschew**: [eh-SHOO] Verb.
To avoid using, participating in, or accepting; to refrain from doing something.

- She **eschewed** the prom because dancing was against her religious beliefs.
- The recluse decided to **eschew** society and settled on a deserted island.

*Synonym:* shun, avoid, evade, forego, elude, abstain
*Antonym:* embrace, pursue, confront

Further Information
- Originated from the Anglo-French word *eschiver* meaning "to frighten away."
- **Eschew** is also related to the Old High German word *sciuhen* which is also related to the English word "shy."
- Other word forms include **eschewal** (n.), **eschewed** (v.) and **eschewing** (v.).

# REVIEW EXERCISE 12

*Match the word with its synonym.*

| | | | | | |
|---|---|---|---|---|---|
| ___ | 1. | emulate | a. | example |
| ___ | 2. | encumbrance | b. | pronounce |
| ___ | 3. | enervate | c. | mystery |
| ___ | 4. | enhance | d. | hindrance |
| ___ | 5. | enigma | e. | boredom |
| ___ | 6. | ennui | f. | imitate |
| ___ | 7. | entourage | g. | weaken |
| ___ | 8. | enunciate | h. | shun |
| ___ | 9. | ephemeral | i. | improve |
| ___ | 10. | epitome | j. | transitory |
| ___ | 11. | erudite | k. | followers |
| ___ | 12. | eschew | l. | scholarly |

*Fill in the blanks with the most appropriate word from list above.* (Word form may need changing.)

1. His self-criticism was an_____ to his own satisfaction with his work.

2. The teacher explained the math _____ written on the whiteboard.

3. The king's_____ accompanied him wherever he went.

4. I must find an _____ math tutor to help me improve my grades.

5. She hoped to _____her successful brother's study habits and earn all A's.

6. As a vegetarian, I _____ any food products that come from animals.

7. The award-winning film is the _____ of classic war movies.

8. The professor's boring lecture filled the class with _____.

9. The marriage was _____, lasting only three weeks.

10. The tour guide's _____ was not good and I couldn't understand a word.

11. The room's attractiveness was _____by the new sofa.

12. The wound did not_____ the robber enough to slow him down during the chase.

# WORD SET 13

**esoteric**: [es-eh-TER-ek] Adjective/Noun.
Intended for or understood by a small group with specialized interests or knowledge. (adj.)
A person or thing that is understood by a small group. (n.)

- The specialized course was very **esoteric**, appealing to a small group of interested students.
- This class is so focused that it seems to be just an exercise in **esoterica**.

*Synonym:* profound, secret, difficult, intricate, complicated, recondite
*Antonym:* exoteric, common, known
Further Information
- Originated from the Greek word *esotero* meaning "inner."
- **Esoterica** and **esoterics** are both acceptable plurals of **esoteric**.
- Related word forms include **esoterically** (adv.) and **esotericism** (n.).


**espouse**: [eh-SPOUZ] Verb.
To adhere to, to advocate.

- The candidate perfectly **espouses** the ideals of the Republican Party.
- Although he was brought up Protestant, he **espoused** Catholicism when he married a Catholic.

*Synonym:* adopt, embrace, support, advocate, defend, back
*Antonym:* disown, discard, reject
Further Information
- Originated from the Old French word *espouser* meaning "to marry."
- An archaic meaning of **espouse** is "to take as a spouse" or "to marry."
- Related word forms include **espouser** (n.), **espoused** (v.) and **espousing** (v.).


**estimable**: [ES-teh-meh-bel] Adjective.
Admirable, deserving of esteem.
Possible to be computed or calculated.

- The **estimable** business performs many community service projects in our city.
- Although the distance on the map may be hard to comprehend, it is **estimable**.

*Synonym:* worthy, creditable, respectable, admirable, praiseworthy, meritorious
*Antonym:* outrageous, undeserving, unworthy
Further Information
- Originated from the Latin word *aestimare* meaning "to value."
- Related words include **estimate** (v.), **estimably** (adv.) and **estimableness** (n.).
- An archaic meaning of **estimable** is "valuable."

**eulogy**: [YOO-leh-gee] Noun.
A highly praising speech or tribute, especially about someone who has died; commendation.

- Despite her tears, she gave a moving **eulogy** at her mother's funeral.
- Her boss added his praise to the warm **eulogies** given by her associates.

*Synonym:* praise, encomium, tribute, compliment, endorsement, commendation
*Antonym:* abuse, criticism, censure

Further Information
- Originated from the Greek word *eulogia* meaning "praise."
- An archaic word for **eulogy** is **eulogium**.
- Not to be confused with **elegy**, which is "a poem or song, especially one written for the dead."


**euphemism**: [YOO-fe-miz-em] Noun.
A milder or more indirect term for a word that is considered offensive or harsh.

- The phrase "to pass away" is a **euphemism** for "to die."
- The little boy asked to "go pee," which is a polite **euphemism** for "urinate."

*Synonym:* expression, alternative, allegory, analogue, metaphor, purism
*Antonym:* dysphemism

Further Information
- Originated from the Greek word *euphemizein* meaning "to use auspicious words."
- Related word forms include **euphemist** (n.), **euphemistic** (adj.) and **euphemistically** (adv.).
- Other words containing the "eu" prefix, which means "well," include **eulogy, euphoria** and **euthanasia**.


**evanescence**: [ev-uh-NES-sents] Noun.
Something that is gradually fading away or vanishing, transitory.

- Because they do not last for long, rainbows are as **evanescent** as they are beautiful.
- As the snow melted into water, it became **evanescent.**

*Synonym:* evaporation, disappearance, transience, dissolution, vanishing, impermanence
*Antonym:* eternity

Further Information
- Originated from the Latin word *evanescere* meaning "to vanish."
- Related word forms include **evanesce** (v.), **evanesces** (n.), **evanescent** (adj.) and **evanescing** (v.).
- **Evanescent** is a more formal way to say "fleeting" or "momentary."

**exacting**: [ig-SAK-ting] Adjective.
Rigorous or making severe demands.
Requiring great attention, effort or care.

- The **exacting** teacher required his students to correctly space an assignment before turning it in.
- The task of placing the cards on top of each other in a house was quite **exacting**.

*Synonym:* demanding, strict, scrupulous, fastidious, severe, meticulous
*Antonym:* simple, easy

Further Information
- Originated from the Latin word *exigere* meaning "to drive out or demand, or to measure."
- Other words derived from the Latin root *agere* include **navigate, mitigate**, **react** and **agent**.
- Related word forms include **exactingly** (adv.) and **exactingness** (n.).

**exasperate**: [ig-ZAS-pe-rayt] Verb.
To annoy, make impatient or angry.

- Although she likes her doctor, it **exasperates** her to have to wait two hours to see him.
- I was **exasperated** when my neighbors played their music late at night.

*Synonym:* annoy, irritate, vex, infuriate, provoke, aggravate
*Antonym:* please, calm, placate

Further Information
- Originated from the Latin word *exasperare* meaning "to make rough."
- Related word forms include **exasperation** (n.), **exasperatedly** (adv.) and **exasperatingly** (adv.).
- In botany, **exasperate** means "having a rough, prickly surface."

**excruciating**: [ik-SKROO-shee-ay-ting] Adjective.
Agonizing or intensely painful; extreme or intense.

- The pain of my migraine was so **excruciating** I had to take a painkiller.
- The experience of sitting on the witness stand was **excruciating** for the young child.

*Synonym:* agonizing, painful, tormenting, harrowing, piercing, distressing
*Antonym:* painless, comfortable, pleasant

Further Information
- Originated from the Latin word *excruciare* meaning "to torture, plague or torment."
- Related word forms include **excruciatingly** (adv.).
- A slang usage of **excruciating** is "very bad."

**exculpate**: [ek-SKUL-payt] Verb.
To clear of blame or guilt.

- After a thorough investigation, the police **exculpated** him, finding no evidence to charge him.
- In court, the defense attorney presented evidence to **exculpate** his client.

*Synonym:* exonerate, acquit, excuse, absolve, clear, vindicate
*Antonym:* condemn, convict, accuse

Further Information
- Originated from the Latin word *exculpare* meaning "without guilt."
- Other words derived from the Latin root *culpa* include **inculpate** and **culpable**.
- Related word forms include **exculpable** (adj.) and **exculpation** (n.).


**exhaustive**: [ig-ZAW-stiv] Adjective.
Thorough, including all possibilities.
Tiring, causing exhaustion.

- The **exhaustive** study still did not come up with a cause for the mysterious disease.
- Building the house was **exhaustive** work for the group of volunteers.

*Synonym:* thorough, complete, full, wearisome, tiresome, jaded
*Antonym:* incomplete, shallow, superficial

Further Information
- Originated from the Latin word *exhaustus* meaning "to draw off or take away."
- Related word forms include **exhaustively** (adv.), **exhaustiveness** (n.) and **exhaustivity** (n.).
- Exhaustive is also related to the Middle High German word *oesen* meaning "to empty."


**expatiate**: [ek-SPAY-shee-ayt] Verb.
To write or speak in detail or at length.

- The author **expatiated** on his travels in Africa during the book signing.
- The long-winded instructor tends to **expatiate** on any subject during class.

*Synonym:* expand, enlarge, elaborate, dilate, amplify, expound
*Antonym:* contract

Further Information
- Originated from the Latin word *exspatiari* meaning "to go out of one's course."
- An archaic meaning of **expatiate** is "to roam or wander freely."
- Other related word forms include **expatiation** (n.), **expatiated** (v.) and **expatiating** (v.).

# REVIEW EXERCISE 13

*Match the word with its synonym.*

| | | | | |
|---|---|---|---|---|
| ___ | 1. | esoteric | a. | acquit |
| ___ | 2. | espouse | b. | annoy |
| ___ | 3. | estimable | c. | adopt |
| ___ | 4. | eulogy | d. | praise |
| ___ | 5. | euphemism | e. | evaporation |
| ___ | 6. | evanescence | f. | secret |
| ___ | 7. | exacting | g. | demanding |
| ___ | 8. | exasperate | h. | elaborate |
| ___ | 9. | excruciating | i. | agonizing |
| ___ | 10. | exculpate | j. | worthy |
| ___ | 11. | exhaustive | k. | expression |
| ___ | 12. | expatiate | l. | thorough |

*Fill in the blanks with the most appropriate word from list above.* (Word form may need changing.)

1.  The scientist_____ the Big Bang Theory for the creation of the universe.

2.  The foreign students in class were confused by the teacher's _____.

3.  The evidence was enough to _____ the suspect from the crime.

4.  The _____ moment did not escape the photographer's lens.

5.  It was _____to watch the video footage of animal abuse.

6.  The _____ medical research could only be understood by a few doctors.

7.  The man was intelligent and liked to _____ on many different subjects.

8.  She sobbed as she listened to her uncle give her father's _____at his funeral.

9.  Her _____client required her to work through the holidays.

10. The _____ teacher asked the principal to suspend the student.

11.  I could not find my keys despite an _____search of my house.

12. The _____ professor won many awards for his Alzheimer's disease research.

# WORD SET 14

**expatriate**: [ek-SPAY-tree-ayt] Verb/Noun/Adjective.
To banish or exile, or to leave one's home country to live elsewhere. (v.)
A person who lives in a foreign country. (n.)
Living in a foreign country. (adj.)

- Candidates for this job should be willing to **expatriate**, as it is in another country. (v.)
- The **expatriate** had moved from his home country of America to Great Britain. (n.)
- The **expatriate** agents were told to go to their home countries and await further orders. (adj.)

*Synonym:* exile, deport, banish, outcast, expel, ostracize
*Antonym:* repatriate, home, allow

Further Information
- Originated from the Latin word *expatriatus* meaning "to leave one's own country."
- Related word forms include **expatriation** (n.).
- **Expatriate** should not be confused with a **migrant**, who "moves to another country for work or better living conditions," or an **immigrant**, who "moves to live permanently in another country."

**expedient**: [ek-SPEE-dee-ent] Adjective/Noun.
Something that is suitable to achieve a specific goal in a given situation. (adj.)
Something that is done or used to achieve a specific goal either temporarily or quickly. (n.)

- It is **expedient** for the candidate to maintain good relationships with both political parties. (adj.)
- We obtained more money through the **expedient** of taking out a loan. (n.)

*Synonym:* convenient, useful, opportune, advantageous, desirable, suitable
*Antonym:* useless, inexpedient, inappropriate

Further Information
- Originated from the Latin word *expedire* meaning "to prepare or be useful."
- Related word forms include **expediently** (adv.).
- **Expedient** is also the brand name of a cloud infrastructure service provider in the United States.

**expiate**: [EK-spee-ayt] Verb.
To make amends for, to get rid of the guilt of something or someone.

- The religious sacrifice was meant to **expiate** the sins of the congregation.
- He had no idea how he would **expiate** the fact that he forgot his wedding anniversary.

*Synonym:* atone, redeem, compensate, redress, absolve, recompense
*Antonym:* embezzle, hock, pawn

Further Information
- Originated from the Latin word *expiare* meaning "to atone for."
- Related words include **expiable** (adj.) and **expiator** (n.).

**explicit:** [ek-SPLIH-set] Adjective.
Clear and without vagueness.
Fully formed or developed.

- She gave her family **explicit** instructions on what to do upon her death.
- The robbers had an **explicit** plan for robbing the bank, which is why they succeeded in doing so.

*Synonym:* definite, clear, exact, unequivocal, unambiguous, unmistakable
*Antonym:* vague, implicit, ambiguous

Further Information
- Originated from the Latin word *explicare* meaning "to unfold."
- In mathematics, **explicit** refers to "an expression containing only independent variables."
- Other word forms include **explicitly** (adv.) and **explicitness** (n.).


**exponent:** [EK-spo-nent] Noun.
In mathematics, a symbol written above to the right of an expression to denote raising to a power.
A person who interprets, supports, or is a representative of something or someone.

- To correctly perform the mathematical equation, you need to understand the **exponent**.
- She has become one of the leading **exponents** of the idea of socialized medicine.

*Synonym:* supporter, advocate, proponent, champion, backer, defender
*Antonym:* enemy, antagonist

Further Information
- Originated from the Latin word *exponere* meaning "to explain or set forth."
- Another word containing the Latin root *ponere* is **proponent.**
- An **exponent** can also mean "one who expounds."


**expunge:** [ek-SPUNJ] Verb.
To obliterate, destroy, or eliminate.

- The tornadoes **expunged** all signs of civilization in the community.
- The professor showed her what to **expunge** from the final draft of her report.

*Synonym:* erase, obliterate, delete, cancel, eradicate, eliminate
*Antonym:* create, build, construct

Further Information
- Originated from the Latin word *expungere* meaning "to mark for deletion."
- Related word forms include **expunger** (n.), **expunging** (v.) and **expunged** (v.).
- In medieval manuscripts, a series of dots, called *puncta delentia,* was used to mark material that needed to be **expunged** from the text.

**expurgate**: [EK-sper-gayt] Verb.
To remove something harmful or offensive from something else.

- The newspaper **expurgated** the abusive language from the fired teacher's remarks prior to publication.
- His name was **expurgated** from the agency's records as if he never worked there.

*Synonym:* censor, expunge, edit, bowdlerize, clean, purge
*Antonym:* permit, allow, authorize

Further Information
- Originated from the Latin word *expurgatus* meaning "to purge."
- Related word forms include **expurgation (**n.) and **expurgator** (n.).
- In 1818 Thomas Bowdler published an expurgated edition of Shakespeare's plays called *The Family Shakespeare*. As a result, **bowdlerize** is now a synonym of **expurgate**.

**extant**: [ek-STANT or EK-stant] Adjective.
Currently in existence or still in existence.

- Football fans will be sad to learn that there is no **extant** copy of the television broadcast of Super Bowl I.
- There are very few **extant** records that survived that period of time.

*Synonym:* existent, existing, present, alive, current, actual
*Antonym:* extinct, dead, defunct

Further Information
- Originated from the Latin word *exstans* meaning "to stand out."
- **Extant** is the opposite of **extinct**, which means "no longer existing."
- An archaic meaning of **extant** is "standing above or standing out."

**extol**: [ek-STOL] Verb.
To give high praise to, to glorify.

- The candidate's military record was **extolled** by the representative speaking about him.
- The fan wrote a letter to her favorite actor **extolling** his acting skills.

*Synonym:* praise, glorify, exalt, celebrate, commend, laud
*Antonym:* criticize, blame, condemn

Further Information
- Originated from the Latin word *extollere* meaning "to lift up."
- **Extol** may also be spelled **extoll**.
- Related word forms include **extoller** (n.) and **extolment** (n.).

**extraneous**: [ek-STRAY-nee-us] Adjective.
Coming from the outside.
Not being an essential part of or having no relevance.

- **Extraneous** light filtered in through the curtains, making it hard to see the screen.
- The DNA obtained at the crime scene was found to be **extraneous** and not related to the crime.

*Synonym:* foreign, irrelevant, extrinsic, alien, unrelated, inappropriate
*Antonym:* appropriate, relevant, pertinent

Further Information
- Originated from the Anglo-French word *estrange* meaning "outside or extra."
- A mathematical meaning of **extraneous** is "a number obtained in solving an equation that is not a solution of that equation."
- Related word forms include **extraneously** (adv.) and **extraneousness** (n.).

**exult**: [eg-ZULT] Verb.
To be very joyful.

- The student **exulted** in the good news that she had won the scholarship.
- Fans **exulted** as their team piled up the touchdowns.

*Synonym:* delight, rejoice, gloat, triumph, glory, celebrate
*Antonym:* lament, mourn, grieve

Further Information
- Originated from the Latin word *exsultare* meaning "to leap up."
- Related word forms include **exultingly** (adv.) and **exulting** (v.).
- An archaic meaning of **exult** is "to jump for joy."

**facetious**: [fuh-SEE-shes] Adjective.
Jokingly inappropriate, meant to be funny or humorous.

- Although we thought she was serious in her remarks, she was only being **facetious**.
- The comedian told **facetious** religious jokes in front of the church members.

*Synonym:* humorous, jocular, witty, funny, comical, playful
*Antonym:* serious, grave, solemn

Further Information
- Originated from the French word *facetieux* meaning "joking remark."
- Other related word forms include **facetiously** (adv.) and **facetiousness** (n.).
- **Facetious** is one of the few English words containing in alphabetical order the vowels a, e, i, o, and u.

# REVIEW EXERCISE 14

*Match the word with its synonym.*

| | | | | |
|---|---|---|---|---|
| ___ | 1. | expatriate | a. | existing |
| ___ | 2. | expedient | b. | irrelevant |
| ___ | 3. | expiate | c. | clear |
| ___ | 4. | explicit | d. | delete |
| ___ | 5. | exponent | e. | delight |
| ___ | 6. | expunge | f. | convenient |
| ___ | 7. | expurgate | g. | exile |
| ___ | 8. | extant | h. | humorous |
| ___ | 9. | extol | i. | advocate |
| ___ | 10. | extraneous | j. | atone |
| ___ | 11. | exult | k. | censor |
| ___ | 12. | facetious | l. | praise |

*Fill in the blanks with the most appropriate word from list above.* (*Word form may need changing.*)

1. He _____ over his wife's pregnancy, because he was so happy.

2. As she described her son to her friends she _____ his virtues.

3. The judge _____ the crimes from the boy's permanent record.

4. Her _____ remarks were inappropriate at her uncle's funeral.

5. I left _____details telling my pet-sitter how to feed my dog.

6. The girl must _____ somehow for breaking the neighbor's window.

7. The rapper _____ offensive words from his song to get airplay.

8. The doctor is an _____of healthy eating and speaks about it often.

9. It is _____that we leave the house quickly before the tornado hits.

10. He is an _____ who left his home country to live in Spain.

11. It was surprising to learn that the species was _____and not extinct.

12. The _____ noise from the next apartment kept me awake at night.

# WORD SET 15

**facile**: [FAH-sel] Adjective.
Easy to accomplish or comprehend.
Ready or fluent.
Often lacking in depth or sincerity, superficial.

- The difficult problem could not have such a **facile** solution.
- The **facile** prose flowed easily from the tongue.
- Her **facile** tears leaked a bit too easily and quickly to be genuine.

*Synonym:* easy, fluent, simple, superficial, smooth, effortless
*Antonym:* difficult, harsh, profound
Further Information
- Originated from the Latin word *facilis* meaning "nimble, easy."
- An archaic meaning of **facile** is "pleasing or mild in disposition or manner."
- Related words include **facilely** (adv.) and **facileness** (n.).

**facilitate**: [feh-SIL-eh-tayt) Verb.
To help to bring about, to make easier.

- The diplomat **facilitated** a peace treaty between the two opposing countries.
- Some believe that cutting taxes will **facilitate** the country's economic growth.

*Synonym:* assist, ease, help, expedite, aid, promote
*Antonym:* hinder, complicate, delay
Further Information
- Originated from the Middle French word *faciliter* meaning "to make easy."
- Related word forms include **facilitative** (adj.).
- **Facilitate** is also derived from the Latin word *facilis* meaning "easy."

**fanciful**: [FANT-si-fel] Adjective.
Marked by imagination and not experience or reason.

- The little girl dreamed up a **fanciful** plan for becoming a princess.
- The **fanciful** tale told by the library's storyteller amused the children.

*Synonym:* fantastic, imaginary, visionary, unreal, whimsical, illusory
*Antonym:* realistic, existent, ordinary
Further Information
- Originated from the Middle English word *fantasie* meaning "imagination."
- Related words include **fancifully** (adj.) and **fancifulness** (n.).
- Obsolete spellings of **fanciful** include **phanciful** and **phancifull**.

**fathom:** [FAH-them] Noun/Verb.
A unit of length equal to six feet, used to measure the depth of water. (n.)
To come to understand. (v.)

- How many **fathoms** below the surface of the water does the shipwreck lie? (n.)
- I can't **fathom** how he escaped punishment for that heinous crime. (v.)

*Synonym:* comprehend, understand, grasp, perceive, get
*Antonym:* misunderstand, mislead, perplex

Further Information
- Originated from the Old English word *faethm* meaning "outstretched arms."
- **Fathom** originally meant "the distance from fingertip to fingertip of outstretched arms."
- Other word forms include **fathomable** (adj.).


**fatuous:** [FAH-chu-es] Adjective.
Foolish.

- The student's **fatuous** questions convinced the teacher that he did not understand the material.
- She was a **fatuous** socialite with a love of shopping and parties.

*Synonym:* silly, asinine, foolish, idiotic, stupid, absurd
*Antonym:* clever, intelligent, smart

Further Information
- Originated from the Latin word *fatuus* meaning "foolish."
- Related word forms include **fatuously** (adv.) and **fatuousness** (n.).
- Other words derived from *fatuus* include **infatuated**.


**feasible:** [FEE-ze-bel] Adjective.
Reasonable, capable of being done or used.

- The president is looking for a **feasible** way to create more jobs for the country.
- Is it **feasible** to expect the construction company to build a house in such a short time?

*Synonym:* possible, practicable, attainable, viable, workable, achievable
*Antonym:* impossible, unsustainable, inconceivable

Further Information
- Originated from the Anglo-French word *faisable* meaning "to make, to do."
- Related word forms include **feasibility** (n.), **feasibly** (adv.) and **feasibleness** (n.).
- A **feasibility** study is "a study of whether an idea or concept is doable."

**felicitous:** [fih-LIH-suh-tus] Adjective.
Well-suited or expressed; pleasant, opportune.

- The chance meeting between them was **felicitous**, as they ended up marrying three years later.
- The recipe included a **felicitous** combination of flavors that meshed quite well.

*Synonym:* happy, fitting, appropriate, good, apt, fit
*Antonym:* improper, inappropriate, unsuitable

Further Information
- Originated from the Old French word *felicite* meaning "happiness."
- Also derived from the Latin root *felix* meaning "fruitful, happy."
- Related word forms include **felicitousness** (n.) and **felicitously** (adv.).


**fetter:** [FEH-tehr] Noun/Verb.
A chain or shackle, a restraint. (n.)
To shackle or restrain. (v.)

- The man felt **fettered** by all his responsibilities. (v.)
- The kidnapped girl had marks on her ankles where **fetters** had been. (n.)

*Synonym:* shackle, chain, restrain, handcuff, manacle, tie
*Antonym:* free, release, loosen

Further Information
- Originated from the Middle English word *feter* meaning "foot."
- Related words include **fettered** (v.) and **fettering** (v.).


**fiat:** [FEE-at] Noun.
A command or authoritative order.

- The leader runs his country by **fiat** and everyone is expected to obey his demands.
- The principal's **fiat** bans the wearing of shorts in school.

*Synonym:* edict, dictum, order, decree, command, mandate
*Antonym:* request

Further Information
- Originated from the Latin word *fieri* meaning "to become, to be done."
- The legal definition of **fiat** is "a decree, or an arbitrary order."
- **Fiat** is also an automotive brand.

**fidelity**: [fuh-DEL-uh-tee] Noun.
The state of being faithful or exact.
The degree to which an electronic device correctly reproduces a visual or audio effect.

- After he admitted to adultery, the man's **fidelity** to his wife was always in question.
- The store was selling the high-**fidelity** version of the recording.

*Synonym:* faithfulness, loyalty, allegiance, devotion, fealty, constancy
*Antonym:* treachery, infidelity, disloyalty
Further Information
- Originated from the Latin word *fidelis* meaning "faithful."
- Other words derived from *fidelis* include **fiduciary** and **confide**.
- A good **fidelity** recording should be "faithful" to the live picture or sound that it reproduces.

**figurative**: [FIG-ye-re-tive] Adjective.
Representing by a figure.
Expressing one thing by relating it to another.

- The **figurative** statue represented the men who died in the war.
- The book was full of **figurative** language that made it a pleasure to read.

*Synonym:* illustrative, metaphorical, nonliteral, allegorical, flowery
*Antonym:* literal, real
Further Information
- Originated from the Middle English word *figuratif* meaning "representing symbolically."
- Related word forms include **figuratively** (adv.) and **figurativeness** (n.).
- **Literal** is the opposite of **figurative** in language.

**finesse**: [fuh-NES] Noun/Verb.
Refinement in structure or texture. (n.)
Skillful handling of a situation. (n.)
To bring about by skillful handling. (v.)

- The intricate details in the jewelry showed extreme **finesse**. (n.)
- He handled the interviewer's tactless questions with **finesse**. (n.)
- He **finessed** his way through the more difficult issues of the situation. (v.)

*Synonym:* skill, tact, adroitness, delicacy, polish, artfulness
*Antonym:* mishandle, clumsiness, ignorance
Further Information
- Originated from the French word *finesse* meaning "subtlety or fineness."
- Other related word forms include **finessed** (v.) and **finessing** (v.).

# REVIEW EXERCISE 15

*Match the word with its synonym.*

____ 1.  facile                a.  illustrative
____ 2.  facilitate            b.  possible
____ 3.  fanciful              c.  assist
____ 4.  fathom               d.  easy
____ 5.  fatuous              e.  order
____ 6.  feasible             f.  skill
____ 7.  felicitous           g.  imaginary
____ 8.  fetter               h.  appropriate
____ 9.  fiat                 i.  faithfulness
____ 10. fidelity             j.  comprehend
____ 11. figurative           k.  silly
____ 12. finesse              l.  restrain

*Fill in the blanks with the most appropriate word from list above. (Word form may need changing.)*

1.  The_____ prevented the slave from walking about freely.

2.  A simile is a type of _____ language.

3.  The boy's _____ choice of not tying his shoe caused him to trip and fall.

4.  I cannot _____ why you would make such a remark at a funeral.

5.  Because I studied all night the exam was _____to me.

6.  The mediator _____ the settlement between the two parties.

7.  The little girl's party had a _____ princess theme.

8.  He has complete _____to the charity for which he raises money.

9.  The kids had a _____time playing indoors since it was raining outside.

10. We hired Jim a tutor to make school more _____ for him.

11.  The champion beat other players by playing the game with _____.

12. Prices on that class of goods have been fixed by government _____.

# WORD SET 16

**flag**: [FLAG] Noun/Verb.
A rectangular piece of fabric used as a symbol. (n.)
To become unsteady or weak or decline in interest or value. (v.)
To signal to stop or to penalize. (v.)
To mark or identify. (v.)

- The **flag** flew at half-staff to commemorate the former president's death. (n.)
- After a long day of hiking around the historical monuments, our interest began to **flag**. (v.)
- He **flagged** down the taxi to get it to stop to pick him up. (v.)
- She **flagged** the spots in the garden where she wished to plant her flowers. (v.)

*Synonym:* banner, signal, languish, weaken, droop, fade
*Antonym:* strengthen
Further Information
- Originated from the Middle English word *flagge* meaning "turf."
- Related words include **flagged** (v.) and **flagging** (v.).

**flagrant**: [FLAY-grant] Adjective.
Conspicuously bad or inconsistent with what is proper or right.

- Sanctions were imposed upon the country due to its **flagrant** violations of human rights.
- His **flagrant** abuse of public office got him kicked out of office.

*Synonym:* blatant, outrageous, atrocious, glaring, shameless, heinous
*Antonym:* discreet, concealed, hidden
Further Information
- Originated from the Latin word *flagrans* meaning "to burn."
- Related word forms include **flagrantly** (adv.).
- An archaic meaning of **flagrant** is "fiery hot or burning."

**fleeting**: [FLEE-ting] Adjective.
Lasting only for a short time, quickly passing.

- Her happiness was **fleeting,** and she was soon back in the throes of depression.
- He had a **fleeting** desire to jump in the mud puddle but was able to restrain himself.

*Synonym:* transient, transitory, ephemeral, passing, temporary, evanescent
*Antonym:* ceaseless, perpetual, endless
Further Information
- Originated from the Old English word *fleotende* meaning "drifting or floating."
- Related words include **fleetingly** (adv.) and **fleetingness** (n.).
- **Fleeting** implies "something that fades so quickly that it is difficult to see or understand."

**foible:** [FOY-bel] Noun.
A minor weakness or flaw.

- She tolerates her husband's **foibles** because of her great love for him.
- The many **foibles** of the politician are often spoken of and written about in the media.

*Synonym:* weakness, failing, fault, imperfection, flaw, frailty
*Antonym:* strength

Further Information
- Originated from the now obsolete French word *foible* meaning "weak."
- A **foible** was once known as "the weakest part of a sword between the point and the middle."
- The plural of **foible** is **foibles**.

**foment:** [FOH-ment] Verb.
To promote the development or growth of something or someone.

- The protester was accused of **fomenting** violence among the crowd.
- The women promised to **foment** a rebellion if they did not receive equal rights.

*Synonym:* provoke, incite, stimulate, excite, instigate, inflame
*Antonym:* tranquilize, allay, soothe

Further Information
- Originated from the Latin word *fomentare* meaning "compress."
- Related word forms include **fomentation** (n.) and **fomenter** (n.).
- The medical definition of **fomentation** is "to apply hot moist substances to relieve pain."

**forbearance:** [for-BER-ents] Noun.
Having patience and leniency.

- The teacher showed great **forbearance** in dealing with the young child's tantrum.
- The director appreciated the audience's **forbearance** while he handled the theatre's audio problems.

*Synonym:* patience, tolerance, restraint, indulgence, kindness, leniency
*Antonym:* impatience, harshness, anger

Further Information
- Originated from the Middle English word *forberen* meaning "to do without or endure."
- The legal definition of **forbearance** is "refraining from enforcing something that is due."
- **Forbearance** may also be spelled **forebearance.**

**foreshadow:** [for-SHAH-dow] Verb.
To suggest, indicate or hint at something beforehand.

- The climax of the plot is **foreshadowed** in the book's first chapter.
- His early interest in cars **foreshadowed** his later career as a racecar driver.

*Synonym:* predict, portend, augur, bode, presage, foretell
*Antonym:* flashback

Further Information
- Originated from the Old English word *forescywa* meaning "shadow."
- Related word forms include **foreshadower** (n.) and **foreshadowing** (v.) or (n.).
- The first known usage of **foreshadow** in English was in the 1570s.


**forfeit:** [FOR-fet] Noun/Verb.
Something lost, especially by an error, neglect of duty or offense. (n.)
The act of losing something especially by abandonment, error or offense. (v.)

- They were required to pay a **forfeit** when they redeemed the item. (n.)
- He **forfeited** his right to trial by jury when he agreed to sentencing by the judge. (v.)

*Synonym:* lose, penalty, fine, loss, relinquish, surrender
*Antonym:* win, gain, victory

Further Information
- Originated from the Anglo-French word *forsfaire* meaning "to commit a crime."
- Related words include **forfeitable** (adj.) and **forfeiter** (n.).
- The plural of **forfeit** is **forfeits**.


**fortify:** [FOR-te-fey] Verb.
To make strong.

- She **fortified** her argument by providing convincing evidence.
- The soldiers **fortified** the city by building high walls.

*Synonym:* strengthen, brace, reinforce, invigorate, energize, support
*Antonym:* weaken, soften, hurt

Further Information
- Originated from the Latin word *fortis* meaning "strong."
- Related word forms include **fort** (n.), **fortress** (n.), **fortification** (n.) and **fortifier** (n.).
- Other words derived from *fortis* include **comfort, effort, forcible, fortitude** and **fortissimo**.

**fortuitous**: [for-TOO-uh-tus] Adjective.
Happening by chance, lucky.

- His presence at the job fair when his prospective new boss walked in was **fortuitous.**
- You could not have arrived at the party at a more **fortuitous** time.

*Synonym:* accidental, fortunate, happy, chance, incidental, lucky
*Antonym:* unlucky, intentional, deliberate

Further Information
- Originated from the Latin word *fors* meaning "chance."
- Other words related to **fortuitous** include **fortuitously** (adv.) and **fortuitousness** (n.).
- Another word related to **fortuitous** and derived from the Latin *fors* is its synonym, **fortunate.**

**fractious**: [FRAK-shes] Adjective.
Troublesome and unruly, irritable.

- The **fractious** crowd outside the courthouse grew violent when the verdict was read.
- The new teacher found the **fractious** students impossible to control.

*Synonym:* peevish, petulant, testy, irritable, refractory, cross
*Antonym:* obedient, agreeable, patient

Further Information
- Originated from the Latin word *frangere* meaning "to break or shatter."
- Related word forms include **fractiously** (adv.) and **fractiousness** (n.).
- Other words derived from *frangere* include **fragile** and **fraction.**

**fray**: [FRAA] Noun/Verb.
A disorderly fight or dispute. (n.)
To wear out. (v.)
To show signs of strain or irritation. (v.)

- Fighting in that nation could easily lure other countries into the **fray**. (n.)
- He picked at the hem of his sweater so often that it **frayed**. (v.)
- The new, ambiguous school rules had **frayed** the students' tempers. (v.)

*Synonym:* fight, ruckus, brawl, fracas, affray, battle
*Antonym:* harmony, agreement

Further Information
- Originated from the Anglo-French word *freir* meaning "to rub."
- Other related word forms include **frayed** (v.) and **fraying** (v.).
- An archaic meaning of **fray** is "to frighten away."

# REVIEW EXERCISE 16

*Match the word with its synonym.*

| | | | | |
|---|---|---|---|---|
| ___ | 1. | flag | a. | fortunate |
| ___ | 2. | flagrant | b. | lose |
| ___ | 3. | fleeting | c. | fight |
| ___ | 4. | foible | d. | weakness |
| ___ | 5. | foment | e. | blatant |
| ___ | 6. | forbearance | f. | passing |
| ___ | 7. | foreshadow | g. | weaken |
| ___ | 8. | forfeit | h. | patience |
| ___ | 9. | fortify | i. | strengthen |
| ___ | 10. | fortuitous | j. | provoke |
| ___ | 11. | fractious | k. | predict |
| ___ | 12. | fray | l. | irritable |

*Fill in the blanks with the most appropriate word from list above. (Word form may need changing.)*

1. He was_____ and chose all six winning lottery numbers.

2. The teacher showed _____ with the young child learning to read.

3. The crowd became _____ when the rapper was late to the stage.

4. The brief rain shower was _____ and did not relieve the humidity.

5. Driving drunk shows _____disregard for others' safety.

6. His one _____ is his weakness for online shopping.

7. Because we didn't have enough team members we had to _____ the game.

8. His lies on their first date _____ problems in their relationship.

9. My attention started to _____ during the third hour of the lecture.

10. She liked to _____ rumors by posting cryptic tweets about her life.

11. You might want to _____ yourself with a protein bar before the long hike.

12. The boys joined in the _____ and started throwing rocks at the other group.

# WORD SET 17

**fringe:** [FRINJ] Noun/Verb.
An ornamental border consisting of short twisted or straight threads. (n.)
The edge of something. (n.)
To border. (v.)

- The **fringe** of my grandmother's antique lampshade has turned brown over the years. (n.)
- Those living on the **fringe** of the city expect to be incorporated into the city limits soon. (n.)
- The vegetation **fringed** the beach. (v.)

*Synonym:* edge, border, rim, periphery, verge, margin
*Antonym:* center, middle, core
Further Information
- Originated from the Old French word *frenge* meaning "thread, hem, border."
- Related words include **fringy** (adj.).
- In Great Britain, **fringe** can refer to "bangs of the hair."


**frugal:** [FROO-gel) Adjective.
Careful about spending money or using supplies.
Simple and without things that are unnecessary.

- The old man was **frugal** in his spending, as he received little money each month.
- The **frugal** meal of bread and cheese was all that the sick girl felt like eating.

*Synonym:* thrifty, economical, sparing, prudent, provident, stingy
*Antonym:* extravagant, lavish, wasteful
Further Information
- Originated from the Latin word *frugalis* meaning "virtuous."
- Frugal also is derived from the Latin word *frux* meaning "fruit or profit."
- Related word forms include **frugality** (n). and **frugally** (adv.).


**furtive:** [FEHR-tiv] Adjective.
Done quietly and secretly to avoid being noticed.

- She **furtively** got the book out of her backpack to read it instead of taking notes during class.
- I gave him a **furtive** look when the teacher asked if anyone had been cheating.

*Synonym:* sneaky, stealthy, secret, underhand, sly, surreptitious
*Antonym:* open, honest, truthful
Further Information
- Originated from the Latin word *furtum* meaning "theft."
- The Latin root *fur* means "thief" and comes from the Greek *phor*, for "thief."
- Related words include **furtively** (adv.) and **furtiveness** (n.).

**gainsay:** [GAYN-say] Verb.
To declare something to be invalid or untrue.

- The politician tried to **gainsay** everything his opponent said at the debate.
- The evidence doesn't **gainsa**y the charge that the man lied to authorities.

*Synonym:* contradict, deny, controvert, dispute, oppose, contravene
*Antonym:* agree, admit, concur

Further Information
- Originated from Old English word *gean* meaning "in opposition to, against."
- Related words include **gainsayer** (n.).
- **Gainsay** is found more in older literature and not as often in modern English.


**gamut:** [GAH-met] Noun.
An entire series or range of related things.

- The play makes the audience feel the **gamut** of human emotions, from sadness to joy.
- The collection of dresses that she chose runs the **gamut** of color.

*Synonym:* spectrum, scale, range, series, progression, extent
*Antonym:* none

Further Information
- Originated from the Latin word *gamma* meaning "the lowest note in the scale."
- In the 11th century, Guido of Arezzo named the first line of his bass staff *gamma* and the first note in the scale *ut*, eventually abbreviated to **gamut**, meaning "scale of meaning."
- A lesser used definition for **gamut** is "the entire series of musical notes."


**garrulous:** [GAH-reh-les] Adjective.
Extremely talkative.

- After drinking a few cocktails, the man became more **garrulous**.
- The boy was always in trouble with the teacher for his **garrulousness** in class.

*Synonym:* talkative, loquacious, chatty, verbose, gabby, wordy
*Antonym:* brief, concise, taciturn

Further Information
- Originated from the Latin word *garrulus* meaning "to talk rapidly or chatter."
- Related word forms include **garrulously** (adv.) and **garrulousness** (n.).
- **Garrulous** has a negative connotation, denoting "rambling, boring chatter or speech."

**gauche** [GOSH] Adjective.
Having no grace, tact or social experience or awareness.

- His **gauche** question about the hostess's age had no place at the dinner party.
- Her loud talking at the theater showed her **gaucheness**.

*Synonym:* crude, graceless, boorish, maladroit, inept, uncouth
*Antonym:* graceful, elegant, debonair

Further Information
- Originated from the French word *gauche* meaning "left."
- **Gauche** originates from the flawed idea that left-handed people are awkward.
- Related word forms include **gaucheness** (n.) and **gauchely** (adv.).

**gawky**: [GAW-kee] Adjective.
(Usually physically) awkward or clumsy.

- The teenage boy's **gawkiness** was evident when he tried to dance at the prom.
- The athlete looked **gawky** on the field but despite appearances, was able to score points.

*Synonym:* awkward, unwieldy, clumsy, rude, coarse, bumbling
*Antonym:* lithe, graceful, agile

Further Information
- Originated from the Anglo-French word *gawk* meaning "left hand."
- Related words include **gawkily** (adv.), **gawk** (n.) and **gawkiness** (n.).
- **Gawky** is another word in which the meaning "left" is given a negative, awkward connotation.

**germane**: [jer-MAYN] Adjective.
Someone or something that is appropriate and relevant or fitting to a subject.

- Her opinion was not **germane** to the discussion of the case.
- Your point is not **germane** to this discussion and I refuse to talk about it further.

*Synonym:* relevant, pertinent, apposite, applicable, apropos, apt
*Antonym:* irrelevant, inapplicable, inappropriate

Further Information
- Originated from the Middle English word *germain* meaning "having the same parents."
- Related word forms include **germanely** (adv.).
- An obsolete meaning of **germane** is "closely akin to."

**gist**: [JIST] Noun.
The main part or point of something.

- Although I didn't overhear every word of their conversation, I caught the **gist** of it.
- The **gist** of his argument didn't make sense with everything else he was saying.

*Synonym:* essence, point, core, heart, pith, kernel
*Antonym:* extension

Further Information
- Originated from the Anglo-French word *gist* meaning "to lie adjacent."
- The legal definition of gist is "the foundation or ground of a legal action."


**glib**: [GLIB] Adjective.
Informal and easy in writing or speech, possibly to the point of insincerity.
Superficial, without depth or substance.

- The politician's **glib** remarks seemed to flow out of his mouth a bit too easily.
- The student offered a **glib** solution to the professor's complex problem.

*Synonym:* smooth, fluent, slick, loquacious, facile, voluble
*Antonym:* quiet, hesitant

Further Information
- Originated from the Low German word *glibberig* meaning "slippery."
- Related word forms include **glibly** (adv.) and **glibness** (n.).
- An archaic meaning of **glib** is "slippery or smooth."


**goosebumps**: [GOOS-bumps] Plural noun.
A temporary roughness of the skin in response to a strong emotion or to cold temperatures.

- Hearing that scary story being read gave me **goosebumps**.
- I can't get rid of these **goosebumps** from being outside in the snow.

*Synonym:* goose pimple, gooseflesh, goose skin
*Antonym:* none

Further Information
- Originated from the Latin words *caro gallinacia* meaning "hen flesh."
- The first usage in English of the term **goosebumps** was likely in the 16th century when the euphemism for having contracted syphilis was "bitten by the Winchester goose."

# REVIEW EXERCISE 17

*Match the word with its synonym.*

___ 1.  fringe           a.  gooseflesh
___ 2.  frugal           b.  crude
___ 3.  furtive          c.  point
___ 4.  gainsay          d.  contradict
___ 5.  gamut            e.  edge
___ 6.  garrulous        f.  talkative
___ 7.  gauche           g.  thrifty
___ 8.  gawky            h.  relevant
___ 9.  germane          i.  range
___ 10. gist             j.  secret
___ 11. glib             k.  awkward
___ 12. goosebumps       l.  fluent

*Fill in the blanks with the most appropriate word from list above.* (Word form may need changing.)

1.  Comments posted must be _____ to the topic at hand.

2.  We wondered how he could be so _____ about the car accident.

3.  The _____ old man loved to tell long, disjointed stories.

4.  The _____ woman clipped hundreds of coupons each week.

5.  Talking with one's mouth full shows _____ table manners.

6.  The store sells a _____ of products from health aids to clothing.

7.  She used _____ tactics to cheat on the exam.

8.  The _____ on those jeans really date them.

9.  She got _____ when her friend whispered in her ear.

10. She _____ her doctor's advice and stopped taking her medication.

11. The _____ teenager often tripped over her own feet.

12. The story was told so confusingly I could not get the _____ of it.

**gourmand**: [gur-MAND] Noun.
A person who loves to eat and drink, usually in large quantities.

- The **gourmand** visited the French countryside only to drink the wine.
- The restaurant was intended more for **gourmands** than for gourmets.

*Synonym:* epicure, glutton, gastronome, foodie
*Antonym: none*

Further Information
- Originated from the Middle French word *gourmand* meaning "glutton."
- Related words include **gourmandism** (n.) and **gourmandize** (v.).
- Don't confuse **gourmand** with **gourmet**, which means "a person who is a connoisseur of good food and wine."

**gradation**: [gra-DAY-shen) Noun.
A series of stages, advancing by degrees or shades.

- There is an obvious **gradation** of color in this painting.
- The tempo **gradations** in this musical piece are very subtle.

*Synonym:* nuance, scale, grade, step, degree, shade
*Antonym: none*

Further Information
- Originated from the Latin word *gradus* meaning "degree or step."
- Related word forms include **gradate** (v.), **gradational** (adj.) and **gradationally** (adv.).

**grandiloquent**: [gran-DIL-uh-kwent] Adjective.
Pompous or inflated in expression or style.

- Although his speech was full of **grandiloquent** language, it lacked new ideas.
- The eulogy was **grandiloquent** and one of which the dead man would have approved.

*Synonym:* bombastic, pompous, inflated, pretentious, overblown, magniloquent
*Antonym:* plain, simple, unpretentious

Further Information
- Originated from the Latin word *grandiloquus* meaning "great speak."
- Other words with the Latin *loqui* root include **eloquent**, **soliloquy** and **loquacious**.
- Related words include **grandiloquence (**n.) and **grandiloquently** (adv.).

**gratuitous:** [gre-TOO-uh-tus] Adjective.
Given without being earned, without cost or without obligation, free.
Not necessary or appropriate.

- Some say there is too much **gratuitous** violence on television.
- Because I hadn't said anything to offend him, his insult was quite **gratuitous**.

*Synonym:* unnecessary, complimentary, free, voluntary, unwarranted, needless
*Antonym:* reasonable, necessary, warranted

Further Information
- Originated from Latin word *gratia* meaning "favor."
- Related words include **gratuitousness** (n.) and **gratuitously** (adv.).
- The legal definition of **gratuitous** is "given without receiving a returned value."

**happy-go-lucky:** [HAH-pee-go-LUH-kee] Adjective.
Carefree and unconcerned.

- The **happy-go-lucky** way she goes through life makes one think she doesn't care about anything.
- I had a **happy-go-lucky** childhood except for a few stressful events.

*Synonym:* carefree, cheerful, easygoing, amused, buoyant, blithe
*Antonym: none*

Further Information
- **Happy-go-lucky** was originally an adverb in the 1630s and was **happy-be-lucky**. At that time the meaning was "haphazard."
- The origin of this word is unknown. It first appeared in English in the 1600s.

**harbinger:** [HAR-ben-jer] Noun/Verb.
Something or someone that signals a big change or foreshadows an event in the future. (n.)
To give a prediction or warning of. (v.)

- Her successful job interview was a **harbinger** of a better future. (n.)
- The uprising **harbingered** the fall of the empire. (v.)

*Synonym:* portent, sign, precursor, omen, herald, presage
*Antonym: none*

Further Information
- Originated from the Anglo-French word *herberge* meaning "camp or lodging."
- An archaic meaning of **harbinger** is "a person who is sent ahead to find lodging."
- The plural of **harbinger** is **harbingers**.

**hardy** [HAR-dee] Adjective.
Brave or bold.
Robust or strong.

- The team has a **hardy** spirit and keeps playing even after many losses.
- The **hardy** soldiers could make it through a long, forced march.

*Synonym:* strong, robust, tough, brave, hale, sturdy
*Antonym:* weak, feeble, shy

Further Information
- Originated from the Old French word *hardir* meaning "to make hard."
- **Hardy** can be used as a botanical term meaning "a plant that can withstand harsh conditions."
- Related word forms include **hardiness** (n.) and **hardily** (adv.).

**haven**: [HAY-ven] Noun.
A safe place; a place offering good conditions or opportunities.

- The women's shelter provided a **haven** for abused mothers and their children.
- The cafe was considered a **haven** for artists as it featured many of their works.

*Synonym:* sanctuary, harbor, refuge, shelter, asylum, retreat
*Antonym:* hazard, risk, danger

Further Information
- Originated from the Old English word *haefen* meaning "harbor."
- **Haven** is also known as "a harbor or port."

**hearken**: [HAR-ken] Verb.
To listen respectfully with attention.

- The church congregation **hearkened** to the evangelist.
- She **hearkened** to the voice of her conscience and opted not to tell a lie.

*Synonym:* listen, hark, heed, attend, hear
*Antonym:* ignore, disregard

Further Information
- Originated from the Old High German word *horechen* meaning "to listen."
- **Hearken** may also be spelled **harken**.
- An archaic meaning of **hearken** is "to hear."

**hedonist**: [HEE-duh-nist] Noun.
A person who is devoted to pursuing pleasure.

- Many religions disagree with the doctrine of **hedonism**.
- Our **hedonist** neighbors like to party all night and sleep during the day.

*Synonym:* sybarite, epicurean, sensualist, debauchee, libertine, immoralist
*Antonym:* ascetic, prude

Further Information
- Originated from the Greek word *hedone* meaning "pleasure."
- Related words include **hedonism** (n.).
- In philosophy, **hedonism** means "only things that are pleasant are inherently good." In psychology, **hedonism** means "behavior is motivated by the avoidance of pain and desire for pleasure."

**hegemony**: [heh-JEH-meh-nee or HEH-jeh-meh-nee] Noun.
The influence or authority a dominant member of a group has over others.

- The chief operating officer of the company has **hegemony** over its employees.
- His wife has a strange **hegemony** over him and must approve his outings with his friends.

*Synonym:* leadership, power, authority, jurisdiction, command, supremacy
*Antonym:* repression, constraint, oppression

Further Information
- Originated from the Greek word *hegemonia* meaning "leader."
- Another word derived from *hegemonia* is **exegesis**, meaning "explanation."
- Related word forms include **hegemonic** (adj.).

**heterogeneous**: [heh-teh-reh-JEE-nee-us] Adjective.
Made up of mixed, dissimilar ingredients.

- My genealogical search showed me that my ancestors were a **heterogeneous** group who originated from all over the world.
- Although they are twins, they are **heterogeneous** in appearance, looking nothing alike.

*Synonym:* diverse, mixed, varied, different, diversified, miscellaneous
*Antonym:* consistent, homogenous, uniform

Further Information
- Originated from the Greek word *heterogenes* meaning "different kind."
- Related words include **heterogeneously** (adv.) and **heterogeneousness** (n.).

# REVIEW EXERCISE 18

## Match the word with its synonym

|     |                   |     |              |
| --- | ----------------- | --- | ------------ |
| ___ 1.  | gourmand          | a.  | listen       |
| ___ 2.  | gradation         | b.  | power        |
| ___ 3.  | grandiloquent     | c.  | glutton      |
| ___ 4.  | gratuitous        | d.  | strong       |
| ___ 5.  | happy-go-lucky    | e.  | unnecessary  |
| ___ 6.  | harbinger         | f.  | sign         |
| ___ 7.  | hardy             | g.  | diverse      |
| ___ 8.  | haven             | h.  | nuance       |
| ___ 9.  | hearken           | i.  | sanctuary    |
| ___ 10. | hedonist          | j.  | pompous      |
| ___ 11. | hegemony          | k.  | cheerful     |
| ___ 12. | heterogeneous     | l.  | sensualist   |

## Fill in the blanks with the most appropriate word from list above. *(Word form may need changing.)*

1. The principal has _____ over all the students in the school.

2. The church was a _____ for those evacuated from the tornado.

3. Some believe the groundhog is a _____ of spring.

4. The _____ attorney tried to persuade the jury with fancy words.

5. The _____ loved to eat at the buffet so he could fill up on his favorite foods.

6. There is a _____ in style from last year's car model to this year's model.

7. The band's audience was _____ and made up of all types of people.

8. He seeks _____ attention from his friends by pulling dangerous stunts.

9. The children played on the playground in a _____ manner.

10. As a _____ he likes to spend money at casinos and clubs.

11. He was a strong, _____ baby, weighing in at 10 pounds at birth.

12. I refuse to _____ my parents' advice.

**heterogenous**: [heh-teh-RAH-jeh-nes] Adjective.
Of foreign origin, not originating within an organism/a body.
Sometimes used as a synonym for heterogeneous.

- The bone transplant was **heterogenous**, as the donated bone was taken from another body.
- The country is a **heterogenous** collection of 26 self-governing nations.

*Synonym:* different, foreign
*Antonym:* homogeneous, autogenic
Further Information

- Originated from the Greek word *heterogenes* meaning "different kind."
- **Heterogenous** is used as a medical term meaning "something that originated outside the body."
- Although not its original intended definition, **heterogenous** is now sometimes used as a synonym for **heterogeneous**, meaning "made up of different parts."

**hierarchy**: [HI-uh-rar-kee) Noun.
A group that is divided into levels and controls an organization.
A system in which people or things having different status are placed at a series of levels.

- The **hierarchy** of this school's administration includes the superintendent, the principal and the vice-principal.
- He worked his way up through the corporate **hierarchy** to become vice-president.

*Synonym:* order, rank, scale, position, class, degree
*Antonym:* declassification, mayhem
Further Information

- Originated from the Old French word *ierarchie* meaning "ranked division of angels."
- Related word forms include **hierarchical** (adj.) and **hierarchically** (adv.).
- A lesser-used definition of **hierarchy** is "a division of angels."

**histrionics**: [his-tree-ah-niks] Noun.
Theatrical, dramatic or emotional behavior designed to achieve an effect.

- The girl ignored her mother's tears as she was used to her **histrionics**.
- When the toddler did not get her way, she started using **histrionics**.

*Synonym:* drama, theatrics, dramatics, melodrama
*Antonym:* none
Further Information

- Originated from the French word *histrionique* meaning "pertaining to an actor."
- Do not confuse **histrionics** with **hysterics**, which are "fits of uncontrollable laughing or crying."

**hodgepodge:** [HAJ-paj] Noun.
A (usually jumbled) mixture of different things.

- The museum contains a **hodgepodge** of art from various periods and countries, with no order or classification system evident.
- The industry leaders were trying to deal with the **hodgepodge** of rules and regulations that attempted to control commerce.

*Synonym:* mess, jumble, mishmash, mixture, medley, melange
*Antonym:* structure, arrangement
Further Information
- Originated from the Old French word *hochepot* meaning "soup or stew."
- **Hodgepodge** was originally spelled **hotchpotch**.

**homogeneous**: [hoh-muh-JEEN-ee-us] Adjective.
Having uniform or similar characteristics. (adj.)

- The world's population is becoming more **homogeneous** as races and nationalities mix.
- The book club shares a **homogeneous** taste in books, so they can always agree what to read.

*Synonym*: alike, comparable, compatible, consistent, equal, same
*Antonym:* different, diverse, heterogeneous
Further Information
- Originated from the Greek words *homos* and *genos* meaning "same kind."
- Related words include **homogeneously** (adv.), **homogeneity** (n.), **homogenize** (v.) and **homogeneousness** (n.).
- **Homogeneous** is occasionally (incorrectly) used as a synonym for **homogenous**, although they have different meanings.

**homogenous**: [huh-MAH-jeh-nus] Adjective.
Body tissues or organs with genetic similarities.

- The host body rejected **homogenous** tissue implants.
- Scientists discussed the difference between **homogenous** structures with common genetic origin and homoplastic structures, which share common environments.

*Synonym:* homologous, identical
*Antonym:* different, dissimilar
Further Information
- Originated from the Greek words *homos* and *genos* meaning "same kind."
- The word **homogenous** is declining in use, even in the medical and science communities.
- Related words include **homogeny** (n.).

**hyperbole** [hi-PER-be-lee] Noun.
Words used to describe something/someone as much better or worse than it is.

- The product's commercial was a **hyperbole** promising rapid and massive weight loss.
- The tale he told us sounded like **hyperbole** but was totally the truth.

*Synonym:* exaggeration, overstatement, embellishment
*Antonym:* understatement, belittlement, disparagement

Further Information
- Originated from the Greek word *hyperballein* meaning "to exceed."
- Hyperbolus was a politician in 5th century B.C. Greece who made exaggerated promises.
- Related word forms include **hyperbolist** (n.).


**iconoclast**: [eye-KAH-neh-klast] Noun.
A person who criticizes widely held beliefs or institutions.

- The man who spoke out against the beliefs of the church was labeled an **iconoclast**.
- The group of 12 jurors had one **iconoclast** who thought the defendant was not guilty.

*Synonym:* rebel, recusant, nonconformist, maverick, dissident, dissenter
*Antonym:* creator

Further Information
- Originated from the Greek word *eikonoklastes* meaning "image destroyer."
- Related words include **icon** (n.), **iconoclastic** (adj.), **iconoclasm** (n.) and **iconoclastically** (adv.).


**idiosyncrasy**: [id-ee-uh-SIN-kreh-see] Noun.
A characteristic of thought or behavior or a feature that is unusual and stands out.

- The girl had an **idiosyncrasy** of twirling her hair every time she told a lie.
- The building's colorful **idiosyncrasy** made it stand out from the white buildings on the street.

*Synonym:* quality, peculiarity, quirk, characteristic, trait, eccentricity
*Antonym:* normality, generalization

Further Information
- Originated from the Greek word *idiosynkrasia* meaning "to blend."
- Related word forms include **idiosyncratic** (adj.) and **idiosyncratically** (adv.).
- In medicine, **idiosyncrasy** means "hypersensitivity" or "an unusual physical or mental characteristic."

**idyllic**: [eye-DIH-lik] Adjective.
Pleasant, charming and picturesque in its simplicity.

- The novelist wrote books loosely based on his **idyllic** childhood.
- I would like to build a home on the **idyllic** hillside.

*Synonym:* pastoral, bucolic, peaceful, rustic, halcyon, ideal
*Antonym:* imperfect, bad, flawed

Further Information
- Originated from the French word *idyllique* meaning "pertaining to a little picture."
- Related words include **idyll** (n.), **idyllical** (adj.) and **idyllically** (adv.).
- An **idyll** can be "a short poem, piece of music or series of events that are simple and pleasant."


**ignominious**: [ig-neh-MIN-ee-us] Adjective.
Causing or deserving of shame or disgrace.

- Becoming a janitor at the school was considered an **ignominious** fate by some of his family.
- The army hoped to wipe out the shame of its **ignominious** defeat.

*Synonym:* shameful, disgraceful, despicable, vile, low, sordid
*Antonym:* honorable, admirable, noble

Further Information
- Originated from the Latin word *ignominiosus* meaning "disgraceful or shameful."
- The Latin root *nomen* means "name" and *in* means "negative," so the literal translation of **ignominious** is "nameless."
- Related word forms include **ignominiously** (adv.) and **ignominiousness** (n.).


**ilk**: [IHLK] Noun.
Kind or sort.

- The old woman and her **ilk** love to sit around gossiping.
- The two men were of the same **ilk** and agreed on many points.

*Synonym:* kind, species, variety, breed, sort, type
*Antonym:* none

Further Information
- Originated from the Old English word *ilca* meaning "the same."
- In Scotland, *ilk* is an adjective that means "same."
- **Ilk** may also be spelled **ilke**.

# REVIEW EXERCISE 19

*Match the word with its synonym.*

| | | | |
|---|---|---|---|
| ___ 1. | heterogenous | a. | peculiarity |
| ___ 2. | hierarchy | b. | peaceful |
| ___ 3. | histrionics | c. | exaggeration |
| ___ 4. | hodgepodge | d. | kind |
| ___ 5. | homogeneous | e. | theatrics |
| ___ 6. | homogenous | f. | rank |
| ___ 7. | hyperbole | g. | identical |
| ___ 8. | iconoclast | h. | comparable |
| ___ 9. | idiosyncrasy | i. | foreign |
| ___ 10. | idyllic | j. | jumble |
| ___ 11. | ignominious | k. | shameful |
| ___ 12. | ilk | l. | rebel |

*Fill in the blanks with the most appropriate word from list above.* (*Word form may need changing.*)

1.   The monkeys were found to have a complex social _____.

2.   His parents forgave his lies, saying that they were mere _____.

3.   My childhood was_____ growing up on a farm.

4.   He hated the photographer and others of his _____.

5.   The team's final defeat was_____, as they had won no games this season.

6.   Marriage involves overlooking each other's _____.

7.   The team is a _____ of players collected from other teams.

8.   The _____ stood up at the meeting and refuted the group's beliefs.

9.   Her brain tumor was considered to be_____, her doctor told her.

10.  The donated heart consisted of _____ tissue, but her body rejected it.

11.   Our family shares a _____ hatred of liver and onions.

12.  Every time I looked at the screaming toddler her_____ increased.

# WORD SET 20

**illiberality**: [ihl-lib-uh-RAL-uh-tee] Noun.
The state or condition of not allowing people to act and think as they choose.

- Some argue that banning smoking in public is the height of **illiberality**.
- The citizens felt the **illiberality** of enforced laws and reforms.

*Synonym:* intolerance, prejudice, racism, bigotry, bias
*Antonym:* open-mindedness, liberality

Further Information
- Originated from the Latin word *illiberalis* meaning "ignoble or stingy."
- Related words include **illiberal** (adj.), **illiberally** (adv.) and **illiberalness** (n.).
- An archaic meaning of **illiberality** is "stinginess."

**imminent**: [IHM-eh-nent] Adjective.
About to happen, ready to take place.

- The toddler playing in the road was in **imminent** danger of being hit by a car.
- The patients with the fatal disease are facing **imminent** death.

*Synonym:* impending, approaching, near, close, coming, immediate
*Antonym:* distant, far-off

Further Information
- Originated from the Latin word *imminens* meaning "to project or threaten."
- Related word forms include **imminently** (adv.).
- Don't confuse **imminent** with **eminent** which means "lofty or noteworthy."

**impair**: [ihm-PAYR] Verb.
To make less or to damage.

- His health was **impaired** by his smoking habit.
- Because his mother drank alcohol while pregnant, his learning ability was **impaired**.

*Synonym:* damage, mar, injure, spoil, harm, weaken
*Antonym:* improve, help, aid

Further Information
- Originated from the Latin word *impejorare* meaning "to make worse."
- Related words include **impairer** (n.) and **impairment** (n.).
- In finance, **impairment** means "assets that have lost value from a prior period."

**impeach:** [im-PEECH] Verb.
To charge a public official with a crime committed while in office.
To cause doubts about the truthfulness of.

- The political party moved for the **impeachment** of the President due to his irregular financial dealings.
- The defense attorney tried to **impeach** the testimony of the victim on the witness stand.

*Synonym:* accuse, incriminate, charge, arraign, blame, indict
*Antonym:* discharge, absolve, exculpate

Further Information
- Originated from the Old French word *empeechier* meaning "to hinder."
- Related words include **impeachment** (n.) and **impeachable** (adj.).
- Only two U.S. presidents have faced **impeachment,** and both were acquitted – Andrew Johnson and Bill Clinton.

**importune**: [im-per-TOON] Verb.
To urge persistently, to repeatedly ask in an annoying way.

- The man sat on the street corner, **importuning** pedestrians to help him.
- The woman from the charity was **importuning** theatregoers in the lobby for contributions.

*Synonym*: beg, press, beseech, urge, entreat, implore
*Antonym:* give

Further Information
- Originated from the Latin word *importunus* meaning "unfavorable or unfit."
- Related words include **importunate** (adj.), **importunely** (adv.), and **importuner** (n.).
- An archaic meaning of **importune** is "to beg for urgently."

**impresario**: [im-pre-SAR-ee-oh] Noun.
The manager or director of a performance or performance company/group.

- The nightclub **impresario** tried to get many people into the audience for concerts.
- The **impresario** spent all his time on the road promoting his concert company.

*Synonym:* entrepreneur, producer, promoter, manager
*Antonym: none*

Further Information
- Originated from the Italian word *impresa* meaning "undertaking."
- Another related word is **emprise** which is "an adventurous enterprise."
- **Impresario** is not related to the word **impress**.

**impute:** [im-PYUT] Verb.
To suggest that someone or something is guilty or responsible.

- The counselor **imputed** the student's failure to laziness.
- The candidate tried to **impute** some heinous remarks to his opponent.

*Synonym:* attribute, ascribe, charge, assign, credit, indict
*Antonym:* defend
<u>Further Information</u>
- Originated from the Latin word *imputare* meaning "to consider."
- Related word forms include **imputation** (n.) **imputability** (n.) and **imputable** (adj.).
- The legal definition of **impute** is "to calculate the value or cost of."


**inane:** [ih-NAYN] Adjective.
Having no meaning, significance or point; empty, silly.

- She complained that there were too many **inane** reality shows on television.
- His **inane** comments are not going to help us to solve our problem.

*Synonym:* silly, foolish, stupid, fatuous, ridiculous, absurd
*Antonym:* clever, smart, intelligent
<u>Further Information</u>
- Originated from the Latin word *inanis* meaning "empty or void."
- Related words include **inanely** (adv.) and **inaneness** (n.).
- In an English dictionary in 1731 the word **inaniloquent**, meaning "prone to empty talk," was published.


**incendiary:** [in-SEN-dee-er-ee] Noun/Adjective.
A person or substance who starts a fire maliciously or is an arsonist. (n.)
A person who incites agitation. (n.)
Something or someone that inflames or excites. (adj.)
Something that is hot or tends to ignite. (adj.)

- The **incendiary** was found as he had used an accelerant in the fire and had traces of it on his clothes. (n.)
- The protests were blamed on outside **incendiaries** trying to overthrow the government. (n.)
- The speech was quite **incendiary** and convinced the protestors to become violent. (adj.)
- As the military vehicle drove over the **incendiary** device, the Humvee exploded. (adj.)

*Synonym:* arsonist, bomb, inflammatory, agitator, combustible, subversive
*Antonym:* unprovocative, incombustible, fireproof
<u>Further Information</u>
- Originated from the Latin word *incendiarius* meaning "conflagration."
- A military term for **incendiary** is "improvised explosive device."

**inchoate**: [in-KOH-ayt] Adjective.
Not completely formed yet, only partly in existence.

- His suspicions that all was not well in the nation were **inchoate**.
- Her feelings of love for him were **inchoate**, as they had been friends until now.

*Synonym:* incipient, rudimentary, embryonic, beginning, undeveloped, formless
*Antonym:* developed, mature, grown

Further Information
- Originated from the Latin word *inchoatus* meaning "to start work on."
- Related words include **inchoately** (adv.) and **inchoateness** (n.).
- The legal definition of **inchoate** is "an activity that is agreed upon but is incomplete or not final."


**incongruous**: [in-KAHN-groo-us] Adjective.
Not suitable, proper, consistent or in harmony.

- The small, skinny girl looked **incongruous** in a military uniform.
- The extremely short man and the very tall woman made an **incongruous** couple.

*Synonym:* incompatible, inconsistent, contradictory, discordant
*Antonym:* congruous, compatible, fitting

Further Information
- Originated from the Latin word *incongruus* meaning "inconsistent."
- Related word forms include **incongruously** (adv.) and **incongruousness** (n.).
- The word **incongruous** was first used in English in 1611, as the opposite of congruous.


**incontrovertible**: [in-kahn-treh-VEHR-teh-bel] Adjective.
Not open to question or doubt.

- The jury felt that the facts of his guilt were **incontrovertible,** so they convicted him.
- The group thought that the facts supporting global warming were **incontrovertible.**

*Synonym:* indisputable, unquestionable, undeniable, irrefutable, certain, sure
*Antonym:* questionable, controversial, debatable

Further Information
- Originated from the Latin word *controversus* meaning "turning against."
- Related word forms include **incontrovertibly** (adv.), **controvert** (v.), **controversy** (n.) and **controversial** (adj.).

# REVIEW EXERCISE 20

*Match the word with its synonym.*

| | | | | |
|---|---|---|---|---|
| ___ | 1. | illiberality | a. | incompatible |
| ___ | 2. | imminent | b. | attribute |
| ___ | 3. | impair | c. | beg |
| ___ | 4. | impeach | d. | inflammatory |
| ___ | 5. | importune | e. | unquestionable |
| ___ | 6. | impresario | f. | damage |
| ___ | 7. | impute | g. | intolerance |
| ___ | 8. | inane | h. | beginning |
| ___ | 9. | incendiary | i. | impending |
| ___ | 10. | inchoate | j. | accuse |
| ___ | 11. | incongruous | k. | producer |
| ___ | 12. | incontrovertible | l. | silly |

*Fill in the blanks with the most appropriate word from list above.* *(Word form may need changing.)*

1. She _____ her husband's laziness for her dinner party's failure.

2. His remarks during the speech were _____ and started a riot.

3. Alcohol _____ his driving ability so his wife drove him home.

4. The weather channel told us that a tornado was _____ and to take cover.

5. The man presented _____ evidence that he did not commit the crime.

6. She thought it was _____ of the obese doctor to tell her to lose weight.

7. The singer also acted as an _____ for the opera company.

8. The child _____ her mother to buy her candy in the store.

9. The new company is _____ and therefore not yet offering all services.

10. The girl acts _____ in class to gain attention from the teacher.

11. The president faced _____ for violating the law.

12. She said the laws enforcing seat belt wearing in the car were the height of _____.

# WORD SET 21

**incorrigibility**: [in-kor-uh-juh-BIL-uh tee] Noun.
The state or condition of not being able to be corrected, reformed or managed.

- The judge told the **incorrigible** youth that he'd end up in jail.
- The **incorrigible** flirt tried to get the phone number of every woman he met.

*Synonym:* unruliness, extremism, intolerance, fanaticism, zeal
*Antonym:* apathy, impartiality, indifference
Further Information
- Originated from the Latin word *incorrigibilis* meaning "to correct."
- Related words include **incorrigible** (adj.), **incorrigibly** (adv.) and **incorrigibleness** (n.).
- The opposite of **incorrigibility** is **corrigibility** which means "able to be corrected or repaired."

**incumbent**: [in-CUM-bent] Noun/Adjective.
The holder of an office. (n.)
Something that must be done. (adj.)
Resting or lying on something else. (adj.)

- With the support of his citizens behind him, the **incumbent** easily beat his challenger in the election. (n.)
- It is **incumbent** upon us to teach our children not to lie. (adj.)
- An **incumbent** geological formation was found in the cave. (adj.)

*Synonym:* necessary, compulsory, officeholder, occupant, obligatory, required
*Antonym:* candidate, unnecessary
Further Information
- Originated from the Latin word *incumbens* meaning "to lie down on."
- **Incumbent** originally meant "a person who held a paid position in a church."

**indoctrinate**: [in-DOK-treh-nayt] Verb.
To teach or instruct, especially the opinions or ideas of a group.

- The cult **indoctrinated** him with their belief system when he joined.
- The citizens were **indoctrinated** not to question their leader.

*Synonym:* teach, train, inculcate, school, drill, instruct
*Antonym:* deprogram, unlearn
Further Information
- Originated from the Anglo-French word *endoctriner* meaning "doctrine."
- Related words include **indoctrination** (n.) and **indoctrinator** (n.).
- Other words containing the Latin root *docere*, meaning "to teach" include **docent, doctrine, docile, document** and **doctor.**

**indolent:** [IN-deh-lent] Adjective.
Not liking to be active or to work, lazy.

- The woman was **indolent,** liking only to go out to lunch with friends and shop.
- The teacher thought the student who refused to take notes in class was very **indolent**.

*Synonym:* lazy, slothful, sluggish, lethargic, idle, listless
*Antonym:* active, industrious, energetic

<u>Further Information</u>
- Originated from the Latin word *indolens* meaning "insensitive to pain."
- Related words include **indolently** (adv.).
- The medical definition of **indolent** is "causing little or no pain, or something that grows slowly or is slow to heal."

**inebriated:** [ih-NEE-bree-ay-ted] Adjective.
Confused as if by alcohol, intoxicated, drunk.

- The **inebriated** man should never have been behind the wheel of a car.
- She was so **inebriated** after the party that she couldn't stand up straight.

*Synonym:* intoxicated, drunk, tipsy, loaded, plastered, boozy
*Antonym:* sober, temperate, clearheaded

<u>Further Information</u>
- Originated from the Latin word *inebriatus* meaning "to intoxicate."
- Related words include **inebriation** (n.) and **inebriate** (v.).
- **Inebriated** is often used as a euphemism to describe oneself as drunk.

**inert:** [ih-NERT] Adjective.
Having no power to move or moving very slowly.

- The **inert** child laid very still in his bed.
- Some people spend their entire lives in a dreamy, **inert** state.

*Synonym:* inactive, sluggish, idle, torpid, listless, languid
*Antonym:* active, animated, lively

<u>Further Information</u>
- Originated from the Latin word *inert* meaning "idle or unskilled."
- Related words include **inertly** (adv.) and **inertness** (n.).
- The chemical definition of **inert** is "something that cannot affect other chemicals when it comes into contact with them."

**inexorable:** [ih-NEKS-er-eh-bel] Adjective.
Unable to be stopped, moved or persuaded; relentless.

- Although she might not have run the race as fast as others, she was making **inexorable** progress towards the finish line.
- The trend of cell phones gradually replacing land lines is **inexorable**.

*Synonym:* relentless, inflexible, stubborn, intransigent, rigid, unrelenting
*Antonym:* flexible, vacillating

Further Information
- Originated from the Latin words *in* meaning "not" and *exorabilis* meaning "capable of being moved."
- Related word forms include **inexorability** (n.), **inexorableness** (n.) and **inexorably** (adv.).
- **Inexorable** first appeared in English in the 1500s.

**infraction:** [in-FRAK-shen] Noun.
An act that breaks a law or rule, a violation.

- If she gets one more **infraction**, the manager will kick her out of the halfway house.
- This minor **infraction** should not harm your chances of getting into college.

*Synonym:* violation, infringement, breach, crime, transgression, trespass
*Antonym:* obedience, compliance, adherence

Further Information
- Originated from the Latin word *infractio* meaning "subduing."
- Related words include **infract** (v.).
- Under U.S. federal law, an **infraction** is less than a misdemeanor, usually punishable by a fine.

**ingenuous:** [in-JEN-yew-es] Adjective.
Displaying childlike innocence and honesty.

- Her questions seemed too **ingenuous** for those of a reporter.
- It was because she was so **ingenuous** that she believed her students' weak excuses.

*Synonym:* naive, artless, guileless, candid, frank, open
*Antonym:* sly, disingenuous, dishonest

Further Information
- Originated from the Latin word *ingennus* meaning "native."
- Two obsolete meanings for *ingenuous* are "honorable or noble" and "ingenious."
- Related word forms include **ingenuously** (adv.).

**ingrained**: [in-GRAYND] Adjective.
Forming a part of the essence of someone or something; worked into the grain or fiber.

- His prejudices were so **ingrained** that they would not be changed easily.
- The woodworking oil became **ingrained** in her skin.

*Synonym:* inherent, innate, inborn, intrinsic, congenital, natural
*Antonym:* superficial

Further Information
- Originated from the French phrase *en graine* meaning "fast-dyed."
- Related words include **ingrain** (v.) and **ingrainedly** (adv.).
- **Ingrained** can also be spelled **engrained.**

**inimical**: [ih-NIH-mih-kel] Adjective.
Likely to cause damage; not friendly.

- The group felt the new laws were **inimical** to a democratic society.
- Some say that lack of ambition is **inimical** to being successful.

*Synonym:* hostile, unfriendly, harmful, antagonistic, adverse, unfavorable
*Antonym:* friendly, good, kindly

Further Information
- Originated from the Latin word *inimicus* meaning "enemy."
- Related word forms include **inimically** (adv.).
- **Inimical** usually refers to a situation or concept being hostile or harmful and not a person.

**injunction**: [in-JUNJK-shen] Noun.
An order from a court of law saying something must or must not be done.

- The family sought an **injunction** against the publication of the book about their uncle.
- The court upheld an **injunction** that barred the protestors from standing within 500 feet of the company.

*Synonym:* mandate, order, instruction, charge, dictate, command
*Antonym:* permission

Further Information
- Originated from the Latin word *injungere* meaning "to enjoin."
- Related word forms include **injunctive** (adj.).
- The original meaning of **injunction** was "an authoritative command."

# REVIEW EXERCISE 21

*Match the word with its synonym.*

| | | | | |
|---|---|---|---|---|
| ___ | 1. | incorrigibility | a. | inherent |
| ___ | 2. | incumbent | b. | inactive |
| ___ | 3. | indoctrinate | c. | violation |
| ___ | 4. | indolent | d. | order |
| ___ | 5. | inebriated | e. | lazy |
| ___ | 6. | inert | f. | train |
| ___ | 7. | inexorable | g. | unruliness |
| ___ | 8. | infraction | h. | necessary |
| ___ | 9. | ingenuous | i. | drunk |
| ___ | 10. | ingrained | j. | naive |
| ___ | 11. | inimical | k. | relentless |
| ___ | 12. | injunction | l. | harmful |

*Fill in the blanks with the most appropriate word from list above.* *(Word form may need changing.)*

1. The school's strict policies seem _____ to academic freedom.

2. The team was making _____ progress towards the championship.

3. She is _____ and sits around the house all day watching TV.

4. The _____ girl asked her date to take her home before she got sick.

5. It was _____ of her to ask a stranger to watch her purse.

6. The driver's _____ of the law earned him a fine for speeding.

7. It is _____ upon parents to set a good moral example for their children.

8. The _____ criminal was sentenced to life in prison.

9. The religious leaders tried to _____ the new recruit with their beliefs.

10. The court issued an _____ prohibiting him from coming near her.

11. The dog lay _____ along the side of the road, appearing dead.

12. A person's morals are usually deeply _____.

# WORD SET 22

**inordinate:** [in-OR-deh-net] Adjective.
Going beyond reasonable limits.

- The college had an **inordinate** number of problems with the new scheduling system.
- We felt that the principal passed an **inordinate** amount of new and unfair school rules.

*Synonym:* excessive, outrageous, exorbitant, extreme, extravagant, immoderate
*Antonym:* frugal, moderate, reasonable

Further Information
- Originated from the Latin word *inordinatus* meaning "to arrange."
- Related words include **inordinately** (adv.) and **inordinateness** (n.).
- An archaic meaning of **inordinately** is "unregulated or disorderly."

**insidious:** [in-SIH-dee-us] Adjective.
Gradually causing harm, or having a gradual effect, subtle.
Awaiting a chance to entrap something or someone.

- The **insidious** disease shows no signs or symptoms in patients until it's too late.
- Psychologists have called stress the **insidious** enemy of our health.

*Synonym:* cunning, deceitful, treacherous, tricky, wily, crafty
*Antonym:* harmless, honest, straightforward

Further Information
- Originated from the Latin word *insidae* meaning "to ambush."
- Related word forms include **insidiously** (adv.) and **insidiousness** (n.).
- The medical definition of **insidious** is "developing gradually before becoming apparent."

**insouciant:** [in-SOO-see-ent] Adjective.
Showing no concern or worry about anything.

- She wandered into class, **insouciant** of the fact that she was late.
- The two boys posed with handguns, attempting to look like **insouciant** rebels.

*Synonym:* nonchalant, unconcerned, indifferent, easygoing, casual, apathetic
*Antonym:* anxious, overprotective, careful

Further Information
- Originated from the French word *in + soucier* meaning "to disturb or trouble."
- Related words include **insouciantly** (adv.) and **insouciance** (n.).
- The literal translation of **insouciant** is "don't trouble or disturb yourself."

**instigate:** [IN-steh-gayt] Verb.
To urge forward, to cause to begin or happen.

- The teenagers tried to **instigate** violence on the street by firing off guns.
- The government has **instigated** an investigation into the case.

*Synonym:* incite, provoke, prompt, excite, urge, move
*Antonym:* prevent, halt, stop

Further Information
- Originated from the Latin word *instigatus* meaning "to urge on."
- Related words include **instigation** (n.), **instigator** (n.) and **instigative** (adj.).
- The word **instigate** was first seen in English in the mid-16th century.

**interlocutor:** [in-ter-LAH-kye-ter] Noun.
A person who takes part in a conversation.

- The man acted as an interpreter and **interlocuto**r for the tour group.
- The diplomat was an **interlocutor** between our government and the other nation's government.

*Synonym*: speaker, talker, conversationalist, questioner, interrogator
*Antonym: none*

Further Information
- Originated from the Latin word *interloqui* meaning "to speak between."
- Related words include **interlocutory** (adj.).
- Other words derived from the *loqui* Latin root include **ventriloquism, circumlocution** and **loquacious**.

**internecine:** [in-ter-NEH-seen] Adjective.
Destructive to both sides in a conflict or group.

- The **internecine** rivalries among members of the political party caused it to falter.
- The war was considered an **internecine** one, in which both sides lost.

*Synonym:* destructive, deadly, lethal, fatal, harmful, mortal
*Antonym:* immortal

Further Information
- Originated from the Latin word *internecinus* meaning "to destroy or kill."
- The modern definition of **internecine** resulted from an error in transcribing the first English dictionary, when Samuel Johnson in 1755 changed the word's original meaning from "deadly" to "assuring mutual destruction."

**intimation:** [in-teh-MAY-shen] Noun.
An indirect suggestion.

- The girl's suicide attempt was the first **intimation** of her serious depression.
- The boss had no **intimation** that his employee was about to resign.

*Synonym:* hint, suggestion, inkling, innuendo, suspicion, allusion
*Antonym:* expression

Further Information
- Originated from the Latin word *intimatus* meaning "to announce."
- Related word forms include **intimater** (n.) and **intimate** (v.) or (adj.).

**intractable**: [in-TRAK-teh-bel] Adjective.
Not easily persuaded, managed or handled.

- The patient experienced **intractable** pain after the operation.
- The **intractable** toddler always does the opposite of what his parents tell him to do.

*Synonym:* uncontrollable, unmanageable, incurable, inflexible
*Antonym:* docile, manageable, tractable

Further Information
- Originated from the Latin word *intractabilis* meaning "not to be handled."
- Related words include **intractability** (n.) and **intractably** (adv.).
- The medical definition of **intractable** is "not easily managed, relieved or cured."

**intransigent:** [in-TRAN-seh-jent] Adjective.
Refusing to compromise or abandon an extreme attitude or position.

- He remained **intransigent** in his refusal to meet with the other nation's leader.
- Because of his **intransigent** attitude, we were unable to come to an agreement.

*Synonym:* stubborn, uncompromising, unreasonable, irreconcilable
*Antonym:* accepting, flexible

Further Information
- Originated from the Spanish word *intransigente* meaning "uncompromising."
- Related word forms include **intransigently** (adv.).
- **Transigent** is not a word and therefore is not the antonym of **intransigent**.

**invective:** [in-VEK-tiv] Adjective/Noun.
Characterized by abuse or insult. (adj.)
Insulting or abusive language or expression. (n.)

- The politician's racist **invective** was welcomed by the like-minded convention audience. (n.)
- The boss often sent **invective** emails to her employees, forcing them to complain to human resources. (adj.)

*Synonym:* vituperation, abuse, denunciation, tirade, scorn, sarcasm
*Antonym:* praise, compliment, flattery

Further Information
- Originated from the Latin word *invectiva* meaning "abusive speech."
- Related words include **invectively** (adv.) and **invectiveness** (n.).
- An **invective** usually implies verbally skillful abusive language, not just a curse.

**inveterate:** [in-VEH-teh-ret] Adjective.
Habitual, always doing something that is expected or specified, always happening.

- She was an **inveterate** smoker and unable to quit the nasty habit completely.
- The politician was an **inveterate** believer in the doctrine of socialism.

*Synonym:* confirmed, chronic, habitual, ingrained, entrenched, set
*Antonym:* occasional

Further Information
- Originated from the Latin word *inveteratus* meaning "of long standing, old."
- Related word forms include **inveterately** (adv.) and **inveterateness** (n.).
- The Latin root *vetus*, or "old" has also inspired the adjective **veteran**.

**invigorate:** [in—VIG-eh-rayt] Verb.
To give energy and life to something or someone.

- The fresh air **invigorated** her and motivated her to take a morning run.
- The goals **invigorated** the hockey team who thought all was lost.

*Synonym:* enliven, energize, animate, revive, stimulate, vitalize
*Antonym:* depress, deaden, debilitate

Further Information
- Originated from the Old French word *envigorer* meaning "vigor."
- Related word forms include **invigoratingly** (adv.), **invigoration** (n.) and **invigorator** (n.).
- **Invigorate** may also be spelled **invigourate**.

# REVIEW EXERCISE 22

**Match the word with its synonym.**

| | | | |
|---|---|---|---|
| ___ | 1. inordinate | a. | chronic |
| ___ | 2. insidious | b. | hint |
| ___ | 3. insouciant | c. | speaker |
| ___ | 4. instigate | d. | stubborn |
| ___ | 5. interlocutor | e. | energize |
| ___ | 6. internecine | f. | deceitful |
| ___ | 7. intimation | g. | nonchalant |
| ___ | 8. intractable | h. | excessive |
| ___ | 9. intransigent | i. | destructive |
| ___ | 10. invective | j. | provoke |
| ___ | 11. inveterate | k. | uncontrollable |
| ___ | 12. invigorate | l. | abuse |

**Fill in the blanks with the most appropriate word from list above.** *(Word form may need changing.)*

1.   She was an _____ joker and never knew when to be serious.

2.   The warfare was _____ and caused losses to both sides.

3.   The group's_____ attitude meant we could not agree on anything.

4.   I don't want to _____ an argument by telling you my true feelings.

5.   The evening's _____ took the stage after the dinner to give a speech.

6.   Even rich countries can face _____ poverty.

7.   She won an _____ amount of awards at the school assembly.

8.   Diabetes is an _____ condition that might not manifest for years.

9.   Her _____ manner belied her worrisome thoughts.

10.   The politician wanted to raise taxes to _____ the economy.

11.   There was no _____ from my doctor that my condition had worsened.

12.   She shouted racist _____ at the family that had moved into her neighborhood.

# WORD SET 23

**inviolable**: [in-VEYE-uh-leh-bel] Adjective.
Too sacred to be denied or broken.
Cannot be violated, invaded or injured.

- The trust between a priest and his parishioner is **inviolable**.
- The new fortress was **inviolable** and kept the enemy out.

*Synonym:* secure, sacrosanct, holy, hallowed, sacred, untouchable
*Antonym:* violable

## Further Information
- Originated from the Latin word *inviolabilis* meaning "untouchable."
- The word **violate** also stems from the Latin root *violare*, meaning "violate."
- Related words include **inviolability** (n.), **inviolableness** (n.) and **inviolably** (adv.).


**irascible**: [ih-RAH-seh-bel] Adjective.
Having a bad temper, easily angered.

- The old man becomes more and more **irascible** as he ages.
- When the boy punched the teacher, it reminded everyone of his **irascibility**.

*Synonym:* irritable, testy, petulant, touchy, cross, short-tempered
*Antonym:* pleasant, easygoing, patient

## Further Information
- Originated from the Latin word *irascibilis* meaning "to become angry."
- The Latin prefix *ira* means "anger."
- Related word forms include **irate** (adj.), **irascibly** (adv.), **irascibility** (n.) and **irascibleness** (n.).


**irresolute**: [ih-reh-zeh-LOOT] Adjective.
Uncertain how to proceed or act.

- The girl was **irresolute** and could not decide between the two housing choices.
- He was **irresolute** when a prompt decision needed to be made.

*Synonym:* indefinite, vacillating, wavering, flexible, undecided, uncertain
*Antonym:* stubborn, resolute, unyielding

## Further Information
- Originated from the Latin word *irresolutus* meaning "not loosened."
- Related words include **irresolutely** (adv.), **irresoluteness** (n.) and **irresolution** (n.).
- **Resolve, resolute and resolution** are all opposites in meaning of **irresolute**.

**irreverence:** [ih-REV-eh-rents] Noun.
A lack of respect.

- The woman's head being uncovered in public showed an **irreverence** towards Islamic principles.
- The boy's **irreverence** for authority foreshadowed that he would be a troublemaker.

*Synonym:* profanity, disrespect, discourtesy, sacrilege, blasphemy, impiety
*Antonym:* sanctuary, helpfulness, reverence

Further Information
- Originated from the Latin word *irreverentia* meaning "disrespect."
- Related words include **irreverent** (adj.), **reverent** (adj.), **reverence** (n.) and **revere** (v.).


**itinerant:** [eye-TIN-er-ent] Adjective/Noun.
Traveling from place to place. (adj.)
One who travels from place to place. (n.)

- The **itinerant** laborer moved from one place to the next looking for available work. (adj.)
- The purpose of the mysterious **itinerant** narrator was not evident in the story. (n.)

*Synonym:* vagabond, nomadic, vagrant, wandering, gypsy, roving
*Antonym:* settled, permanent, stationary

Further Information
- Originated from the Latin word *itinerari* meaning "to journey."
- Related words include **itinerantly** (adv.).
- The Latin word *itinerari* also gave us the English word **errant**, "meaning one who likes to travel."


**jettison:** [JEH-teh-zen] Verb/Noun.
To drop or get rid of. (v.)
A sacrifice of cargo to lighten a ship's load. (n.)

- We had to **jettison** our plans to go out after school because we had to go to detention. (v.)
- When the captain thought the ship was sinking, he ordered a **jettison** of the ship's cargo. (n.)

*Synonym:* discard, reject, scrap, dump, ditch, eliminate
*Antonym:* adopt

Further Information
- Originated from the Middle English word *jetteson* meaning "act of throwing overboard."
- Related word forms include **jettisonable** (adj.).
- **Jettison** was sometimes written as **jetsam** in early English.

**juxtapose:** [JUK-stuh-poz] Verb.
To put different things beside each other either to compare/contrast them or to create effect.

- In the art gallery, simple drawings were **juxtaposed** with professional Renaissance paintings.
- It is hard to classify the program, as it **juxtaposes** serious news pieces with celebrity fluff.

*Synonym:* compare, contrast, relate, join, pair, merge
*Antonym:* division, gap
Further Information
- It is believed that **juxtapose** originated as a back-formation from the noun **juxtaposition**.
- **Juxtaposition** comes from the Latin word *juxta,* meaning "near" and the English word *position*.
- Related word forms include **juxtaposition** (n.), **juxtaposed** (v.), and **juxtaposing** (v.).


**kindle:** [KIN-del] Verb.
To start a fire.
To stir up or bring into being.
To cause to glow.

- The Boy Scouts tried to find the driest wood possible to **kindle** the fire.
- Going to the art museum really **kindled** the child's interest in and love of modern art.
- His face **kindled** with happiness when she accepted his proposal.

*Synonym:* fire, ignite, inflame, provoke, stimulate, excite
*Antonym:* extinguish, dampen, smother
Further Information
- Originated from the Old Norse word *kynda* meaning "fire."
- Related words include **kindling** (n.) or (v.), **kindler** (n.) and **kindled** (v.).
- **Kindle** also means "to bring forth young," and the term is usually used with rabbits being born.


**knell:** [NEHL] Noun/Verb.
The toll of a bell, especially rung slowly to indicate disaster or death. (n.)
A signal of the end or failure of something. (n.)
To summon or ring, especially in an ominous manner or for a death or disaster. (v.)

- We heard the **knell** signaling the funeral for the statesman had ended. (n.)
- Losing that player might be a death **knell** for the rest of the team's season. (n.)
- The church bells **knelled** to let everyone know that the king had died. (v.)

*Synonym:* ring, toll, chime, peal, sound, dirge
*Antonym:* none
Further Information
- Originated from the Old English word *cnyll* meaning "sound made by a bell struck slowly."
- Other foreign words related to knell include the Dutch *knal*, Swedish *knall*, Danish *knald* and Welsh *cnull*.

**labyrinth**: [LAH-beh-renth] Noun.
A maze or something extremely complex in arrangement.

- We lost our way in the **labyrinth** of city streets.
- The government's decisions were often delayed in the **labyrinth** of councils and committees.

*Synonym:* maze, tangle, puzzle, web, jungle, complication
*Antonym:* straight

Further Information
- Originated from the Latin word *laborintus* meaning "maze."
- Related words include **labyrinthine** (adj.).
- The medical definition of **labyrinth** is "a complicated structure of human anatomy."

**laceration**: [lah-seh-RAY-shen] Noun.
A deep, raggedly torn wound.

- She suffered **lacerations** on her face from the car accident.
- The medical examiner noted that the body showed many signs of bruising and **laceration**.

*Synonym:* cut, gash, wound, slash, hurt, injury
*Antonym:* closure

Further Information
- Originated from the Latin word *lacerationem* meaning "a tearing or mutilation."
- Related word forms include **lacerate** (v.).
- The term **laceration** is often used in medicine.

**laconic**: [leh-KAH-nik] Adjective.
Using few words in writing or speech.

- The girl was very **laconic** in the principal's office, not saying much to defend herself.
- The **laconic** musician rarely speaks in public.

*Synonym:* brief, terse, concise, pithy, succinct, compact
*Antonym:* wordy, talkative, verbose

Further Information
- Originated from the Greek word *lakonikos* meaning "terseness of speech."
- Related word forms include **laconically** (adv.).
- *Laconia* was an ancient country in southern Greece, whose capital city was Sparta. Spartans were famous for their "terseness of speech."

# REVIEW EXERCISE 23

*Match the word with its synonym.*

|   |   |   |   |
|---|---|---|---|
| ___ | 1. inviolable | a. | cut |
| ___ | 2. irascible | b. | nomadic |
| ___ | 3. irresolute | c. | discard |
| ___ | 4. irreverence | d. | ignite |
| ___ | 5. itinerant | e. | irritable |
| ___ | 6. jettison | f. | toll |
| ___ | 7. juxtapose | g. | terse |
| ___ | 8. kindle | h. | secure |
| ___ | 9. knell | i. | indefinite |
| ___ | 10. labyrinth | j. | disrespect |
| ___ | 11. laceration | k. | relate |
| ___ | 12. laconic | l. | maze |

*Fill in the blanks with the most appropriate word from list above.* *(Word form may need changing.)*

1. The loss of Texas sounded the death _____ to the party's hopes.

2. If you_____ the two items, you can clearly see the difference.

3. Your_____ for authority has labeled you a rabble-rouser.

4. It is your _____ right to expect to feel safe in public.

5. The little boy suffered _____ of the leg when he fell off his bike.

6. He has an _____ temper and blows up at the littlest things.

7. She was_____ and hesitant in the face of a crisis.

8. We_____ our holiday plans when our father did not receive a bonus.

9. The _____ salesman traveled all over the country selling his wares.

10. The politician's _____ speech contrasted with his opponent's verbosity.

11. She hopes to _____ romance with her mate by booking a second honeymoon.

12. She went through a _____ of corridors before finding her professor's office.

# WORD SET 24

**lampoon:** [lam-POON] Noun/Verb.
A piece of writing that mocks a well-known thing or person. (n.)
To make fun of. (v.)

- The cartoon **lampoons** the politicians of our day.
- The editorial was more like a **lampoon** against social policies the writer dislikes.

*Synonym:* parody, burlesque, caricature, mock, satirize, spoof
*Antonym:* support

Further Information
- Originated from the French word l*ampons* meaning "let us drink."
- Related words include **lampooner** (n.) and **lampoonery** (n.).
- **Lampoon** was first used as a noun in English in 1645. It was used as a verb about 10 years later.


**languor:** [LAHN-ger] Noun.
A usually pleasant, dreamy feeling of tiredness and inactivity, relaxation.

- She drove home in a state of **languor** after the massage.
- We **languorously** enjoyed a lazy Sunday afternoon at home.

*Synonym:* relaxation, sluggishness, torpor, laziness, dreaminess
*Antonym:* energy, enthusiasm, alacrity

Further Information
- Originated from the Latin word *languorem* meaning "faintness or lassitude."
- Other commonly used word forms include **languorous** (adj.), **languorously** (adv.) and **languorousness** (n.).


**largesse:** [lar-JESS] Noun.
The act of giving away money or the quality of a person who gives away money.

- The philanthropist is known for his **largesse**.
- The developing country depends on the **largesse** of others to survive.

*Synonym:* charity, gift, donation, generosity, munificence, bounty
*Antonym:* avarice, greed, parsimony

Further Information
- Originated from the Latin word *largus* meaning "large, abundant or generous."
- **Largesse** may also be spelled **largess**.
- Do not confuse **largesse** with **largeness**.

**lassitude**: [LAH-seh-tood] Noun.
A condition of tiredness or laziness.

- One of the symptoms of her disease is **lassitude**, which explains why she's always tired.
- Neither **lassitude** nor illness prevented her from finishing her work.

*Synonym:* listlessness, lethargy, weariness, sluggishness, fatigue
*Antonym:* enemy, vigor, alacrity
Further Information

- Originated from the Latin word *lassitudo* meaning "weary."
- The medical definition of **lassitude** is "a condition of weariness, fatigue or debility."
- **Lassitude** can also mean "negligence."

**latent**: [LAY-tent] Adjective/Noun.
Present but not active or able to be seen. (adj.)
A fingerprint that is barely visible but can be developed to study. (n.)

- Your musical talent will remain **latent** without proper instruction.
- The crime scene investigators attempted to pick up **latent** prints from the scene. (n.)

*Synonym:* dormant, concealed, hidden, inactive
*Antonym:* active, alive, obvious
Further Information

- Originated from the Greek word *lanthanein* meaning "to escape notice"
- Related words include **latently** (adv.).
- **Latent** is often used in medicine and legal realms, in both cases meaning "something that is existing in hidden form."

**laud**: [LAWD] Verb/Noun.
To praise. (v.)
An offer of solemn praise to God. (n.)

- The valedictorian was **lauded** for his academic accomplishments. (v.)
- The words of the hymn included, "All glory, **laud** and honor to Thee." (n.)

*Synonym*: praise, acclaim, admire, exalt, celebrate, extol
*Antonym:* abhor, blame, condemn
Further Information

- Originated from the Latin word *laudare* meaning "to praise."
- Related words include **laudable** (adj.).
- William **Laud** was archbishop of Canterbury in the 1600s and persecuted the Puritans, leading to the English-Scottish Civil War. He was impeached and executed.

**levity:** [LEH-veh-tee] Noun.
A lack of seriousness or steadiness.

- Although the trauma was serious, they managed to find some **levity** in the situation.
- Some teachers dismiss her intelligence because she displays too much **levity**.

*Synonym:* frivolity, flippancy, lightness, giddiness, buoyancy, flightiness
*Antonym:* permanence, seriousness, gravity

Further Information

- Originated from the Latin word *levis* meaning "light in weight."
- **Levity** was once used as a scientific term for "a physical force pulling in the opposite direction of gravity."
- Related word forms include **levitate** (v.).


**levy:** [LEH-vee] Noun/Verb.
An amount taxed or assessed. (n.)
To collect by legal authority. (v.)
To enlist for military service or to carry on war. (v.)

- The **levy** that they told us to pay for the small piece of property was way too high. (n.)
- The government **levied** a tax on alcohol and cigarettes. (v.)
- The country's government **levied** war against its enemy. (v.)

*Synonym:* tax, duty, tariff, toll, impost, charge
*Antonym:* veto, demote, displace

Further Information

- Originated from the Anglo-French word *leve* meaning "raising."
- Related words include **levier.** (n.)
- In finance, a **levy** is "the seizure of property to repay a debt."


**liability:** [ley-eh-BIL-eh-tee] Noun.
Something for which one is obligated.
A disadvantage or drawback.

- As tenants, we had **liability** for anything in the structure of the apartment that was damaged.
- His shyness is a real **liability** when he gets on stage.

*Synonym:* obligation, responsibility, burden, encumbrance, accountability, debt
*Antonym:* asset, aid, privilege

Further Information

- Originated from the Old French word *lier* meaning "to bind."
- Related words include **liable** (adj.) and **liableness** (n.).
- The financial definition of **liability** is "a claim on a person's or company's assets."

**libertarian**: [lih-ber-TER-ee-en] Noun/Adjective.
A person who believes in individual liberty, especially of action or thought. (n.)
Characterized by the belief of free will and liberty. (adj.)

- Her **libertarian** ideas for the school include getting rid of the rules and regulations. (adj.)
- He is a **libertarian** who says that genetic testing raises privacy and legal concerns. (n.)

*Synonym:* permissive, enlightened, freethinker, tolerant, liberal, independent
*Antonym:* authoritarian

Further Information
- Originated from the Latin word *liber* meaning "free."
- **Libertarian** was coined in English in 1789 from *liberty* and the *arian* suffix which means "a believer or advocate of."


**libertine**: [LIH-ber-teen] Noun/Adjective.
A person who is not restrained by morality or convention. (n.)
Unhindered by moral restraint. (adj.)

- The man was considered a **libertine** because he lived with four women. (n.)
- His **libertine** attitudes got him in trouble with the church elders. (adj.)

*Synonym:* lecher, debauchee, sensualist, freethinking, profligate, debauched
*Antonym:* chaste, moral, ethical

Further Information
- Originated from the Latin word *liber* meaning "free."
- Related word forms include **libertinage** (n.) and **libertinism** (n.).
- When it first appeared in 14th century English, the word **libertine** originally meant "freedman."


**linchpin**: [LINCH-pin] Noun.
A locking pin that is inserted crosswise.
Something that critically holds together parts that function as a unit.

- The **linchpin** came out of the wheel and the carriage overturned.
- The captain is considered to be the **linchpin** that holds the whole team together.

*Synonym:* anchor, mainstay, keystone, backbone
*Antonym:* none

Further Information
- Originated from the Middle English words *lyns* and *pin* meaning "axle" and "pin."
- The plural of **linchpin** is **linchpins.**
- **Linchpin** may also be spelled **lynchpin.**

# REVIEW EXERCISE 24

*Match the word with its synonym.*

_____ 1.  lampoon            a.  tax
_____ 2.  languor            b.  frivolity
_____ 3.  largesse           c.  concealed
_____ 4.  lassitude          d.  enlightened
_____ 5.  latent             e.  listlessness
_____ 6.  laud               f.  parody
_____ 7.  levity             g.  generosity
_____ 8.  levy               h.  obligation
_____ 9.  liability          i.  relaxation
_____ 10. libertarian        j.  praise
_____ 11. libertine          k.  anchor
_____ 12. linchpin           l.  lecher

*Fill in the blanks with the most appropriate word from list above.* *(Word form may need changing.)*

1.  Her _____ matches her beauty, as she gives millions to charity.

2.  The soldier was _____ for his courage on the battlefield.

3.  The government will_____ a tax on sodas and other beverages.

4.  His _____ ideas include legalizing certain street drugs.

5.  There are _____ dangers if you disobey the rules.

6.  The playboy was known as quite a _____ with women.

7.  Our mother is the _____ of this family and holds it together.

8.  Her beauty was seen as a _____ in her profession, which valued intelligence.

9.  The politician's speech was written to _____ his opponent.

10. Her _____ felt out of place at the solemn funeral.

11. During the long hot bath, she felt a delicious _____ settle over her.

12. He felt a sense of _____ that he knew meant he was getting sick.

# WORD SET 25

**lithe**: [LEYTH] Adjective.
Easily bent, having easy flexibility and grace.

- The **lithe** dancer moved easily across the stage.
- The middle-aged woman felt awkward among the **lithe** young girls on the beach.

*Synonym:* flexible, limber, agile, nimble, supple, pliant
*Antonym:* stiff, awkward, clumsy

Further Information
- Originated from the Old English word *lithe* meaning "gentle."
- Related words include **litheness** (n.) and **lithely** (adv.).
- An obsolete meaning of **lithe** is "calm or mild."

**loquacious**: [lo-KWAY-shes] Adjective.
Full of smooth, easy talk; wordy.

- The politician was known for his **loquaciousness**, especially at press conferences.
- The normally **loquacious** Mrs. Smith said very little when I met with her today.

*Synonym:* talkative, chatty, garrulous, wordy, verbose, gabby
*Antonym:* quiet, laconic, speechless

Further Information
- Originated from the Latin word *loqui* meaning "to speak."
- Other commonly used word forms include **loquaciously** (adv.) and **loquaciousness** (n.).
- Other words related to the Latin word *loqui* include v**entriloquism, soliloquy, eloquent** and **colloquial**.

**lucid**: [LOO-sed] Adjective.
Expressed clearly; Easy to understand.

- His writing style is **lucid** and to the point.
- In his **lucid** moments, the frail centenarian would talk excitedly about his past.

*Synonym:* clear, plain, understandable, intelligible, distinct, rational
*Antonym:* unclear, murky, confusing, ambiguous

Further Information
- Originated from the Latin word *lucere* meaning "to shine."
- Related words include **lucidly** (adv.), **luminous** (adj.) and **lucidity** (n.).
- Do not confuse with **lucent** which means "glowing with light."

**maelstrom**: [MAYL-strem] Noun.
A confusing, turbulent situation.
A dangerous area of water moving very fast in a circle.

- He was caught in a **maelstrom** of emotions after learning that he won the award but beat his brother.
- The **maelstrom** produced by the hurricane was powerful and dangerous to ships at sea.

*Synonym:* vortex, whirlpool, eddy, turbulence, confusion, stir
*Antonym:* calm, quiet

Further Information
- Originated from the Dutch word *maalstroom* meaning "to grind" and "stream."
- **Maelstrom** was a channel off the coast of Norway with dangerous tidal currents.
- **Charybdis**, from Greek mythology, meaning "a large whirlpool/sea monster that eats ships" is also a synonym of **maelstrom.**

**malleable**: [MAHL-yeh-bel Adjective.
Capable of being shaped, stretched or influenced.

- Her personality was so **malleable** that she would change her opinions like the weather.
- The iron was **malleable** once it was heated.

*Synonym:* pliable, pliant, ductile, plastic, tractable, supple
*Antonym:* stiff, rigid, firm

Further Information
- Originated from the Latin word *malleabilis* meaning "to hammer."
- Related words include **malleability** (n.).
- The first usage of **malleable** was to describe metals that could be reshaped when beaten with a hammer.

**masticate**: [MAS-teh-kayt] Verb.
To chew.

- The old woman's mouth worked in her sleep, as if she were **masticating** something.
- The cat refused to thoroughly **masticate** her food, resulting in her vomiting it up.

*Synonym*: chew, munch, gnaw, chomp, crunch, nibble
*Antonym: none*

Further Information
- Originated from the Greek word *mastichan* meaning "to gnash the teeth."
- Related words include **mastication** (n.) and **masticator** (n.).

**maudlin:** [MAWD-len] Adjective.
Displaying or expressing too much emotion in a silly, sentimental way.

- After his third glass of wine, he became **maudlin** and weepy.
- The drama was described by critics as being too **maudlin** for modern tastes.

*Synonym:* sentimental, mawkish, mushy, schmaltzy, romantic, sappy
*Antonym:* unemotional, calm, numb

Further Information
- Originated from the Biblical character *Mary Magdalene*, as she was a "weeping penitent."
- **Magdalene** was the original word until it was altered in the 16th century to **maudlin.**
- Related words include **maudlinly** (adv.) and **maudlinness** (n.).


**maverick:** [MAV-rik] Noun/Adjective.
An independent animal or person who does not go along with the group. (n.)
Not following the rules or customs of a group. (adj.)

- He was a real **maverick**, setting off on his own and leaving his group behind. (n.)
- The candidate was too much of a **maverick** politician for her party to support her. (adj.)

*Synonym:* nonconformist, unorthodox, unconventional, rebel, radical, dissenter
*Antonym:* conformist, perfectionist

Further Information
- Originated from *Samuel A. Maverick*, an 1870 pioneer who did not brand his calves.
- Originally, **maverick** referred to "an unbranded calf allowed to roam freely."
- **Maverick** was a popular U.S. television show in the late 1950s/early 1960s.


**mendacious:** [men-DAY-shus] Adjective.
Based on lies, dishonest.

- The children readily believed his **mendacious** tales of adventure, but we adults knew better.
- The politician was described by the press as a **mendacious** philanderer.

*Synonym:* deceitful, false, lying, untruthful, dishonest, hypocritical
*Antonym:* true, veracious, straightforward

Further Information
- Originated from the Latin word *mendacium* meaning "to lie."
- Related words include **mendaciously** (adv.) and **mendaciousness** (n.).
- **Mendacious** usually describes "one who lies over and over, intentionally and habitually."

**mercurial**: [mer-KYUR-ee-el] Adjective.
Changing moods often, unpredictably and quickly.

- Her **mercurial** temperament has won her few friends.
- She showed her **mercurial** self, changing her mind about who her date for the dance would be.

*Synonym:* fickle, erratic, capricious, changeable, inconstant, unstable
*Antonym:* consistent, calm, unchangeable

Further Information
- Originated from the Roman god *Mercury*, noted for eloquence, cunning and swiftness.
- **Mercurial** originally meant "having elegance, quickness and ingenuity related to the god/planet Mercury."
- Related words include **mercurially** (adv.) and **mercurialness** (n.).
- The medical definition of **mercurial** is "a product containing mercury."

**metamorphosis**: [met-uh-MOR-feh-ses] Noun.
A change of physical form, character, appearance or circumstances.

- The butterfly is the result of the **metamorphosis** of a caterpillar.
- The website underwent a complete **metamorphosis** and is almost unrecognizable.

*Synonym:* transformation, alteration, change, mutation, transfiguration, modification
*Antonym:* unchanging, stagnation, stable

Further Information
- Originated from the Greek word *metamorphoun* meaning "to transform."
- The plural of **metamorphosis** is **metamorphoses**.
- In Greek mythology, many myths end in a **metamorphosis**.

**modicum**: [MOD-eh-kem] Noun.
A small amount or quantity.

- You expect to see at least a **modicum** of sadness at someone's funeral.
- If she had a **modicum** of decency, she wouldn't have worn a dress that short to church.

*Synonym:* dash, bit, particle, iota, crumb, speck
*Antonym:* abundance, lot

Further Information
- Originated from the Latin word *modicus* meaning "moderate."
- Other words with the modus root include **modulate, modern, modify** and **model**.
- **Modicum** was originally a Scottish word before it was adopted into English.

# REVIEW EXERCISE 25

**Match the word with its synonym.**

| | | | | |
|---|---|---|---|---|
| ___ | 1. | lithe | a. | erratic |
| ___ | 2. | loquacious | b. | unconventional |
| ___ | 3. | lucid | c. | chew |
| ___ | 4. | maelstrom | d. | dash |
| ___ | 5. | malleable | e. | turbulence |
| ___ | 6. | masticate | f. | flexible |
| ___ | 7. | maudlin | g. | talkative |
| ___ | 8. | maverick | h. | sentimental |
| ___ | 9. | mendacious | i. | clear |
| ___ | 10. | mercurial | j. | pliable |
| ___ | 11. | metamorphosis | k. | transformation |
| ___ | 12. | modicum | l. | dishonest |

**Fill in the blanks with the most appropriate word from list above.** *(Word form may need changing.)*

1.  Her _____ mood shifts scared her young children.

2.  The baby has not learned to _____ solid food and almost choked.

3.  He had a_____, graceful stride as he walked across the stage.

4.  The _____ girl got in trouble for chattering to a friend during class.

5.  Exercising caused him to experience a great _____ of his body.

6.  He was considered a _____ in the corporate world as he led in his own way.

7.  Don't let her have more than three drinks or she'll become _____.

8.  Write your essay in a clear, _____ style so we can understand it.

9.  Although she did not show it, she felt a _____ of emotions.

10. His facial features were quite _____, helping his acting ability.

11. The student told a _____ story to explain why he was cheating.

12. I only need a _____ of money to support my basic needs.

# WORD SET 26

**morass**: [meh-RAS] Noun.
A swamp or marsh.
A confusing or overwhelming situation or mixture.

- The attorney was challenged trying to find a solution for the legal **morass** of his client.
- As he was walking back from the lake, he became stuck in a **morass** he didn't know was there.

*Synonym:* quagmire, chaos, mess, tangle, swamp, bog
*Antonym:* desert, order
Further Information
- Originated from the Old French word *maresc* meaning "marsh."
- Related words include **morassy** (adj.).
- Although **morass** literally means "swamp," it's more commonly used in a figurative sense today to describe "a situation in which one does not want to get stuck."


**mores**: [MOR-ez] Noun.
Morally binding custom, attitudes or manners of a group.

- Social **mores** of the tribe required men and women to sit on different sides of the room.
- The man had no concept of societal **mores** and did not know the proper way to act on a date.

*Synonym:* etiquette, culture, custom, manners, decorum, morals
*Antonym: none*
Further Information
- Originated from the Latin word *mos* meaning "custom."
- **Mores** is a commonly used term in sociology.
- Although it looks like the word **more, mores** should be pronounced with two syllables.


**moribund**: [MOR-eh-bund] Adjective.
Dying or in the process of dying, being inactive or becoming obsolete.

- Because of the Internet, many say traditional newspapers are **moribund**.
- The consultant is credited with reviving what had been a **moribund** corporation.

*Synonym:* dying, expiring, stagnant, fading, declining, going
*Antonym:* alive, active, thriving
Further Information
- Originated from the Latin word *mori* meaning "to die."
- Related words include **moribundity** (n.).
- The medical definition of **moribund** is "approaching death."

**multifarious:** [mul-tee-FER-ee-us] Adjective.
Having a great variety, diverse

- This country is a composite of **multifarious** nationalities and customs.
- The school has a **multifarious** student population.

*Synonym:* diverse, manifold, various, assorted, miscellaneous, varied
*Antonym:* homogenous, identical

Further Information
- Originated from the Latin word *multifariam* meaning "in many places."
- Related words include **multifariousness** (n.).
- In the 15th century the word **multifary**, meaning "in many ways," appeared, and then disappeared, in written English.


**munificent:** [myu-NIH-feh-sent] Adjective.
Liberal in giving, generous.

- The millionaire is known for being **munificent** and donating large sums to many charities.
- The former student donated a **munificent** amount of money to the university.

*Synonym:* generous, charitable, philanthropic, bountiful, lavish, unselfish
*Antonym:* greedy, stingy, frugal

Further Information
- Originated from the Latin word *munificus* meaning "generous."
- Related words include **munificence** (n.) and **munificently** (adv.).
- **Munificent** was formed when English speakers in the 1500s changed **munificence** to **munificent**.


**nadir:** [NAY-der] Noun.
The lowest and deepest point, usually associated with despair or adversity.

- When she lost her job, she wondered if she was at the **nadir** of her career.
- After he spent all his money he found that his fortune was at its **nadir**.

*Synonym:* bottom, base, sole, foot, depths, minimum
*Antonym:* zenith, acme, peak

Further Information
- Originated from the Arabic word *nazir* meaning "opposite the zenith."
- In astronomy, the **nadir** is "a point on the sphere directly opposite the zenith and below the observer."
- John Donne first used the word **nadir** to mean "lowest point" in a 1627 sermon.

**nascent:** [NAH-sent] Adjective.
Having recently come into existence.

- A **nascent** socialist movement is starting in the country as a reaction to conservatism.
- Online dating was once a **nascent** idea and is now the norm for many people.

*Synonym:* incipient, emerging, beginning, initial, inaugural, introductory
*Antonym:* last, dying, moribund

Further Information
- Originated from the Latin word *nascens*, meaning "to be born."
- Other words related to the Latin word *nascens* include **nature, native, nation, innate** and **natal.**
- In chemistry, **nascent** means "relating to a substance at the moment of its formation with greater reactivity than normal."


**nefarious:** [neh-FER-ee-us] Adjective.
Blatantly breaking with traditions and laws of conduct; wicked, evil.

- The con man pulled off a **nefarious** scheme to rob people of their money.
- The dictator's government was accused of **nefarious** activities such as financing drug traffickers.

*Synonym:* villainous, criminal, atrocious, wicked, vile, vicious
*Antonym:* honorable, virtuous, ethical

Further Information
- Originated from the Latin word *nefas* meaning "crime."
- Related word forms include **nefariously** (adv.) and **nefariousness** (n.).
- **Nefarious** is often used to describe "actions, plans or conspiracies that are immoral or criminal."


**neophyte:** [NEE-uh-feyt] Noun.
A beginner, a new convert, a novice.

- The awestruck **neophyte** walked down the red carpet among her acclaimed peers.
- It was obvious from his answers to debate questions that the candidate was a **neophyte** at politics.

*Synonym:* beginner, novice, rookie, amateur, apprentice, newcomer
*Antonym:* professional, expert

Further Information
- Originated from the Greek word *neophytos* meaning "newly planted."
- **Neophyte** was first widely seen in print in English in a 16<sup>th</sup> century Bible translation.
- In Christianity, especially Catholicism, **neophyte** refers to "a person who has recently become a Christian/Catholic and has been baptized."

**nepotism:** [NEH-peh-ti-zem] Noun.
The unfair practice of a powerful person giving jobs and/or favors to relatives.

- The man claimed he was a victim of **nepotism** because he lost the job to the boss's daughter.
- Although widely frowned upon, **nepotism** runs rampant in the administration, with many staffers sharing last names.

*Synonym:* bias, partiality, favoritism, partisanship, preference, inclination
*Antonym:* equity, justice

Further Information
- Originated from the Latin word *nepos* meaning "grandson, nephew."
- Related words include **nepotistic** (adj.).
- The word **nepotism** was first seen after the publication of a book on favoritism among popes in 1667, *Il Nepotismo di Roma*, translated as "The History of the Popes' Nephews."

**notoriety:** [no-teh-REYE-eh-tee] Noun.
The state of being very widely known, especially for something bad.

- The criminal achieved **notoriety** for kidnapping dozens of children in the country.
- This model year and make of car has a certain **notoriety** for brake problems.

*Synonym:* fame, renown, repute, infamy, celebrity, distinction
*Antonym:* anonymity, obscurity

Further Information
- Originated from the Latin word *notorius* meaning "widely or fully known."
- Related words include **notorious** (adj.) and **notoriousness** (n.).
- The negative connotation of **notoriety** did not appear in its meaning until the 17th century.

**obdurate:** [AHB-dur-et] Adjective.
Stubborn and resistant to changing one's opinion or behavior.

- The candidate was **obdurate**, refusing to alter his opinion on the issue.
- He was so **obdurate** in his position that he did not want to go on vacation.

*Synonym:* stubborn, inflexible, rigid, uncompromising, unyielding, obstinate
*Antonym:* abundance, lot

Further Information
- Originated from the Latin word *obduratus* meaning "to harden."
- Other words that trace back to the Latin root *durus* include **endure**, **dour, durable,** and **during**.
- An obsolete meaning of **obdurate** is "physically toughened or hardened."

# REVIEW EXERCISE 26

*Match the word with its synonym.*

___ 1. morass          a. novice
___ 2. mores           b. emerging
___ 3. moribund        c. dying
___ 4. multifarious    d. diverse
___ 5. munificent      e. generous
___ 6. nadir           f. stubborn
___ 7. nascent         g. quagmire
___ 8. nefarious       h. villainous
___ 9. neophyte        i. favoritism
___ 10. nepotism       j. custom
___ 11. notoriety      k. bottom
___ 12. obdurate       l. renown

*Fill in the blanks with the most appropriate word from list above.* (Word form may need changing.)

1. Her abrasive manner garnered her much unwanted _____.

2. Company morale has reached a _____ due to the many layoffs.

3. She was a _____ who was too eager to try to reform the dangerous criminal.

4. A _____ of red tape is preventing us from getting a mortgage.

5. It is interesting to study the _____ of various social tribes and groups.

6. Although they argued, he remained _____ in his opinion.

7. The _____ record store carried quite a variety of genres of music.

8. The principal ordered some new computers to replace our _____ ones.

9. The _____ embryo is too small yet to see via ultrasound.

10. The rich boss gave his employees some surprisingly _____ gifts.

11. Because of his _____ actions, he was feared among members of the mob.

12. The college was accused of _____ for hiring the dean's son as professor.

# WORD SET 27

**obfuscate:** [AHB-feh-skayt] Verb.
To confuse or make obscure.

- Her arguments during the debate **obfuscated** the main issue.
- The writer tends to **obfuscate** the main topic with unnecessary details.

*Synonym:* confuse, obscure, cloud, muddle, darken, perplex
*Antonym:* interpret, clarify, explain

Further Information
- Originated from the Latin word *obfuscare* meaning "in the way" and "dark brown."
- Related words include **obfuscatory** (adj.) and **obfuscation** (n.).
- The Latin root *ob* means "in the way" and is also found in words such as **obscure**.


**obsequious:** [ahb-SEE-kwee-us] Adjective.
Too eagerly attentive, fawning.

- The student is **obsequious** to all his teachers, hoping to flatter his way into good grades.
- The **obsequious** praise she received angered her brother, who knew she deserved none of it.

*Synonym:* servile, sycophantic, humble, fawning, subservient, toadying
*Antonym:* disobedient, arrogant, assertive

Further Information
- Originated from the Latin word *obsequium* meaning "compliance."
- Related word forms include **obsequiously** (adv.) and **obsequiousness** (n.).
- Other words with the Latin root *sequi*, which means "to follow," include **sequel, consequence** and **non sequitur**.


**obstreperous:** [ahb-STREH-peh-rus] Adjective.
Aggressively noisy, unruly and hard to control.

- After he had too many drinks at the party, he became **obstreperous**.
- Children who were placed on the attention deficit disorder drug were less **obstreperous**.

*Synonym:* boisterous, disorderly, unruly, noisy, rowdy, vociferous
*Antonym:* quiet, obedient, tractable

Further Information
- Originated from the Latin word *obstrepere* meaning "to clamor against."
- Related words include **obstreperousness** (n.) and **obstreperously** (adv.).
- The literal translation of **obstreperous** is "to make a noise against" or "to rebel against."

**obviate**: [AHB-vee-ayt] Verb.
To anticipate and prevent something from happening.

- If the diplomats come up with a peaceful solution it would **obviate** the need for war.
- Studying well for the test the night before **obviates** the need to cram just before the test.

*Synonym:* prevent, preclude, avert, avoid, forestall, hinder
*Antonym:* ask, need, involve
<u>Further Information</u>
- Originated from the Latin word *obviare* meaning "to hinder or block."
- Related words include **obviation** (n.) and **obvious** (adj.).
- Remember, only things that haven't yet occurred can be **obviated**.

**occult**: [uh-KULT] Verb/Adjective/Noun.
To cover from view. (v.)
Secret, not easily understood, hidden. (adj.)
Related to mysticism or magic. (adj.)
Something that involves a supernatural influence. (n.)

- During a lunar eclipse, the earth **occults** the moon. (v.)
- The mystic studied **occult** knowledge before opening her psychic business. (adj.)
- The **occult** carcinoma was not detected until it was too late. (adj.)
- The **occult** is regarded by some religious people as heretical. (n.)

*Synonym:* mysterious, mystic, secret, obscure, esoteric, arcane
*Antonym:* known, natural
<u>Further Information</u>
- Originated from the Latin word *occultus* meaning "secret, concealed, hidden."
- Related words include **occulter** (n.), **occultation** (n.) and **occultism** (n.).
- **Occult** is not related to the word "cult."

**onerous**: [O-neh-res] Adjective.
Causing a burden, especially a distasteful one.
Being under legal obligations that outweigh any advantages.

- When the student vomited in the hall, the janitor had the **onerous** task of cleaning up the mess.
- The **onerous** contract that was once beneficial now kept him tied to a team he loathed.

*Synonym:* burdensome, difficult, laborious, hard, arduous, strenuous
*Antonym:* easy, light, effortless
<u>Further Information</u>
- Originated from the Latin word *onerosus* meaning "burden."
- Related words include **onerously** (adv.) and **onerousness** (n.).
- Other words derived from the Latin root *onus* include **exonerate** and **oneration**.

**opaque:** [o-PAYK] Adjective.
Blocking light.
Hard to explain or understand.

- The curtains were so **opaque** they blocked all the sunlight that would come in the window.
- The professor's jargon and convoluted speech was **opaque** to me.

*Synonym:* dark, obscure, hazy, cloudy, unclear, murky
*Antonym:* transparent, clear, translucent

Further Information
- Originated from the Latin word *opacus* meaning "dark or shaded."
- Related words include **opacity** (n.), **opaquely** (adv.) and **opaqueness** (n.).
- A less-used meaning of **opaque** is "stupid or obtuse."

**opprobrium:** [uh-PRO-bree-um] Noun.
Something that causes public shame or disgrace, or the actual disapproval/criticism itself.

- Some felt that the criminal didn't deserve the **opprobrium** the public heaped on him.
- The ex-convict was the **opprobrium** of our community.

*Synonym:* shame, disgrace, infamy, disrepute, obloquy, odium
*Antonym:* pride, dignity, honor

Further Information
- Originated from the Latin word *opprobrare* meaning "to reproach."
- Related word forms include **opprobrious** (adj.).
- Another lesser used related word is **exprobrate**, meaning "to criticize strongly."

**orthodox:** [OR-theh-dahks] Adjective/Noun.
Conforming to accepted, established doctrine or approaches. (adj.)
A person who conforms. (n.)

- She took the **orthodox** approach to teaching, lecturing and using a textbook. (adj.)
- He is an **orthodox** who believes in a literal interpretation of scripture. (n.)

*Synonym:* traditional, conventional, standard, customary, mainstream, normal
*Antonym:* unorthodox, unconventional, irregular

Further Information
- Originated from the Greek word *orthodoxos* meaning "having the right opinion."
- Related words include **orthodoxly** (adv.).
- **Orthodox** can also refer to a branch of Judaism and several branches of Christianity, including Greek and Russian Orthodox.

**ostentatious**: [ah-sten-TAY-shus] Adjective.
Attracting attention by showing off cleverness or wealth.

- The **ostentatious** mansions that were set along the oceanfront cost millions of dollars.
- His **ostentatious** show of wealth did not impress us, as we knew he was not generous.

*Synonym:* showy, pretentious, flamboyant, flashy, gaudy, pompous
*Antonym:* modest, humble, reserved

Further Information
- Originated from the Latin word *ostentare* meaning "to display."
- Related words include **ostentation** (n.).
- **Ostentatious** may be applied to "people who show off by spending money or to buildings or things that are too luxurious and pretentious."


**ostracism**: [AHS-treh-sih-zem] Noun.
Excluding something or someone by general consent of a group.

- Victims of that disease unfortunately often experience **ostracism**.
- The new girl was **ostracized** by the popular crowd at the school because she was different.

*Synonym:* exile, banishment, exclusion, expulsion, deportation, expatriation
*Antonym:* inclusion

Further Information
- Originated from the Greek word *ostrakismos* meaning "to banish."
- Related words include **ostracize** (v.).
- In ancient Athens, Greece, **ostracism** was a banishment of someone agreed upon by popular vote.


**palliate**: [PAL-ee-ayt] Verb.
To moderate the effects or intensity of something, making it less harsh or painful.

- The essential oils will not cure the disease but may **palliate** its symptoms.
- Women's groups and clubs helped to **palliate** the homemaker's loneliness.

*Synonym:* mitigate, soften, relieve, alleviate, assuage, soothe
*Antonym:* agitate, blame

Further Information
- Originated from the Latin word *palliare* meaning "to conceal."
- Related words include **palliative** (adj.), **palliation** (n.) and **palliator** (n.).
- **Palliative** care is often referred to as hospice care and is designed to keep the dying comfortable without attempting to cure their illness or disease.

# REVIEW EXERCISE 27

*Match the word with its synonym.*

| | | | | | |
|---|---|---|---|---|---|
| ___ | 1. | obfuscate | a. | showy | |
| ___ | 2. | obsequious | b. | obscure | |
| ___ | 3. | obstreperous | c. | prevent | |
| ___ | 4. | obviate | d. | fawning | |
| ___ | 5. | occult | e. | confuse | |
| ___ | 6. | onerous | f. | relieve | |
| ___ | 7. | opaque | g. | shame | |
| ___ | 8. | opprobrium | h. | burdensome | |
| ___ | 9. | orthodox | i. | exile | |
| ___ | 10. | ostentatious | j. | boisterous | |
| ___ | 11. | ostracism | k. | mystic | |
| ___ | 12. | palliate | l. | conventional | |

*Fill in the blanks with the most appropriate word from list above.* (Word form may need changing.)

1. The diamonds she wore around her neck were too _____ for my tastes.

2. The terrorist act attracted international _____.

3. She is interested in witchcraft and the _____.

4. The politicians _____ the real issue in favor of rumors and innuendo.

5. She tried to _____ her own faults by exposing the faults of her friend.

6. The salesperson was _____ to me as he was trying to make a sale.

7. The children were too _____ for their grandmother to watch.

8. Her poetry was too _____ and I couldn't understand its meaning.

9. Helping a friend move was one of the most _____ favors I've ever done.

10. The district boss coming to our site _____ our need to travel to him.

11. She looked for a more _____ solution to the problem.

12. The deposed leader was _____ by the citizens of his country.

# WORD SET 28

**panacea**: [pa-nuh-SEE-uh] Noun.
A remedy for all difficulties or problems; something/someone that will make a situation better.

- There is no **panacea** to cure your disease, but we can palliate its symptoms.
- The politician could not offer a **panacea** to fix the nation's economy.

*Synonym:* remedy, cure, elixir, drug, antidote, medicine
*Antonym:* toxin, poison, venom

Further Information
- Originated from the Greek word *panakes* meaning "all-healing."
- Related words include **panacean** (adj.).
- **Panacea** was the Greek goddess of healing.

**pandemonium**: [pan-deh-MOH-nee-um] Noun.
Tumult, a wild uproar.

- There was complete **pandemonium** in the classroom when the teacher stepped out for a bit.
- **Pandemonium** broke out when the celebrity was spotted at the parade.

*Synonym:* chaos, uproar, commotion, tumult, bedlam, confusion
*Antonym:* peace, calm, order

Further Information
- Originated from the Greek word *daimonion* meaning "inferior divine power."
- Related words include **pandemoniac** (n.), **pandemoniacal** (adj.) and **pandemonian** (adj.).
- When capitalized, **Pandemonium** refers to "the capital of Hell in John Milton's *Paradise Lost*" or it may describe in general "the lowest regions of Hell."

**parable**: [PAHR-eh-bel] Noun.
A short story that exemplifies a moral or religious ideal.

- The Bible teacher taught the children the **parable** of the Good Samaritan.
- The trader's rise and fall is the **parable** of the greed of the 1980s.

*Synonym:* fable, allegory, story, legend, anecdote, myth
*Antonym:* fact, nonfiction

Further Information
- Originated from the Latin word *parabola* meaning "comparison."
- Other words derived from *parabola* include **palaver** and **parole**.
- **Parabola** in geometry is "a comparison between a fixed point and a straight line."

**paradigm**: [PAHR-eh-deym] Noun.
A model or example for something.
A group of ideas or theory about how something should be done.

- The businesswoman had become the **paradigm** of a successful woman.
- The terrorist attack prompted the government to create a new **paradigm** for homeland security.

*Synonym:* example, pattern, archetype, prototype, ideal
*Antonym: none*

Further Information
- Originated from the Greek word *paradeigma* meaning "to show side by side."
- Related words include **paradigmatic** (adj.) and **paradigmatically** (adv.).
- The term **paradigm shift** means "a change in one's underlying ideas or theories."


**paradox**: [PAHR-eh-daks] Noun.
Something or someone that contradicts itself but may be true.
A statement that seems to contradict itself but might be true.

- It seems to be a **paradox** that poverty can exist in such a rich country.
- Some see it as a **paradox** that many comedians find despair in their personal lives.

*Synonym:* absurdity, enigma, contradiction, inconsistency, ambiguity, mystery
*Antonym:* certainty, axiom, normality

Further Information
- Originated from the Greek word *paradoxos* meaning "contrary to expectation."
- Related words include **paradoxical** (adj.).
- There are many famous **paradoxes** in medicine and philosophy.


**paragon**: [PAHR-eh-gahn] Noun.
A model of perfection, an outstanding example.

- The girl was a **paragon** of virtue and never did anything that went against her morals.
- The country was upheld as a **paragon** of democracy.

*Synonym*: epitome, perfection, model
*Antonym:* imperfection

Further Information
- Originated from the Italian word *paragone* meaning "touchstone."
- A **paragon** may also describe "a perfect diamond of at least 100 carats."
- An obsolete meaning of **paragon** is "a companion or a match."

**pariah** [peh-REYE-eh] Noun.
A person who is rejected or hated by others.

- The whistleblower quickly became the **pariah** of the company.
- In this story, the **pariah** becomes a hero.

*Synonym:* outcast, castaway, derelict, tramp, outsider, exile
*Antonym:* none
<u>Further Information</u>
- Originated from the Tamil word *paraiyan* meaning "drummer."
- In Tamil or Malaysia, the **pariah** was "a drummer who was of the lower strata of society."
- A **pariah** may also mean "a member of a low caste in southern India."

**parsimonious**: [par-seh-MOH-nee-us] Adjective.
Being frugal, stingy or restrained.

- The **parsimonious** old man ate only canned food, as fresh food was more expensive.
- The tourists were **parsimonious** and did not want to pay more than $100 per night for lodging.

*Synonym:* stingy, miserly, penurious, frugal, selfish
*Antonym:* generous, extravagant, selfless
<u>Further Information</u>
- Originated from the Latin word *parsimonia* meaning "perfect stem."
- Related word forms include **parsimony** (n.) and **parsimoniously** (adv.).
- In sports, **parsimonious** usually describes "a team that doesn't give up many goals or points."

**patent**: [PAH-tent] Adjective/Noun/Verb.
Readily visible, obvious. (adj.)
Unobstructed, allowing free passage. (adj.)
A written document that secures the right from others making, using or selling an invention. (n.)
To obtain such a document. (v.)

- The politician's **patent** lies were easily pointed out by his opponent during the debate. (adj.)
- There is a **patent** opening that allows us to get through the underground cave. (adj.)
- She was seeking a **patent** on her invention before bringing it to the marketplace. (n.)
- He **patented** the product so that no one could copy his ideas. (v.)

*Synonym:* obvious, manifest, apparent, clear, evident, unmistakable
*Antonym:* hidden, ambiguous, unclear
<u>Further Information</u>
- Originated from the Latin word *patens* meaning "to be open."
- Related words include **patently** (adv.) and **patentable** (adj.).
- An archaic meaning of **patent** is "exposed or accessible."

**pathological**: [pah-the-LAH-jih-kel] Adjective.
Caused by, changed by or indicative of disease.
Being extreme or abnormal, unwholesome.

- Doctors agreed that the **pathological** changes seen in the patient's tumor were not a good sign.
- The boy was a **pathological** liar who could not tell the truth if his life depended upon it.

*Synonym:* diseased, morbid, unhealthy, unsound
*Antonym:* healthy

Further Information
- Originated from the Greek word *pathos* meaning "disease."
- Related words include **pathology** (n.) and **pathologically** (adv.).
- In medicine, **pathological** can also mean "related to the study of disease."


**paucity**: [PAW-seh-tee] Noun.
Smallness of quantity or number.

- His name has a **paucity** of vowels and is hard for others to pronounce.
- Unfortunately, there is a **paucity** of answers to the problem of rush hour traffic congestion.

*Synonym:* insufficiency, dearth, lack, scarcity, shortage, deficiency
*Antonym:* plethora, abundance, opulence

Further Information
- Originated from the Latin word *paucus* meaning "little."
- **Paucity** was first seen in written English in the 15th century.


**pecuniary**: [peh-KYU-nee-er-ee] Adjective
Related to, consisting of or measured in money.

- The reasons for their divorce were **pecuniary** and, while not romantic, made financial sense.
- The company's chief financial officer was accused of crimes of **pecuniary** indecency.

*Synonym:* financial, monetary, fiscal, economic, commercial
*Antonym:* nonfinancial

Further Information
- Originated from the Latin word *pecunia* meaning "money."
- Related words include **pecuniarily** (adv.).
- In Latin, *pecus* meant "cattle," and was close to *pecunia*, or "money," as cattle were a trading commodity.

# REVIEW EXERCISE 28

**Match the word with its synonym.**

| | | | | |
|---|---|---|---|---|
| ___ | 1. | panacea | a. | financial |
| ___ | 2. | pandemonium | b. | obvious |
| ___ | 3. | parable | c. | outcast |
| ___ | 4. | paradigm | d. | contradiction |
| ___ | 5. | paradox | e. | example |
| ___ | 6. | paragon | f. | unhealthy |
| ___ | 7. | pariah | g. | remedy |
| ___ | 8. | parsimonious | h. | chaos |
| ___ | 9. | patent | i. | story |
| ___ | 10. | pathological | j. | epitome |
| ___ | 11. | paucity | k. | scarcity |
| ___ | 12. | pecuniary | l. | stingy |

**Fill in the blanks with the most appropriate word from list above.** *(Word form may need changing.)*

1. I can't get a loan because of my poor _____ history.

2. He is a _____ gambler who bets on every competition imaginable.

3. The _____ of the boy who cried wolf is designed to teach us not to lie.

4. Is chicken soup really a _____ for the common cold?

5. The economic _____ of this nation says price determines demand.

6. There is a _____ of common sense among many in the government.

7. He was injured in the _____ of the riot.

8. In an odd _____, the medicine made her sicker before it cured her.

9. He is the _____ of the family and is never invited to family gatherings.

10. The girl was _____ with her spending, rarely buying new clothes.

11. He should get a _____ on his invention before his idea is stolen.

12. The nun is considered a_____ of virtue by the church members.

# WORD SET 29

**pejorative**: [pi-JOR-eh-tiv] Noun/Adjective.
A word or phrase with negative connotations. (n.)
A word or remarks that have negative connotations. (adj.)

- To conservatives, the word "liberal" is a **pejorative** term. (adj.)
- The word that was a racial slur was a **pejorative** that no one wanted him to repeat. (n.)

*Synonym:* disparaging, deprecatory, derisive, derogatory, uncomplimentary
*Antonym:* complimentary, positive, praising
Further Information
- Originated from the Latin word *pejoratus* meaning "to aggravate or make worse."
- Related words include **pejoratively** (adv.).
- Synonyms of the noun form of **pejorative** are **dyslogism** and **dysphemism.**

**penchant**: [PEN-chent] Noun.
A liking or inclination for something or someone.

- Because she has a **penchant** for Chinese food, we took her to the new Asian restaurant.
- My **penchant** for wandering around new neighborhoods has fueled my love of travel.

*Synonym:* inclination, predilection, partiality, fondness, liking, taste
*Antonym:* disinclination, indifference, aversion
Further Information
- Originated from the French word *pencher* meaning "to incline."
- A **penchant** is also "a card game."
- In the card game **penchant**, "the act of holding a queen and jack of different suits" is also called a **penchant**.

**penurious**: [peh-NUR-ee-us] Adjective.
Showing extreme frugality or stinginess.
Very poor or impoverished

- The **penurious** old man died owning few possessions despite the large sums of money hidden in his house.
- The **penurious** beggar asked anyone he came across on the street for money.

*Synonym:* penniless, poor, parsimonious, miserly, stingy, frugal
*Antonym:* affluent, prosperous, generous
Further Information
- Originated from the Latin word *penuriosus* meaning "want."
- Related word forms include **penuriously** (adv.) and **penuriousness** (n.).

**peregrination**: [per-eh-greh-NAY-shun] Noun.
A trip, especially one taken on foot.

- His many **peregrinations** were filmed for a television program on the travel network.
- We took a **peregrination** across the countryside when we visited Ireland.

*Synonym:* journey, trip, expedition, trek, jaunt, excursion
*Antonym: none*

Further Information
- Originated from the Latin word *peregrinus* meaning "foreign."
- Related words include **peregrinate** (v.) and **peregrine** (adj.).
- The original meaning of **peregrination** was "a trip on foot taken by a pilgrim."


**perfidious:** [per-FIH-dee-us] Adjective.
Disloyal, faithless, treacherous.

- The candidate argued that the education bill was **perfidious** since it also increased taxes on the middle class.
- The **perfidious** military attack took the country's citizens by surprise.

*Synonym:* treacherous, dishonest, traitorous, false, disloyal, deceitful
*Antonym:* loyal, faithful, devoted

Further Information
- Originated from the Latin word *perfidiosus* meaning "faithless, dishonest."
- Related words include **perfidy** (n.), **perfidiously** (adv.) and **perfidiousness** (n.).
- **Perfidious** was first seen in the English language in 1572.


**perfunctory**: [per-FUNK-teh-ree] Adjective.
Lacking in enthusiasm or interest, seeming routine or superficial.

- His **perfunctory** speech was given out of obligation, not interest in the cause.
- It seemed a **perfunctory** courtesy when he opened her car door for her.

*Synonym:* indifferent, cursory, negligent, thoughtless, careless, superficial
*Antonym:* attentive, careful, prudent

Further Information
- Originated from the Latin word *perfungi* meaning "to accomplish."
- Related word forms include **perfunctorily** (adv.) and **perfunctoriness** (n.).
- **Perfunctory** may also mean "done as a formality only."

**pernicious:** [per-NIH-shes] Adjective.
Highly destructive.

- Telling lies can be **pernicious** to a relationship.
- The **pernicious** fire destroyed most of the homes in the neighborhood.

*Synonym:* harmful, deleterious, destructive, injurious, baneful, noxious
*Antonym:* benevolent, good, salubrious

Further Information
- Originated from the Latin word *pernicies* meaning "destruction."
- Related word forms include **perniciously** (adv.) and **perniciousness** (n.).
- An archaic meaning of **pernicious** is "wicked."

**perspicacious:** [per-speh-KAH-shes] Adjective.
Able to understand things that are not obvious or are difficult to understand.

- He was **perspicacious** and found the solution to the problem quickly and easily.
- She was **perspicacious** enough to realize the situation was about to change.

*Synonym:* discerning, perceptive, astute, intelligent, shrewd, sagacious
*Antonym:* ignorant, dense, dull

Further Information
- Originated from the Latin word *perspicere* meaning "to look through."
- Related word forms include **perspicacity** (n.) and **perspicaciously** (adv.).
- **Perspicacious** can also be used as a synonym for "savvy."

**pert:** [PERT] Adjective.
Disrespectful and bold.
Perky and attractive.

- The **pert** pharmacist rudely brushed off the customer's questions and went back to work.
- The **pert** cashier greeted customers warmly as they entered the store.

*Synonym:* saucy, sassy, fresh, impertinent, impudent, forward
*Antonym:* dull, lifeless, bland

Further Information
- Originated from the Latin word *apertus* meaning "open."
- Related words include **pertly** (adv.) and **pertness** (n.).
- An archaic meaning of **pert** is "clever."

**perturbed**: [per-TURBED] Verb/Adjective.
To disturb or confuse. (v.)
To be alarmed or confused by something. (adj.)

- News of the impending storm **perturbed** him greatly. (v.)
- He was **perturbed** at the idea of being reprimanded for something he did not do. (adj.)

*Synonym:* disturbed, upset, agitated, annoyed, troubled, uneasy
*Antonym:* peaceful, relaxed, calm

Further Information
- Originated from the Latin *per* meaning "thoroughly" and *tubare* meaning "to disturb."
- Related words include **perturbable** (adj.) and **perturb** (v.).
- In physics and astronomy, perturbed means "to cause disturbance by gravitational interaction."


**peruse:** [peh-ROOZ] Verb.
To carefully examine and consider.
To look over in a casual, leisurely manner.

- She **perused** the genealogical records looking for the name of her great-grandfather.
- In his spare time, he likes to **peruse** the yellow pages just for something to do.

*Synonym:* study, scrutinize, read, examine, scan, inspect
*Antonym:* skim, overlook

Further Information
- Originated from the Middle English word *peruse* meaning "to use up."
- Related word forms include **perusal** (n.) and **peruser** (n.).
- Note that **peruse** has two contradictory meanings – "a careful read" or "a quick scan."


**philanthropic**: [fil-en-THRAH-pik] Adjective.
Related to the act of giving money and time to the needy.

- He was honored at the dinner for his **philanthropic** work in the community.
- Giving money to the homeless showed that his intentions were **philanthropic**.

*Synonym:* benevolent, charitable, humanitarian, generous, beneficent, altruistic
*Antonym:* greedy, narcissistic, selfish

Further Information
- Originated from the Greek word *philanthropia* meaning "love for mankind."
- Related words include **philanthropically** (adv.) and **philanthropical** (adj.).
- **Philanthropic** implies "doing things for or giving things to people whom one doesn't know."

# REVIEW EXERCISE 29

*Match the word with its synonym.*

| | | | | |
|---|---|---|---|---|
| ___ | 1. | pejorative | a. | scrutinize |
| ___ | 2. | penchant | b. | disturbed |
| ___ | 3. | penurious | c. | dishonest |
| ___ | 4. | peregrination | d. | perceptive |
| ___ | 5. | perfidious | e. | charitable |
| ___ | 6. | perfunctory | f. | inclination |
| ___ | 7. | pernicious | g. | trip |
| ___ | 8. | perspicacious | h. | disparaging |
| ___ | 9. | pert | i. | destructive |
| ___ | 10. | perturbed | j. | stingy |
| ___ | 11. | peruse | k. | indifferent |
| ___ | 12. | philanthropic | l. | impertinent |

*Fill in the blanks with the most appropriate word from list above.* *(Word form may need changing.)*

1. He was _____ enough to buy the stock when its price was the lowest.

2. She _____ the help wanted ads, scouring the newspaper for a job.

3. He used a _____ term to describe the fact that she is overweight.

4. To my dismay, she has a _____ for champagne and drinks it to excess.

5. Traitors are known for being _____.

6. After his boring speech, the audience's applause was _____.

7. The billionaire is quite _____ and gives millions away to the poor each year.

8. The old woman was _____, denying herself simple pleasures of life.

9. His _____ took him across some beautiful countryside.

10. The girl who was described as _____ did not know if that was a good or bad trait.

11. Some say that idleness is _____ because it gets you into trouble quickly.

12. The teacher was _____ by her class's lack of interest in the project.

**phlegmatic**: [fleg-MAH-tik] Adjective.
Not easily angered or upset; unemotional.

- The taxi driver, who was a **phlegmatic** middle-aged man, was not easily surprised by riders.
- Rush-hour commuting requires a **phlegmatic** temperament.

*Synonym:* apathetic, indifferent, stoic, listless, languid, lethargic

*Antonym:* fervent, active

Further Information
- Originated from the Greek word *phlegein* meaning "to burn."
- Related words include **phlegmatically** (adv.).
- In ancient Greece, **phlegm** was "water," one of the four fluids that controlled human temperaments (along with blood, black bile and yellow bile).


**pithy**: [PIH-thee] Adjective.
Using few words in an effective, clever way.

- Newspaper headlines should be short and **pithy** in order to be most effective.
- Her essay was short and **pithy**, which was the opposite of what the teacher requested.

*Synonym:* terse, compact, succinct, concise, laconic, short

*Antonym:* verbose, wordy, long-winded

Further Information
- Originated from the Old English word *pipa* meaning "essential part."
- Related word forms include **pith** (n.), **pithily** (adv.) and **pithiness** (n.).
- In botany, **pith** is "the central strand of sponge-like tissue in the stem of a vascular plant."


**placate**: [PLAY-kayt] Verb.
To calm the anger of, to soothe.

- After I backed into the woman's car, I tried to **placate** her by offering to pay for repairs.
- The company held a series of meetings to attempt to **placate** its investors after the merger.

*Synonym:* pacify, appease, mollify, propitiate, soothe, calm

*Antonym:* enrage, annoy, irritate

Further Information
- Originated from the Latin word *placatus* meaning "soothed, quiet."
- Related word forms include **placater** (n.), **placatingly** (adv.), **placation** (n.), **placative** (adj.) and **placatory** (adj.).
- **Please** is another word related to **placate**.

**placid**: [PLAH-sed] Adjective.
Calm and free from disturbances.

- The **placid** lake was still and beautiful under the moonlight.
- Her face was **placid** as she sat waiting for him, despite the turmoil inside her head.

*Synonym:* calm, serene, tranquil, peaceful, quiet, still
*Antonym:* agitated, angry, excited

Further Information
- Originated from the Latin word *placere* meaning "to please."
- Related words include **placidity** (n.), **placidly** (adv.) and **placidness** (n.).
- **Placid** can have a negative connotation that implies "calmness because of stupidity."


**platitude**: [PLAH-teh-tyud] Noun.
A remark that expresses an old, unoriginal, trite idea.

- The politician used a monotone voice to deliver **platitudes** to the public after the disaster.
- We are tired of hearing the usual **platitudes** about watching our weight.

*Synonym:* truism, cliche, banality, saying, bromide
*Antonym: none*

Further Information
- Originated from the French word *plat* meaning "flat."
- Related words include **platitudinous** (adj.) and **platitudinal** (adj.).
- **Platitude** was first seen in English in the early 1800s.


**plaudit**: [PLAW-det] Noun.
An act of applause or enthusiastic approval.

- Their daughter received many **plaudits** for her academic achievements.
- The actors bowed to the enthusiastic **plaudits** of the audience.

*Synonym:* acclaim, praise, applause, cheer, ovation, approval
*Antonym:* disapproval, reproach, complaint

Further Information
- Originated from the Latin word *plaudite* meaning "applaud."
- Other related words include **applaud, applause, explode,** and **plausible**.
- Plaudit is short for the word **plaudite**, meaning "an actor's request for applause" in the 1600s.

**plenitude:** [PLEH-neh-tyud] Noun.
Having an abundance or completeness.

- The farmer's market offered a **plenitude** of fresh fruits and vegetables.
- There is a **plenitude** of that material in the world, so it should be easy enough to obtain.

*Synonym:* plenty, profusion, abundance, wealth, opulence, plethora
*Antonym:* deficiency, paucity, dearth

Further Information
- Originated from the Latin word *plenitudinem* meaning "abundance, fullness, completeness."
- Related word forms include **plenitudinous** (adj.) and **plenty** (adj.).
- **Plenitude** is often misspelled as **plentitude**.


**plethora**: [PLETH-er-uh] Noun.
Having more than enough of something.

- You can find a **plethora** of books on that subject at your local library.
- The school's **plethora** of rules and regulations can be quite confusing to new students.

*Synonym:* surfeit, excess, surplus, overabundance, superfluity, plenitude
*Antonym:* scarcity, deficiency, want

Further Information
- Originated from the Greek word *plethora* meaning "to be full."
- Related words include **plethoric** (adj.).
- Note that **plethora** and **plenitude** are synonyms of each other. The only slight difference is **plenitude** implies "fullness," while **plethora** implies "an overabundance."


**polarized:** [PO-leh-reyzd] Verb/Adjective.
To cause something or someone to separate into opposite groups. (v.)
To cause something to vibrate in a pattern (v.)
Related to directions of vibration. (adj.)

- The public's opinion has **polarized** on that issue. (v.)
- My sunglasses are **polarized** and therefore reduce the sun's glare. (adj.)
- He attempted to **polarize** the light waves during the experiment. (v.)

*Synonym:* opposing, antithetical, contradictory, contrary
*Antonym:* none

Further Information
- Originated from the Latin word *polaris* meaning "polar."
- Related words include **polarize** (v.), **polarity** (n.) and **polarization** (n.).
- The adjective form of **polarized** is used most often in physics.

**ponderous**: [PON-deh-res] Adjective.
Heavy and clumsy.
Dull and lifeless.

- The elephants in the circus were **ponderous**.
- We fell asleep during his **ponderous** lecture.

*Synonym:* massive, weighty, heavy, leaden, burdensome, hefty
*Antonym:* light, airy, weightless

Further Information
- Originated from the Latin word *pondus* meaning "weight."
- Related words include **ponderously** (adv.) and **ponderousness** (n.).
- The original meaning of **ponderous** was "serious" but it is no longer used.


**portent:** [POR-tent] Noun.
A foreshadowing of a (usually bad) coming event, omen.

- We knew that the thunder was just the **portent** of the approaching storm.
- Some people see a crow as a **portent** of death.

*Synonym:* presage, sign, foreboding, foreshadowing, prophecy, omen
*Antonym: none*

Further Information
- Originated from the Latin word *portentum* meaning "a sign."
- Related word forms include **portentous.** (adj.)
- The archaic meaning of **portent** is "a prodigy" or "something amazing."


**posthumous**: [PAHST-hyu-mus] Adjective.
After death.

- The author's best novels were published **posthumously**, so he never got to enjoy their fame.
- My grandmother died last year but received a **posthumous** award this year for her generosity.

*Synonym:* postmortem, late, belated, postdiluvian
*Antonym:* early, antemortem

Further Information
- Originated from the Latin word *posthumus* meaning "late-born, coming after."
- Related words include **posthumously** (adv.) and **posthumousness** (n.).
- The original literal meaning of **posthumous** was "born after the father's death."

# REVIEW EXERCISE 30

*Match the word with its synonym.*

___ 1.   phlegmatic        a.   postmortem
___ 2.   pithy              b.   plenty
___ 3.   placate            c.   contradictory
___ 4.   placid             d.   heavy
___ 5.   platitude          e.   banality
___ 6.   plaudit            f.   pacify
___ 7.   plenitude          g.   terse
___ 8.   plethora           h.   indifferent
___ 9.   polarized          i.   calm
___ 10.  ponderous          j.   praise
___ 11.  portent            k.   excess
___ 12.  posthumous         l.   sign

*Fill in the blanks with the most appropriate word from list above.* *(Word form may need changing.)*

1.   The four-hour movie was so _____ that it put her to sleep.

2.   The record store offers a _____ of musical styles.

3.   The new movie opened to the _____ of the critics.

4.   Although he was known to be_____, we saw tears in his eyes.

5.   Despite being valedictorian, she gave quite a _____ speech at graduation.

6.   The changes to the movie did little to _____ the critics.

7.   She was tired of hearing everyone's _____ at her mother's funeral.

8.   He received _____ acclaim for his last album, released after his death.

9.   The _____ water on the lake is calming to view.

10.  The dining room table held a _____ of his favorite foods on his birthday.

11.   The candidate's extremely liberal views caused _____ among party members.

12.  Some believe the black cat to be a _____ of bad luck.

# WORD SET 31

**potentate**: [PO-ten-tayt] Noun.
A person with the power to rule over others.

- Although the soldiers did not agree with the **potentate**, they followed his orders.
- How many **potentates** have there been in the British monarchy?

*Synonym:* king, monarch, sovereign, emperor, ruler, royalty
*Antonym:* servant, peasant
Further Information
- Originated from the Latin word *potentatus* meaning "power."
- Other English words descended from *potentatus* include **omnipotent**, **impotent** and **potent**.
- **Potentate** was first seen in English in the 15th century.

**precipitate**: [pree-SIP-ih-tayt] Verb/Adjective/Noun.
To cause to happen. (v.)
Moving heedlessly and rapidly. (adj.)
A product resulting from a course of action or an event. (n.)

- An invasion of the enemy country would certainly **precipitate** a full-scale war. (v.)
- The **precipitate** that fell from the clouds was in the form of rain and hail. (n.)
- The **precipitate** marriage ended as quickly as everyone had predicted it would. (adj.)

*Synonym:* hasty, rash, sudden, impetuous, hurried, abrupt
*Antonym:* slow, deliberate
Further Information
- Originated from the Latin word *praecipitat* meaning "to throw headlong."
- Related word forms include **precipitator** (n.), **precipitately** (adv.), **precipitative** (adj.) and **precipitateness** (n.).
- In chemistry, a **precipitate** is a noun meaning "a solid separated from a solution."

**preclude**: [pree-KLOOD] Verb.
To make impossible to happen.

- Unfortunately, an emergency will **preclude** me from accepting that job.
- The move **precludes** him from being able to attend the neighborhood school.

*Synonym:* prevent, prohibit, hinder, forbid, stop, impede
*Antonym:* allow, permit, encourage
Further Information
- Originated from the Latin word *praecludere* meaning "to close."
- Related word forms include **preclusion** (n.) and **preclusive** (adj.).
- An archaic meaning of **preclude** is "to close."

**precocious** [pree-KO-shus] Adjective.
Characterized by early or advanced development.

- The young musician displayed a **precocious** talent for music.
- She earned her first patent at the **precocious** age of 10.

*Synonym:* intelligent, advanced, premature, forward, smart, bright
*Antonym:* delayed, late

Further Information
- Originated from the Latin word *praecoquere* meaning "to boil before."
- Related words include **precocity** (n.), **precociously** (adv.) and **precociousness** (n.).
- In botany, **precocious** means "blossoming before leaves appear."

**predilection:** [pred-el-EK-shen] Noun.
A preference for or liking of something.

- The man obviously has a **predilection** for redheads as four of his five wives have had red hair.
- She has a **predilection** for spicy food and therefore loves to eat at Mexican restaurants.

*Synonym:* partiality, inclination, penchant, liking, preference, fondness
*Antonym:* dislike, aversion, disinclination

Further Information
- Originated from the Latin word *praedilectus* meaning "to prefer."
- *Praedilectus* is based on the Latin verb *legere* which means "to read."
- Other words descended from *legere* include **legume, sacrilege, lesson** and **collect**.

**predisposition:** [pre-dis-peh-ZIH-shen] Noun.
A tendency or inclination towards something/someone.

- That teacher has a **predisposition** to find fault in even her brightest students.
- Some say humanity has as much of a **predisposition** towards evil as it does towards goodness.

*Synonym:* bent, tendency, proclivity, bias, leaning
*Antonym:* disinclination

Further Information
- Originated from the Latin word *disponere* meaning "to put in order or arrange."
- Other related words include **predispose** (v.) and **predisposal** (n.).
- In medicine, **predisposition** means "susceptibility to a disease."
- **Predisposition** is close in meaning to **predilection**; however, **predilection** means "a liking towards something/someone based on temperament," while **predisposition** implies "a tendency (not necessarily a liking or positive feeling) towards something or someone."

**prelude:** [PRAY-lood] Noun/Verb.
An introductory performance preceding a more important one. (n.)
To serve as an introduction. (v.)

- The committee's discussions were a **prelude** to the meeting on the peace treaty. (n.)
- The short song **preluded** the longer musical performance. (v.)

*Synonym:* introduction, preface, preamble, overture, foreword, prologue
*Antonym:* conclusion, ending, closing

Further Information
- Originated from the Latin word *praeludere* meaning "to compose a beginning."
- Related word forms include **preludial** (adj.).
- **Prelude** may also be pronounced PREH-lood.

**premonition:** [prem-eh-NISH-en] Noun.
A sight or feeling that something (usually negative) is about to happen.

- She had a **premonition** that the teacher would surprise the class with a pop quiz.
- He had a **premonition** that his dog would get hurt in some way today.

*Synonym:* intuition, foreboding, vision, omen, portent
*Antonym:* unawareness, oblivion

Further Information
- Originated from the Latin word *praemonitus* meaning "to forewarn."
- Related words include **premonitory** (adj.) and **premonitorily** (adv.).
- **Premonition** is usually related to "a feeling that something bad is about to happen."

**preponderance:** [prih-PON-der-ens] Noun.
Superiority in influence, importance or weight.

- The **preponderance** of evidence against the defendant suggests she is guilty.
- There is a **preponderance** of males signed up for computer club at our school.

*Synonym:* superiority, dominance, ascendancy, prevalence, supremacy, advantage
*Antonym:* inferiority

Further Information
- Originated from the Latin word *praeponderans* meaning "make heavier."
- Related words include **preponderancy** (n.).
- **Preponderance** and **preponderancy** are interchangeable; both are acceptable for use.

**presage**: [pri-SAJ or PREH-sij] Noun/Verb.
A warning of a future occurrence or event, a sign. (n.)
To warn in advance, to predict. (v.)

- The dark clouds **presaged** a thunderstorm. (v.)
- Some people see a black cat as a **presage** of bad luck. (n.)

*Synonym:* prognostication, misgiving, presentiment, sign, forecast, foreshadow
*Antonym: none*

Further Information
- Originated from the Latin word *praesagire* meaning "to perceive beforehand."
- Related words include **presageful** (adj.).
- **Presage** and **premonition** are close in meaning. However, **premonition** implies "a vision of the future", while **presage** means "a sign of a future occurrence."


**prevaricate:** [prih-VAR-eh-kayt] Verb.
To speak or write in an evasive manner, to lie.

- Please tell us exactly what happened in detail, and do not **prevaricate**.
- He will not admit his guilt, choosing instead to **prevaricate**.

*Synonym:* equivocate, lie, palter, fib, quibble, dodge
*Antonym: none*

Further Information
- Originated from the Latin word *praevaricari* meaning "to straddle."
- Related word forms include **prevarication** (n.) and **prevaricator** (n.).
- **Prevaricate** was once used to mean "to delay, procrastinate or behave indecisively."


**pristine**: [pris-TEEN] Adjective.
Remaining pure, free or clean.
Of the earliest condition or time, original or primitive.

- The baby's skin was so **pristine**, her mother wished it could stay that way forever.
- The walls of our new house are **pristine** without paint or wallpaper.

*Synonym:* clean, pure, immaculate, original, early, primordial
*Antonym:* dirty, mucky, impure

Further Information
- Originated from the Latin word *pristinus* meaning "prior, former, original, early."
- Related words include **pristinely** (adv.).
- **Pristine** originally meant "early or original," but has also come to mean "fresh and clean."

# REVIEW EXERCISE 31

*Match the word with its synonym.*

| | | | |
|---|---|---|---|
| ___ 1. | potentate | a. | superiority |
| ___ 2. | precipitate | b. | foreshadow |
| ___ 3. | preclude | c. | intuition |
| ___ 4. | precocious | d. | tendency |
| ___ 5. | predilection | e. | prevent |
| ___ 6. | predisposition | f. | clean |
| ___ 7. | prelude | g. | king |
| ___ 8. | premonition | h. | advanced |
| ___ 9. | preponderance | i. | hasty |
| ___ 10. | presage | j. | preference |
| ___ 11. | prevaricate | k. | lie |
| ___ 12. | pristine | l. | introduction |

*Fill in the blanks with the most appropriate word from list above.* *(Word form may need changing.)*

1. Little did we know that the argument would _____ a divorce.

2. I had a _____ that you were about to call me.

3. His backpack was heavy due to the _____ of books it carried.

4. Because of his genetics, he has a _____ to the disease.

5. Tell me if you cheated on the test, and please don't _____.

6. The _____ child was able to read before she was a year old.

7. She has a _____ for old dolls, evidenced by her vast collection of them.

8. Do you often _____ the future in your dreams?

9. The _____ of the musical piece is harder to play than the body.

10. Going to the movies now does not _____ you from going out again later.

11. The _____ snow was white and blanketed the earth.

12. The citizens rose up against the dictatorial rule of their _____.

# WORD SET 32

**privation**: [pri-VAY-shen] Noun.
Lacking the things that are needed to exist.

- During the war, the citizens endured years of **privation**.
- Many believe that crime is caused by economic **privation** of the poor.

*Synonym:* hardship, poverty, want, need, destitution, indigence
*Antonym:* luxury, opulence, abundance
Further Information
- Originated from the Latin word *privatus* meaning "to deprive."
- **Privation** is often used interchangeably with **deprivation**. **Privation**, however, implies "lacking what is needed to exist" and **deprivation** means "lacking things necessary for a good, healthy life."

**probation**: [pro-BAY-shen] Noun.
A test/trial period of a person's fitness (for a job, membership in a group, etc.).
The suspension of a convicted offender's sentence and subsequent freedom under supervision.

- The judge sentenced the defendant to two years' **probation** instead of jail time.
- Because I started a new job, I am on **probation** for the first 90 days, after which time I will receive full benefits if my work is acceptable.

*Synonym:* test, trial, experiment, inquest
*Antonym: none*
Further Information
- Originated from the Latin word *probation* meaning "to test."
- Related word forms include **probational** (adj.), **probationally** (adv.) and **probationary (**adj.).
- Under the law, **probation** is "a period of time or situation in which a person who has committed a crime is allowed to stay out of prison if they maintain good behavior."

**probity**: [PRO-beh-tee] Noun.
Tried and proven integrity or uprightness of character, complete honesty.

- She is the perfect choice for president, as her **probity** is beyond question.
- The professor enjoys a reputation for **probity** among his colleagues.

*Synonym:* integrity, virtue, goodness, rectitude, morality, righteousness
*Antonym:* deceit, dishonesty, corruption
Further Information
- Originated from the Latin word *probus* meaning "upright, good."
- A **Probus** club is a local group of retired business people with high moral character.

**proclivity** [pro-CLIV-eh-tee] Noun.
A natural tendency or inclination, usually towards something bad.

- The young man shows a **proclivity** towards aggression.
- She has a **proclivity** towards exaggeration.

*Synonym:* bent, tendency, propensity, leaning, inclination, predilection
*Antonym:* repulsion, disinclination, objectivity

Further Information
- Originated from the Latin word *proclivis* meaning "inclined."
- Note the close meanings: **proclivity** implies "a tendency towards something bad." **Predilection** implies "a liking for something based on one's temperament." **Predisposition** implies "a tendency or susceptibility towards something/someone."

**prodigious:** [preh-DIJ-es] Adjective.
Impressively great in size, degree or quantity.

- The store generates profits in **prodigious** amounts.
- Building the highway system was a **prodigious** feat of engineering.

*Synonym:* enormous, immense, gigantic, huge, tremendous, colossal
*Antonym:* tiny, microscopic, small

Further Information
- Originated from the Latin word *prodigiosus* meaning "portentous."
- Other related words include **prodigiously** (adv.) and **prodigiousness** (n.).
- An obsolete definition of **prodigious** is "ominous or portentous."

**profuse:** [preh-FYOOS] Adjective.
Pouring forth in large quantities without restraint.

- She was **profuse** in her thanks when we helped her with household chores.
- The boy was admitted to the hospital with **profuse** bleeding after the accident.

*Synonym:* abundant, exuberant, lavish, copious, luxuriant, plentiful
*Antonym:* sparse, scarce, frugal

Further Information
- Originated from the Latin word *profusus* meaning "to pour forth."
- Other related words include **profusely** (adv.), **profusion** (n.) and **profuseness** (n.).
- **Profuse** can also mean "produced in large quantities, abundant."

**progeny:** [PRO-jeh-nee] Noun.
A child of a parent or parents; descendants.
A result or product of something.

- The man's numerous **progenies** now have **progeny** of their own, making him a grandfather.
- This television series is the **progeny** of a successful series of books.

*Synonym:* issue, offspring, family, child, descendant, issue
*Antonym:* ancestor, precursor, parent

Further Information
- Originated from the Latin word *progignere* meaning "to beget."
- Related word forms include **progenitor** (n.).
- Other descendants of the Latin root *gignere* include **congenital, benign, genius, engine, germ, indigenous** and **ingenuous**.


**proliferate:** [preh-LIHF-eh-rayt] Verb.
To increase at a fast rate.

- The virus **proliferated** at a surprising and terrifying rate.
- The fear was that nuclear weapons might **proliferate** in the country if not halted by others.

*Synonym:* multiply, increase, propagate, reproduce, procreate, breed
*Antonym:* decrease, decline

Further Information
- Originated from the French word *prolifere* meaning "procreative."
- Related words include **proliferative** (adj.), **proliferation** (n.) and **proliferator** (n.).
- In biology, **proliferate** means "to grow or reproduce new parts or cells rapidly."


**promulgate:** [PROM-ul-gayt] Verb.
To make known to the public, to officially announce or decree.

- The store **promulgated** a new policy regarding smoking in the break rooms.
- The school's new regulations were **promulgated** by the principal at the assembly.

*Synonym:* publish, announce, proclaim, broadcast, advertise, declare
*Antonym:* conceal, hide

Further Information
- Originated from the Latin word *promulgare* meaning "to bring to public knowledge."
- Related words include **promulgation** (n.) and **promulgator** (n.).
- An archaic predecessor of **promulgate** is **promulge**.

**propitious**: [preh-PISH-es] Adjective.
Showing signs of a favorable outcome or presenting favorable circumstances.

- This might not be a **propitious** time to start a new business.
- The circumstances were not **propitious** for a labor strike.

*Synonym:* auspicious, opportune, favorable, advantageous, promising, lucky
*Antonym:* unfavorable, unfriendly, inauspicious

Further Information
- Originated from the Latin word *propitius* meaning "to perceive beforehand."
- **Propitious** derives from the Middle English *propycyous* which came from the Latin *propitius*.
- Related words include **propitiously** (adv.) and **propitiousness** (n.).

**prosaic:** [pro-ZAY-ik] Adjective.
Lacking in imagination, ordinary, dull.

- She could transform something as **prosaic** as chicken into a gourmet meal.
- When he asked if I was hurt in a fight, I told him the **prosaic** truth that I fell down the stairs.

*Synonym:* dull, boring, commonplace, tedious, humdrum, ordinary
*Antonym:* imaginative, interesting

Further Information
- Originated from the Latin word *prosa* meaning "prose."
- Related word forms include **prosaically** (adv.).
- The original meaning of **prosaic** was "characteristic of prose," the opposite of which was **poetic**.

**proscribe**: [pro-SKREYB] Verb.
To prohibit or forbid.

- In that culture, women are **proscribed** from walking in public without their heads covered.
- The author's books are **proscribed** in that country because of his controversial views.

*Synonym:* prohibit, ban, forbid, interdict, disallow, outlaw
*Antonym:* allow, permit, approve

Further Information
- Originated from the Latin word *proscribere* meaning "to put up someone's name as outlawed."
- Related words include **proscriber** (n.).
- In ancient Rome, to **proscribe** was "to announce the name of a person condemned to death."

# REVIEW EXERCISE 32

*Match the word with its synonym.*

___ 1. privation          a. advantageous
___ 2. probation          b. trial
___ 3. probity            c. multiply
___ 4. proclivity         d. dull
___ 5. prodigious         e. hardship
___ 6. profuse            f. integrity
___ 7. progeny            g. prohibit
___ 8. proliferate        h. abundant
___ 9. promulgate         i. tendency
___ 10. propitious        j. enormous
___ 11. prosaic           k. offspring
___ 12. proscribe         l. announce

*Fill in the blanks with the most appropriate word from list above.* *(Word form may need changing.)*

1. The lecture was _____ and put the students to sleep.

2. He offered _____ apologies for the mistake.

3. The judge was a man of unquestioned _____.

4. She has a _____ appetite for sweets.

5. The new leader promised to end poverty and _____ in the country.

6. The superintendent _____ all religious books in the school library.

7. After his release from prison he was on _____ for two years.

8. She proudly took her _____ to her extended family's reunion.

9. The child shows a _____ towards violence.

10. The country's new constitution was _____ last month.

11. Cells _____ and the cancer grew and spread.

12. The most _____ time for the attack had passed.

# WORD SET 33

**puerile**: [PYOOR-il] Adjective.
Immature, silly, trivial, childish.

- Many find the comedian's sense of humor rather **puerile**.
- Her **puerile** act of stomping away in a huff when she's angry shows her immaturity.

*Synonym:* immature, childish, silly, callow, foolish, infantile
*Antonym:* mature, clever, adult

## Further Information
- Originated from the Latin word *puerilis* meaning "child, boy."
- Related words include **puerilely** (adv.), **puerility** (n.) and **puerileness** (n.).
- An archaic meaning of **puerile** is "juvenile" or "belonging to childhood."

**pugnacious**: [pug-NAY-shes] Adjective.
Inclined to argue or fight, combative, belligerent.

- The boss was in a **pugnacious** mood when he spoke with his employees after the strike.
- The **pugnacious** youth likes to pick fights with everyone.

*Synonym:* combative, hostile, bellicose, belligerent, quarrelsome, contentious
*Antonym:* peaceful, friendly, amicable

## Further Information
- Originated from the Latin word *pugnax* meaning "to fight."
- Related word forms include **pugnaciousness** (n.), **pugnaciously** (adv.) and **pugnacity (**n.).
- **Pugnacious** usually suggests "a characteristic of a person who enjoys personal or physical combat."

**punctilious**: [pungk-TIL-ee-es] Adjective.
Attentive to small details in conduct or action, precise.

- She was **punctilious** with her manners when she had dinner at her grandparents' house.
- The genealogist was **punctilious** about his research into family trees.

*Synonym:* scrupulous, meticulous, painstaking, careful, conscientious, fastidious
*Antonym:* careless, informal

## Further Information
- Originated from the Italian word *puntiglioso* meaning "fine point."
- Related words include **punctiliously** (adv.) and **punctiliousness** (n.).

**quandary:** [KWON-deh-ree] Noun.
A situation or circumstance that is uncertain or causes problems or confusion.

- He was in a **quandary** about whether he should go on vacation or stay home.
- When the girl was presented with many options, she was in a **quandary** about which job to accept.

*Synonym:* dilemma, difficulty, predicament, pickle, plight, problem
*Antonym*: certainty, advantage

Further Information
- The origin of quandary is unknown. It is thought to have originated from the Latin word *quando* meaning "when."
- **Quandary** was originally pronounced with an accent on the second syllable.

**quibble:** [KWIB-el] Noun/Verb.
To argue. (v.)
A trivial objection raised in an argument. (n.)

- They **quibbled** about where to go on vacation. (v.)
- His only **quibble** with the choice they made for the trip was that it rained there every day. (n.)

*Synonym:* squabble, dodge, cavil, prevaricate, equivocate, bicker
*Antonym:* agree, approve

Further Information
- The origin of **quibble** is unknown but believed to have derived from the English word *quib*, meaning "avoiding the point at issue."
- Other related words include **quibbling** (adj.) and **quibbler** (n.).
- An archaic meaning of **quibble** is "a pun."

**quixotic**: [kwik-SOT-ik] Adjective.
Idealistic or unrealistically optimistic with no regard to practicality.

- The politician ran a **quixotic** campaign but lost to his opponent.
- The teacher supports her students' ideas even if they are **quixotic**.

*Synonym:* idealistic, romantic, visionary, unrealistic, impractical, fanciful
*Antonym:* practical, pragmatic, realistic

Further Information
- Originated from the 1605 novel *Don Quixote de la Mancha* by Cervantes. **Quixote** was an unrealistic idealist. His name is Spanish and literally translates to "thigh."
- Related words include **quixotical** (adj.), **quixotically** (adv.) and **quixotism** (n.).

**quotidian:** [kwo-TID-ee-en] Adjective.
Commonplace, everyday; recurring daily.

- Cell phones have become part of our **quotidian** existence.
- Unfortunately, employees plotting against each other is **quotidian** in almost every company.

*Synonym:* everyday, workaday, routine, daily, ordinary, diurnal
*Antonym:* unusual, extraordinary, amazing

Further Information
- Originated from the Latin word *quotidie* meaning "each day."
- In medicine, **quotidian** can be used as a noun that means "something that occurs every day," such as a fever.
- On medical prescriptions, the letters "q.d." mean "once a day," or in Latin, "quaque die."


**rabid**: [RAB-id] Adjective.
Affected by the disease rabies.
Uncontrollable or raging, violent.
Extremely enthusiastic.

- He was subjected to a series of shots after the dog bit him, just in case it was **rabid**.
- The **rabid** crowd holding protest signs surged as the candidate exited the car.
- The singer has maintained a **rabid** fan base even though his mainstream popularity has waned.

*Synonym:* mad, wild, fanatical, frenzied, frantic, furious
*Antonym:* moderate, delighted, happy

Further Information
- Originated from the Latin word *rabidus* meaning "to rave."
- Related words include **rabidly** (adv.) and **rabidity** (n.).


**raiment:** [RAY-ment] Noun.
Clothing or garments.

- The boy complained of lacking suitable **raiment** for the first day of school.
- She appeared in spotless **raiment** despite the raging storm.

*Synonym:* apparel, garb, clothing, attire, dress, garment
*Antonym:* none

Further Information
- Originated from the Middle English word *arrayment* meaning "to array."
- **Raiment** is rarely used in modern English, being a more ancient, poetic term for "clothing."

**recalcitrant**: [ree-KAL-seh-trent] Adjective/Noun.
Resistant to authority or guidance. (adj.)
Hard to manage. (adj.)
Not responsive to treatment. (adj.)
A person who is resistant to authority, stubborn or hard to manage. (n.)

- The **recalcitrant** boy keeps getting into trouble at school despite his many detentions. (adj.)
- The economic crisis is a **recalcitrant** problem that the government is trying to manage. (adj.)
- She has severe **recalcitrant** pneumonia that has resisted all attempts at treatment. (adj.)
- He is a **recalcitrant** who never seems to learn from his mistakes and is in jail again. (n.)

*Synonym:* stubborn, refractory, obstinate, unruly, intractable, unmanageable
*Antonym:* compliant, submissive, desirous
<u>Further Information</u>
- Originated from the Latin word *recalcitrare* meaning "to be disobedient."
- Related words include **recalcitrance** (n.).
- In chemistry, **recalcitrant** means "resistant to chemical decomposition."


**recant**: [ree-KANT] Verb.
To take back or retract a previously held statement or belief.

- The witness **recanted** her statement against the suspect since she wasn't sure he was the thief.
- The former religious leader **recanted** his beliefs when he left the church.

*Synonym:* retract, withdraw, revoke, recall, rescind, repudiate
*Antonym:* confirm, affirm, reiterate
<u>Further Information</u>
- Originated from the Latin word *recantare* meaning "to sing."
- Related word forms include **recantation** (n.) and **recanter** (n.).
- **Recant** implies "taking back something that you once believed or taught others."


**recondite**: [REK-en-dit] Adjective.
Hard to understand; concealed, hidden.

- To him, geometry is a **recondite** subject.
- The ancient report with **recondite** language was impossible to grasp.

*Synonym:* abstruse, obscure, arcane, dark, mysterious, esoteric
*Antonym:* simple, straightforward, comprehensible
<u>Further Information</u>
- Originated from the Latin word *recondere* meaning "to put away."
- Related words include **reconditely** (adv.) and **reconditeness** (n.).
- **Condite** is an obsolete verb that means "to preserve."

# REVIEW EXERCISE 33

*Match the word with its synonym.*

___  1.  puerile                a.  stubborn
___  2.  pugnacious             b.  squabble
___  3.  punctilious            c.  combative
___  4.  quandary               d.  dilemma
___  5.  quibble                e.  wild
___  6.  quixotic               f.  clothing
___  7.  quotidian              g.  everyday
___  8.  rabid                  h.  obscure
___  9.  raiment                i.  immature
___  10. recalcitrant           j.  meticulous
___  11. recant                 k.  idealistic
___  12. recondite              l.  retract

*Fill in the blanks with the most appropriate word from list above. (Word form may need changing.)*

1.  The children were _____, resisting the substitute teacher's requests for order.

2.  The musician's _____ fans swarmed him after the concert.

3.  The adopted girl started a _____ quest to find her biological mother.

4.  The man _____ his unlawful confession after his lawyer arrived.

5.  Many thought the students' behavior was _____ as they were teenagers.

6.  He becomes _____ and rude when he has too much to drink.

7.  He was _____ about being on time to all his classes.

8.  Although she loved him, his proposal of marriage put her in a _____.

9.  Mathematicians have almost solved a _____ problem.

10. Don't _____ over a couple of dollars – just pay the entire bill.

11. He drove home through the _____ traffic.

12. The necessities of life include food, shelter and _____.

# WORD SET 34

**redolent**: [RED-el-ent] Adjective.
Having or giving off a fragrance or odor.
Suggestive or reminiscent.

- The kitchen was **redolent** with onions after he cooked some with hamburger.
- The album is a throwback **redolent** of the music of the 1950s.

*Synonym:* fragrant, evocative, sweet, aromatic, perfumed, odorous
*Antonym:* odorless, unscented
Further Information
- Originated from the Latin word *olere* meaning "to smell."
- Related words include **redolently** (adv.), **redolence** (n.) and **redolency** (n.).
- Another related word also from *olere* is **olfactory**, which means "of the sense of smell."


**redoubtable**: [ree-DOWT-eh-bel] Adjective.
Causing awe or fear.
Worthy of honor or respect.

- The candidate is a **redoubtable** debater who can easily make mincemeat of his opponent.
- The boxer is facing the most **redoubtable** opponent of his entire career.

*Synonym:* formidable, dire, fearful, gruesome, appalling, ghastly
*Antonym:* sad, pathetic
Further Information
- Originated from the Anglo-French word *reduter* meaning "to dread."
- Related word forms include **redoubtableness** (n.) and **redoubtably** (adv.).
- **Redoubtable** first appeared in the English language in the 15th century.


**relegate**: [REL-eh-gayt] Verb.
To assign or classify someone/something to a place of insignificance.
To send into exile.
In sports, to move to a lower position in the league.

- In that country, women are **relegated** to only nursing and teaching jobs.
- He was **relegated** from his own country to another.
- The football team was **relegated** to the lower division last year.

*Synonym:* demote, banish, dismiss, transfer, exile, deport
*Antonym:* promote, upgrade, advance
Further Information
- Originated from the Latin word *legare* meaning "to send with a commission."
- Related words include **relegation** (n.).

**remiss:** [ree-MISS] Adjective.
Negligent or lacking in attending to duty.

- He has been **remiss** in paying child support to his ex-wife.
- It was **remiss** of me to forget to pay the bill.

*Synonym:* neglectful, negligent, careless, inattentive, thoughtless, heedless
*Antonym*: thoughtful, overprotective

Further Information
- Originated from the Latin word *remittere* meaning "to send back."
- **Remissly** (adv.) and **remissness** (n.) are related word forms.
- **Remiss** implies "carelessness shown through neglect."


**repertoire:** [REP-er-twar] Noun.
A list of songs, plays, readings, etc. that a performer or company is prepared to perform.
A list of skills, devices or methods a person uses in his/her practice or occupation.

- She has added considerably to her violin **repertoire**.
- Some interesting and unusual plays are in that quarterback's **repertoire**.

*Synonym:* abilities, capabilities, experience, proficiencies, talents
*Antonym: none*

Further Information
- Originated from the Latin word *repertorium* meaning "list."
- **Repertoire** may also be written as **repertory**, although in modern English, **repertory** means "the company that presents a list of works," while **repertoire** is "the list of works itself."


**repose**: [ree-POS] Noun/Verb.
The state of being at rest or free from worry. (n.)
To lay oneself down or to rest. (v.)

- Her face while in **repose** looked much younger. (n.)
- Two heads **repose** upon the same pillow. (v.)

*Synonym:* rest, ease, peace, relaxation, serenity, tranquility
*Antonym:* agitation, disturbance, struggle

Further Information
- Originated from the Latin word *repausare* meaning "to cause to rest."
- Related words include **reposal** (n.) and **reposer** (n.).
- An archaic meaning for **repose** is "to rely."

**reprobate:** [REP-re-bayt] Noun/Adjective/Verb.
A person without morals. (n.)
Morally unprincipled or shameless. (adj.)
To condemn or disapprove of strongly. (v.)

- The hardened **reprobate** was let out of prison after 20 years. (n.)
- The woman disowned her **reprobate** son after he committed another crime. (adj.)
- He **reprobated** her for being naive, making her cry. (v.)

*Synonym:* sinful, immoral, corrupt, miscreant, profligate, depraved
*Antonym:* moral, approbate
Further Information
- Originated from the Latin word *reprobare* meaning "to reprove."
- Related words include **reprobation** (n.) and **reprobative** (adj.).
- When used as a verb with God as subject, **reprobate** means "to banish to eternal damnation."


**repudiate:** [ree-PYOO-dee-ayt] Verb.
To reject the authority or validity of.
To disown (as in a child or spouse) or refuse to deal with.

- The policeman **repudiated** the charges that were brought against his son.
- She **repudiated** her husband and threw him out of her house.

*Synonym:* deny, renounce, reject, disavow, disclaim, refuse
*Antonym:* bear, accept, admit
Further Information
- Originated from the Latin word *repudium* meaning "a separation or divorce."
- Related words include **repudiation** (n.) and **repudiator** (n.).
- In finance, **repudiate** means "to refuse to recognize or pay a debt."


**requisition:** [rek-weh-ZIH-shen] Noun/Verb.
A formal written request. (n.)
Requesting something, usually in writing. (v.)

- Put in a **requisition** for a new desk chair since yours is no longer comfortable. (n.)
- Human resources **requisitioned** more computers for our office, as we are running out. (v.)

*Synonym:* demand, request, order, claim, solicit, require
*Antonym:* give
Further Information
- Originated from the Latin word *requiere* meaning "to search."
- Related words include **requisite** (n.).
- **Requisition**'s legal definition is "taking property by a public authority for a public use."

**rescind**: [ree-SIND] Verb.
To repeal or make void.

- After she did not fulfill the terms of the contract, he **rescinded** it.
- My grandmother **rescinded** her invitation to us for dinner tonight, as she has a cold.

*Synonym:* cancel, revoke, annul, repeal, void, nullify
*Antonym:* allow, approve, mandate

Further Information
- Originated from the Latin word *scindere* meaning "to split."
- Related words include **rescindable** (adj.) and **rescindment** (n.).
- Other words derived from *scindere* include **exscind**, meaning "to cut off," and **prescind**, meaning "to withdraw attention."

**restive**: [RES-tiv] Adjective.
Uneasily impatient or hard to control, unsettled.

- The crowd was becoming **restive** as they waited for the band to take the stage.
- She spent a **restive** night worrying about the next day's geography test.

*Synonym:* restless, unruly, fidgety, edgy, uneasy, nervous
*Antonym:* calm, relaxed, collected

Further Information
- Originated from the French word *rester* meaning "to remain."
- Related word forms include **restively** (adv.) and **restiveness** (n.).
- **Restive** can also mean "refusing to move" if used to describe an animal.

**reticent**: [RET-eh-sent] Adjective.
Reserved or restrained, keeping one's thoughts to oneself.

- He is **reticent** about his opinions, preferring to keep them to himself.
- She has been **reticent** about her feelings regarding the move.

*Synonym:* reserved, shy, taciturn, uncommunicative, timid, silent
*Antonym:* chatty, communicative, loquacious

Further Information
- Originated from the Latin word *reticere* meaning "to keep silent."
- Related words include **reticently** (adv.) and **reticence** (n.).
- Some people have incorrectly used **reticent** as meaning "unwilling or reluctant." However, this usage is not technically correct.

# REVIEW EXERCISE 34

*Match the word with its synonym.*

| | | | | |
|---|---|---|---|---|
| ___ | 1. | redolent | a. | request |
| ___ | 2. | redoubtable | b. | rest |
| ___ | 3. | relegate | c. | formidable |
| ___ | 4. | remiss | d. | reserved |
| ___ | 5. | repertoire | e. | abilities |
| ___ | 6. | repose | f. | fragrant |
| ___ | 7. | reprobate | g. | revoke |
| ___ | 8. | repudiate | h. | demote |
| ___ | 9. | requisition | i. | deny |
| ___ | 10. | rescind | j. | negligent |
| ___ | 11. | restive | k. | immoral |
| ___ | 12. | reticent | l. | restless |

*Fill in the blanks with the most appropriate word from list above.* (Word form may need changing.)

1. The children were _____, waiting for the clown to take the stage.

2. The candidate _____ the remarks made by her opponent.

3. The company will _____ the bonuses as they experienced a loss.

4. The flowers were _____ and their sweet scent filled the room.

5. It would be _____ of me not to congratulate you on the win.

6. The body was lying in _____ in the casket.

7. I faced a _____ opponent in the debate last night.

8. She certainly has a lot of skills in her _____.

9. Should we _____ her to the back of the classroom for her talking?

10. He is known as the town _____ because he's always in trouble.

11. She was _____ about her past, refusing to discuss it.

12. Put in a _____ for more paper towels for the breakroom.

# WORD SET 35

**rue**: [ROO] Verb/Noun.
To feel regret for. (v.)
A sorrow or regret. (n.)

- Mark my words - you will **rue** the day when you stabbed me in the back. (v.)
- I am full of **rue** now that my love has gone. (n.)

*Synonym:* regret, lament, sorrow, grieve, mourn, repent
*Antonym:* praise
Further Information
- Originated from the Germanic word *hrewan* meaning "to be sad."
- Related words include **rued** (v.) and **ruing** (v.).
- **Rue** means "street" in French but is not related to the English **rue**.

**ruminate**: [ROO-men-ayt] Verb.
To reflect on over and over in one's mind.

- He **ruminated** for weeks about how to tell his boss he was quitting his job.
- The elderly man sat and **ruminated** a lot about things that had happened in his life.

*Synonym:* meditate, ponder, reflect, muse, contemplate, deliberate
*Antonym:* ignore, neglect
Further Information
- Originated from the Latin word *ruminatus* meaning "to chew the cud."
- Related word forms include **rumination** (n.) and **ruminatively** (adv.).
- When used with an animal, **rue** means "to chew repeatedly for a long time."

**rustic**: [RUS-tik] Adjective.
Relating to the country.
Simple and unsophisticated.

- She loved the beautiful **rustic** setting where her new house was built.
- He is a **rustic** fellow, having lived a simple and uncomplicated life.

*Synonym:* rural, pastoral, countrified, bucolic, country, agrarian
*Antonym:* urban, polished, city
Further Information
- Originated from the Latin word *rusticus* meaning "country."
- Related words include **rusticity** (n.) and **rustically** (adv.).
- In architecture, **rustic** means "having a rough finish."

**sacrosanct:** [SAK-reh-sangkt] Adjective.
Sacred and holy.
Immune from violation or criticism.

- The church is believed by many to be a **sacrosanct** place.
- The Bill of Rights is a **sacrosanct** document that should always be protected.

*Synonym:* divine, sacred, inviolable, holy, hallowed, blessed
*Antonym:* nonreligious, profane, irreligious

Further Information
- Originated from the Latin word *sacrosanctus* meaning "hallowed by a sacred rite."
- Other words derived from the Latin root *sanctus* include **sanctimony, sanctuary** and **sanctify**.
- Related words include **sacrosanctity** (n.).


**salubrious:** [seh-LOO-bree-us] Adjective.
Favorable to health.

- The mountain air is **salubrious** and seems to have cleared up my sinuses.
- There is a **salubrious** effect on human beings from getting sunlight daily.

*Synonym:* healthful, healthy, beneficial, wholesome, good, salutary
*Antonym:* unwholesome, unhealthy, harmful

Further Information
- Originated from the Latin word *salus* meaning "health."
- Related words include **salubriously** (adv.), **salubriousness** (n.) and **salubrity** (n.).
- **Salubrious** is often used to describe "the healthful effects of the air or the climate."


**sanctimonious**: [sangk-teh-MO-nee-us] Adjective.
Hypocritically devout or pious.

- The speech that the politician gave was uncharacteristically **sanctimonious**.
- She might really be that religious, but I have a feeling she's just being **sanctimonious**.

*Synonym:* hypocritical, pharisaic, self-righteous, pious, unctuous, insincere
*Antonym:* non-judgmental

Further Information
- Originated from the Latin word *sanctimonia* meaning "sacredness."
- Related words include **sanctimony** (n.) and **sanctimoniously** (adv.).
- An archaic meaning for **sanctimonious** is "being holy."

**sanguine:** [SANG-gwin] Adjective.
Cheerfully optimistic and confident.
Having a reddish color.

- She was **sanguine** about her chances of getting the job.
- His **sanguine** complexion was the result of having just finished a workout.

*Synonym:* confident, hopeful, cheerful, optimistic, upbeat, self-confident
*Antonym:* pessimistic, depressed, sad
Further Information
- Originated from the Latin word *sanguineus* meaning "blood-red."
- Related words include **sanguinity** (n.) and **sanguinely** (adv.).
- An archaic usage of **sanguine** is "having blood as the dominant humor of the body," or "passionate."

**satiate:** [SAY-shee-ayt] Verb.
To satisfy or provide with more than enough.

- The huge Thanksgiving meal **satiated** my hunger.
- Sugar-free foods don't **satiate** me as they leave me wanting more.

*Synonym:* satisfy, sate, gorge, glut, fill, stuff
*Antonym:* deprive, insatiate
Further Information
- Originated from the Latin word *satis* meaning "sufficient."
- Related words include **satiation** (n.) and **satiated** (v. or adj.).
- An archaic usage of **satiate** is as an adjective meaning "filled to satisfaction."

**saturate:** [SACH-er-ayt] Verb.
To soak so that no more may be absorbed.

- The recipe said to **saturate** the chicken with a marinade of oil and herbs.
- I left the window open and the rain **saturated** my carpet.

*Synonym:* permeate, soak, drench, immerse, imbue, douse
*Antonym:* dry, dehydrate
Further Information
- Originated from the Latin word *satur* meaning "sated."
- Related words include **saturator** (n.) and **saturable** (adj.).
- In chemistry, **saturate** means "to cause a substance to join with the greatest possible amount of another substance."
- In economics, **saturate** means "to supply the market with a service or good in the amount consumers are willing and able to purchase."

**savor**: [SAY-ver] Noun/Verb.
A specific smell or taste. (n.)
A distinctive characteristic. (n.)
To smell or taste. (v.)
To appreciate fully. (v.)

- The dish carries the **savor** of fresh garlic. (n.)
- During our vacation, we enjoyed the **savors** of the countryside. (n.)
- He **savored** the smell of the ocean on his last day of vacation. (v.)
- She **savored** life's pleasures. (v.)

*Synonym:* relish, enjoy, taste, flavor, tang, zest
*Antonym:* dislike, disgust

Further Information
- Originated from the Latin word *sapere* meaning "to taste."
- Related words include **savorer** (n.) and **savorous** (adj.).
- **Savor** is spelled **savour** in Great Britain.

**scathing:** [SKAY-thing] Adjective.
Very critical and severe.

- The skits on the comedy show offered a **scathing** commentary on the political scene.
- His **scathing** criticism of the book convinced me not to read it.

*Synonym:* mordant, caustic, sarcastic, acrimonious, harsh, biting
*Antonym:* mild

Further Information
- Originated from the German word *schaden* meaning "to injure or damage."
- Related word forms include **scathingly** (adv.).
- **Scathing** implies "stinging, severe attacks."

**schism**: [SKIZ-em] Noun.
A separation into factions.

- The church was divided by a **schism**, with each side holding different beliefs.
- The political **schism** in the country was never more evident than during the election.

*Synonym:* split, division, rift, rupture, breach, separation
*Antonym:* union, harmony, unity

Further Information
- Originated from the Greek word *skhizein* meaning "to split."
- **Schism** has been spelled **scicme, cisme** and **sisme** in English at various times in history.

# REVIEW EXERCISE 35

*Match the word with its synonym.*

| | | | |
|---|---|---|---|
| ___ 1. | rue | a. | soak |
| ___ 2. | ruminate | b. | healthy |
| ___ 3. | rustic | c. | cheerful |
| ___ 4. | sacrosanct | d. | regret |
| ___ 5. | salubrious | e. | sacred |
| ___ 6. | sanctimonious | f. | harsh |
| ___ 7. | sanguine | g. | relish |
| ___ 8. | satiate | h. | meditate |
| ___ 9. | saturate | i. | rural |
| ___ 10. | savor | j. | split |
| ___ 11. | scathing | k. | hypocritical |
| ___ 12. | schism | l. | satisfy |

*Fill in the blanks with the most appropriate word from list above.* (Word form may need changing.)

1.  His _____ criticism of her report brought tears to her eyes.

2.  This mountain air is _____ and will make you feel better.

3.  She _____ the sponge with water to clean the kitchen counters.

4.  You should _____ on your problem to come up with a solution.

5.  She was _____ about her chances of winning the award.

6.  You will _____ the day you told me to leave.

7.  He is _____, praying in church each week yet living immorally the rest of the time.

8.  The old man lives in a _____ log cabin in the woods.

9.  There is a _____ in the group, with both sides holding different beliefs.

10. Although I was very hungry, my appetite was _____ by a big dinner.

11. Some believe the law is _____ and cannot ever be changed or altered.

12. _____ the years you are in school before you must work every day.

# WORD SET 36

**scurrilous**: [SKER-eh-less] Adjective.
Using coarse language, vulgar, abusive, defamatory.

- The politician was defamed by a **scurrilous** piece in the newspaper.
- She launched into a **scurrilous** attack against her boss, which was overheard by management.

*Synonym:* abusive, vulgar, obscene, coarse, foul, lewd
*Antonym:* polite, courteous, charming

Further Information
- Originated from the Latin word *scurrilis* meaning "buffoonlike."
- In Latin, a *scurra* was a buffoon. "Buffoonlike" meant "jeering."
- Related words include **scurrilously** (adv.).

**secular**: [SEK-ye-ler] Adjective.
Worldly, not spiritual, not related to religion.

- She prefers to use a **secular** rather than a religious curriculum in her homeschooling.
- Some say society is becoming more **secular** every day.

*Synonym:* worldly, earthly, terrestrial, profane, temporal, lay
*Antonym:* divine, holy, sacred

Further Information
- Originated from the Latin word *saecularis* meaning "of an age."
- Related word forms include **secularly** (adv.).
- **Secular** can also be used as a noun to describe "a member of secular clergy or a layperson."

**sedulous**: [SEH-jeh-les] Adjective.
Resulting from persistent and careful efforts.

- The detective was able to solve the murder after a **sedulous** investigation of the facts.
- Because of her **sedulous** work, she was able to earn all A's.

*Synonym:* industrious, assiduous, diligent, persevering, persistent, tireless
*Antonym:* unorganized, negligent

Further Information
- Originated from the Latin word *sedulo* meaning "sincerely or diligently."
- Related words include **sedulousness** (n.) and **sedulously** (adv.).
- **Sedulous** implies "a painstaking, detailed effort."

**sentient**: [SENT-shent] Adjective.
Responsive to sensory impressions.

- It was believed that the new artificial intelligence could one day become a **sentient** being.
- Animals are recognized as **sentient** beings in some states, making their abuse a crime.

*Synonym:* sensitive, feeling, awake, cognizant, conscious, aware
*Antonym:* insentient, inanimate, unconscious

Further Information
- Originated from the Latin word *sentiens* meaning "to perceive."
- Other words derived from *sentiens* include **sensual, sentimental,** and **sentiment**.
- Related words include **sentiently** (adv.).

**serendipity**: [ser-en-DIH-peh-tee] Noun.
The luck of finding valuable or good things that one has not looked for.

- It was **serendipity** that led me to the coffee house, where I met my future husband.
- Thanks to the **serendipity** of genetics, I have never had trouble staying slim.

*Synonym:* fluke, happenstance, chance, luck, coincidence, fortuity
*Antonym:* misfortune, bad luck, mishap

Further Information
- The word **serendipity** was coined by English author Horace Walpole in 1754 who formed it from a Persian fairy tale, "The Three Princes of Serendip." The book's heroes always made accidental discoveries of things for which they were not looking.
- Related words include **serendipitous** (adj.).

**shibboleth**: [SHIB-beh-leth] Noun.
An old-fashioned idea that is commonly repeated and believed but may seem untrue.
A way of speaking or words that identify a person as belonging to a special group.

- Some teachers still cling to the old **shibboleths** of education.
- When the group started talking to each other, **shibboleths** started passing through their lips.

*Synonym:* catchword, truism, motto, slogan, byword, platitude
*Antonym: none*

Further Information
- Originated from the Hebrew word *shibboleth* meaning "stream."
- **Shibboleth** was first seen in the Bible's Book of Judges. Soldiers were asked to say the word **shibboleth** before crossing the Jordan River. If they mispronounced it, they would be killed.

**sinecure:** [SI-neh-kyur] Noun.
A position or office that requires little to no work or effort and provides pay.

- His father obtained a **sinecure** for her in his company, ensuring she would have to work little.
- The man's appointment to the position seemed more of a **sinecure** to his fellow employees.

*Synonym:* position, office, station, cinch
*Antonym:* none

Further Information
- Originated from the Latin words *sine cura* meaning "without cure."
- **Sinecure** originally meant "a position in the church that did not require one to tend to the church members' souls."

**skepticism:** [SKEP-teh-sih-zem] Noun.
An attitude of doubting the truth of something.

- The treaty between the two countries was met with **skepticism** by most observers.
- The candidate's extremely liberal views prompted **skepticism** even among her followers.

*Synonym:* incredulity, doubt, disbelief, distrust, uncertainty, mistrust
*Antonym:* trust, faith, certainty

Further Information
- Originated from the Greek word *sceptic* meaning "member of an ancient Greek school of philosophy that doubted the existence of real knowledge."
- Related words include **skeptic** (n.), **skeptical** (adj.) and **skeptically** (adv.).
- **Skepticism** now means "refraining from belief without concrete evidence."

**slovenly:** [SLAH-ven-lee] Adjective.
Untidy, especially in one's personal appearance.

- The man lived alone and often held **slovenly** habits.
- Her **slovenly** appearance at the interview shocked the interviewer.

*Synonym:* sloppy, unkempt, dirty, untidy, messy, slipshod
*Antonym:* neat, stylish, clean

Further Information
- Originated from the German word *sloven* meaning "put on clothes carelessly."
- Related words include **slovenliness** (n.) and **slovenly** (adv.).
- **Slattern** and **slut** are two words that are also descended from *sloven*.

**solicitous**: [seh-LISS-seh-tes] Adjective.
Showing concern for someone or something.
Being full of fears or concern.

- He **solicitously** asked after his grandmother's health.
- Since the tornado destroyed our home, we are quite **solicitous** about our future.

*Synonym:* thoughtful, concerned, attentive, anxious, troubled, mindful
*Antonym:* inconsiderate, disinterested, uncaring

Further Information
- Originated from the Latin word *solicitus* meaning "restless, uneasy, full of anxiety."
- Related words include **solicitousness** (n.) and **solicitously** (adv.).
- **Solicitous** is not related to the word **solicit,** which means "to seek through persuasion."

**soluble**: [SAHL-yeh-bel] Adjective.
Able to be dissolved.
Able to be solved or explained.

- Foods that are high in **soluble** fiber are good for one's health.
- The teacher was impatient with the class as he knew the questions he posed were **soluble**.

*Synonym:* dissolvable, solvable, explicable, dissoluble
*Antonym:* insoluble, unsolvable

Further Information
- Originated from the Latin word *solvere* meaning "to loosen or dissolve."
- **Soluble** is often used as a term in chemistry.

**soporific**: [sah-peh-RIF-ik] Adjective.
Tending to cause sleep.

- The speaker's voice held a **soporific** effect, putting me to sleep in class.
- Some say that turkey is **soporific**, explaining the need for Thanksgiving after-dinner naps.

*Synonym:* narcotic, hypnotic, sedative, soporiferous, somniferous, sleepy
*Antonym:* union, harmony, unity

Further Information
- Originated from the Latin word *sopor* meaning "deep sleep."
- The French word *soporifique* was most likely the predecessor to the English **soporific,** which appeared in 1665.
- The English word **soporiferous** was once an adjective used to mean "characterized by excessive sleep." However, it was replaced by **soporific** in the 1600s.

# REVIEW EXERCISE 36

*Match the word with its synonym.*

___ 1.  scurrilous
___ 2.  secular
___ 3.  sedulous
___ 4.  sentient
___ 5.  serendipity
___ 6.  shibboleth
___ 7.  sinecure
___ 8.  skepticism
___ 9.  slovenly
___ 10. solicitous
___ 11. soluble
___ 12. soporific

a.  concerned
b.  doubt
c.  worldly
d.  abusive
e.  truism
f.  diligent
g.  luck
h.  sleepy
i.  sloppy
j.  feeling
k.  office
l.  solvable

*Fill in the blanks with the most appropriate word from list above.* *(Word form may need changing.)*

1.  The party host was very _____ of his guests, anticipating their needs.

2.  His position is merely a _____--a way to pass the time and get paid.

3.  The vitamin is _____ in water.

4.  The _____ editorial about the politician ran in today's newspaper.

5.  Is that science textbook _____ or religious?

6.  Do you view your dog as a _____ being?

7.  His _____ paid off, earning him commendations for his work.

8.  Her voice singing the baby a lullaby is quite _____, even to adults.

9.  The principal's belief that school morale would improve was met with _____.

10. Many Eastern _____ about health and wellness have proven to be true.

11. It is _____ that I ran into you here today when I didn't even look for you.

12. You should not have shown up at school looking so _____.

**spartan**: [SPAR-ten] Noun.
Characterized by strict self-denial or self-discipline.
Characterized by simplicity and frugality.

- The **spartan** lifestyle of the Amish does not allow them to have a phone in the house.
- The elderly couple enjoys a **spartan** life, with few comforts of home and no luxuries.

*Synonym:* austere, severe, harsh, stern, disciplined, stark
*Antonym:* luxurious, plush, opulent

Further Information
- Originated from the Greek word *Sparta.*
- In ancient Greece, **Sparta** had a reputation for its citizens living a severe, disciplined way of life.
- If **Spartan** is capitalized, it refers to a native of **Sparta**.

**spate**: [SPAYT] Noun.
A sudden flood.
A large amount of something occurring in a short time.
A sudden, strong outburst or outpouring of something.

- The river was in **spate** after the days of heavy rain.
- There was a **spate** of terrorist attacks occurring in a few short days.
- Our objections to his argument evoked a **spate** of anger from him.

*Synonym:* flood, surge, deluge, torrent, rush, flow
*Antonym:* drip, dribble, drought

Further Information
- Originated from the Scottish word *spate* meaning "a sudden flood."
- **Spate** acquired its secondary meaning, a large quantity, in 1600s English.

**specious**: [SPEE-shes] Adjective.
Deceptively attractive or genuine.

- Her voice was soft and filled with **specious** humility.
- His **specious** reasoning was what got us into trouble in the first place.

*Synonym:* false, ostensible, deceptive, fallacious, spurious, superficial
*Antonym:* sincere, valid, real

Further Information
- Originated from the Latin word *speciosus* meaning "beautiful or plausible."
- Related words include **speciousness** (n.) and **speciously** (adv.).
- An obsolete meaning of **specious** is "showy."

**spectrum:** [SPEK-trum] Noun.
An entire range of waves (such as light or radio).
A complete range of different things or people.

- Infrared light lies beyond the end of the visible light **spectrum**.
- We hold a broad **spectrum** of assets in our financial portfolio.

*Synonym:* rainbow, range, gamut, series, scale, scope
*Antonym:* individual

Further Information
- Originated from the Latin word *spectrum* meaning "an appearance or image."
- Related words include **specter** (n.).
- The plural of **spectrum** is **spectra**.


**sportive:** [SPOR-tiv] Adjective.
Playful and lively.

- The school's curriculum incorporates **sportive** gymnastics.
- He enjoyed her **sportive** personality and fun-loving instincts.

*Synonym:* flirty, playful, frolicsome, merry, jocular, frisky
*Antonym:* solemn

Further Information
- Originated from the Old French word *desport* meaning "pleasure, enjoyment."
- Related words include **sportively** (adv.) and **sportiveness** (n.).
- **Sportive** may less commonly mean "of or relating to sports."


**stoical**: [STO-ik-el] Adjective.
Unaffected by or indifferent to pleasure or pain.

- The **stoical** courage of the pioneers is something to admire.
- She was **stoical** and resigned, while her husband was emotional and extroverted.

*Synonym*: aloof, detached, imperturbable, calm, cool, dispassionate
*Antonym:* emotional, feeling, sentimental

Further Information
- Originated from the Greek word *stoikos* meaning "of the portico."
- The **Stoic** philosophy in Ancient Greece was created by Zeno of Citium and he taught it at a public hall called the Stoa Poikile.
- **Stoicism**, as a philosophy, teaches self-control, with passion as the root of all evil.
- **Stoical** is interchangeable with **stoic**. Both can be used as adjectives.

**stolid:** [STAH-led] Adjective.
Unemotional, showing no sensitivity or sensibility.

- My grandfather was known as being a **stolid,** serious man for his entire life.
- The meetings we had to attend were **stolid** and stuffy and almost put us to sleep.

*Synonym:* impassive, apathetic, unexcitable, unemotional, insensitive
*Antonym:* emotional, sentimental, ardent
Further Information
- Originated from the Latin words *stolidus* meaning "dull and stupid."
- Related words include **stolidity** (n.), **stultify** (v.) and **stolidly** (adv.).
- **Stolid** was originally used to mean "a lack of smarts." This meaning changed by the 1800s.
- **Stoic** and **stolid** are synonyms, although **stoic** implies "braving life without complaining," while **stolid** implies "someone who isn't easily excited."


**strident:** [STRI-dent] Adjective.
Marked by harsh, loud, unpleasant sounds.
Assertively commanding attention.

- The professor's **strident** voice is hard to listen to for an hour.
- She is a **strident** advocate for women's rights.

*Synonym:* harsh, raucous, shrill, grating, loud, blatant
*Antonym:* soft, melodious, low
Further Information
- Originated from the Latin word *stridens* meaning "to make a harsh noise."
- Related words include **stridently** (adv.).
- **Strident** implies "an insistent, discordant sound or quality."


**stymie:** [STI-mee] Verb.
To stand in the way of something/someone, to stop something from happening.

- We were **stymied** by the absence of clues in our quest for evidence of the crime.
- Because he acted without authorization, the entire plan has been **stymied.**

*Synonym:* hinder, thwart, obstruct, foil, impede, block
*Antonym:* assist, help, aid
Further Information
- Originated from the Scottish word *stimie* meaning "to obstruct a golf shot."
- **Stymie** started being used in England and North America in the 19th century, first in the original, Scottish sense of the word, and then as a word meaning "to impede."
- Related words include **stymied** (v.) and **stymieing** (v.).

**subterfuge**: [SUB-ter-fyuj] Noun.
Deception by tricks designed to avoid, escape or conceal.

- The journalist used **subterfuge** to get juicy material for her story.
- She claimed to be an actress, a **subterfuge** to get into the theatre without paying for a ticket.

*Synonym:* trick, stratagem, artifice, ruse, deception, ploy
*Antonym:* honesty

Further Information
- Originated from the Latin word *subterfugium* meaning "to escape or evade."
- The *fugere* root, meaning "to flee," is also found in words such as **refuge, refugee** and **fugitive**.
- **Subterfuge** implies "adopting a plan or telling a lie to escape guilt or to gain a goal."

**succinct**: [suh-SINGKT] Adjective.
Compact and precise without wasted words.

- She wrote him a **succinct** letter breaking up with him.
- The prosecutor's closing arguments were **succinct** and to the point.

*Synonym:* brief, terse, laconic, concise, compact, short
*Antonym:* wordy, lengthy, verbose

Further Information
- Originated from the Latin word *succinctus* meaning "having one's clothes gathered by a belt."
- Related words include **succinctly** (adv.) and **succinctness** (n.).
- An archaic meaning of **succinct** is "close-fitting."

**supercilious**: [soo-per-SIL-ee-us] Adjective.
Characteristic of thinking/acting like one is better or more important than someone else.

- The clerk in the expensive clothing store was **supercilious** to her clientele.
- The teacher spoke to the class in a **supercilious**, haughty voice.

*Synonyms:* arrogant, haughty, contemptuous, disdainful, superior, scornful
*Antonym:* humble, modest, meek

Further Information
- Originated from the Latin word *supercilium* meaning "eyebrow."
- Related words include **superciliary** (adj.) and **superciliously** (adv.).
- **Superciliary** now means "of the eyebrow," while **supercilious** means "haughty."

# REVIEW EXERCISE 37

*Match the word with its synonym.*

____ 1.   spartan           a.   obstruct
____ 2.   spate             b.   playful
____ 3.   specious          c.   haughty
____ 4.   spectrum          d.   surge
____ 5.   sportive          e.   severe
____ 6.   stoical           f.   artifice
____ 7.   stolid            g.   false
____ 8.   strident          h.   range
____ 9.   stymie            i.   harsh
____ 10.  subterfuge        j.   detached
____ 11.  succinct          k.   concise
____ 12.  supercilious      l.   impassive

*Fill in the blanks with the most appropriate word from list above.* *(Word form may need changing.)*

1.   His feelings ran the _____ from joyfulness to sorrow.

2.   Her opponents relished every opportunity to _____ her during the game.

3.   The_____ detective didn't get excited easily.

4.   The _____ editor acted like he was better than his reporters.

5.   She was wearing a _____ dress and looked like she was having fun.

6.   Her argument is a _____ one, which is why I don't agree with her.

7.   Her speech was _____and easy for the class to comprehend.

8.   The hotel room was rather _____, lacking even a television.

9.   My long-suffering grandma is_____ and doesn't let anything bother her.

10.  The spy lured his target to the hotel room under _____.

11.  _____ criticism from members of the group caused us to change plans.

12.  There was a _____ of fires that wiped out the whole neighborhood.

**supine**: [SOO-peyn] Adjective.
Lying on the back facing upward.
Willing to be controlled by others, weak.

- The baby always sleeps in a **supine** position in her crib.
- The **supine** group is afraid to act against their leader.

*Synonym:* listless, inert, flat, sluggish, recumbent, passive
*Antonym:* active, flirty, proactive

Further Information
- Originated from the Latin word *supinus* meaning "under, up to."
- Related words include **supinely** (adv.) and **supineness** (n.).
- An archaic meaning of **supine** is "leaning or sloping backward."

**supplicate**: [SUP-pleh-kayt] Verb.
To ask for humbly and earnestly.

- The homeless man **supplicated** passersby for change to purchase food.
- The defense attorney **supplicated** for his client's freedom during his closing argument.

*Synonym:* beseech, beg, entreat, implore, request, appeal
*Antonym: none*

Further Information
- Originated from the Latin word *supplicare* meaning "to beg on one's knees"
- Related words include **supple** (adj.), **supplication** (n.) and **supplicant** (n. or adj.).
- An archaic meaning of **supplicate** is "to conjure."

**surfeit**: [SER-fet] Noun/Verb.
An overabundance or excess. (n.)
To supply to overabundance. (v.)

- Your health will suffer if you **surfeit** yourself. (v.)
- A **surfeit** of salty foods is bad for your health. (n.)

*Synonym:* plethora, glut, surplus, excess, oversupply, superfluity
*Antonym:* lack, need, want

Further Information
- Originated from the Anglo-French word *surfaire* meaning "to overdo."
- An archaic meaning of **surfeit** is "to indulge to satiety in gratification."

**surmise:** [ser-MEYZ] Noun/Verb.
An idea or thought based on little evidence. (n.)
To form an idea or thought based on little evidence. (v.)

- My **surmise** that he was going to ask me out today turned out to be correct. (n.)
- He **surmised** that the teacher would give them a quiz today since she hadn't in a while. (v.)

*Synonym:* suppose, guess, conjecture, assume, presume, believe
*Antonym:* knowledge, measurement, calculation

Further Information
- Originated from the French word *surmettre* meaning "to accuse."
- Related words include **surmiser** (n.) and **surmisable** (adj.).
- The early definition of **surmise** in the 15th century was "a charge or formal accusation."

**surreptitious:** [ser-ep-TIH-shes] Adjective.
Done in secret or stealthily.

- The boss had a **surreptitious** relationship with his employee.
- The mother carried out a **surreptitious** search of her son's belongings.

*Synonym:* furtive, clandestine, stealthy, secret, sneaky, covert
*Antonym:* open, overt, public

Further Information
- Originated from the Latin word *surreptus* meaning "to snatch secretly."
- Related words include **surreptitiously** (adv.).
- **Surreptitious** implies "behavior or action done in secret that may violate a law or custom, usually with skillful avoidance of being noticed."

**swarthy:** [SWOR-thee] Adjective.
Of a dark color or complexion.

- The foreign travelers had **swarthy** complexions and stood apart from the pale natives.
- The pirate in the story was described as having a **swarthy** appearance.

*Synonym:* dark, dusky, ebony
*Antonym:* light, pale, ashen

Further Information
- Originated from the German word *schwarz* meaning "black or dark-colored."
- Related words include **swarthiness** (n.).
- **Swarthy** was originally written as **swart** or **swarty** before the spelling was changed in the late 1500s.

**synchronous:** [SIN-kreh-nes] Adjective.
Happening or existing at exactly the same time.

- The **synchronous** loss of my grandmother and arrival of our child emotionally affected us all.
- The children started **synchronously** flailing their arms in a group temper tantrum.

*Synonym:* concurrent, contemporaneous, coincident, coexistent, simultaneous, concomitant
*Antonym:* asynchronous

Further Information
- Originated from the Greek words *syn* and *chronos* meaning "together" and "time."
- Related words include **synchronousness** (n.), **synchronicity** (n.) and **synchronously** (adv.).
- In describing digital communications, **synchronous** means "a common timing signal that tells when individual bits of data are transmitted allowing for higher rates of data transfer."


**taciturn:** [TAH-seh-turn] Adjective.
Quiet, reluctant to talk.

- The girl was quiet, almost **taciturn**, which made it hard for her to find friends.
- Their **taciturn** leader only speaks to give orders.

*Synonym:* silent, reserved, reticent, uncommunicative, speechless, mute
*Antonym:* talkative, loquacious, chatty

Further Information
- Originated from the Latin word *tacere* meaning "to be silent."
- Related words include **tacit** (adj.), **taciturnly** (adv.) and **taciturnity** (n.).
- **Taciturn** was first seen in English writing in a 1734 play by James Miller.


**tangential:** [tan-JENT-shel] Adjective.
Touching lightly.
Divergent or digressive.

- The teacher's lecture went off on **tangential** matters and didn't stick to the topic at hand.
- The matter the candidate raised was only **tangential** to the discussion.

*Synonym:* digressive, peripheral, extraneous, divergent, rambling, unrelated
*Antonym:* relevant, central, core

Further Information
- Originated from the Latin word *tangentem* meaning "to touch."
- Related words include **tangent** (n. or adj.) and **tangentially** (adv.).
- In geometry, a **tangent** is "a straight line that touches a curve at one single point."

**tantamount:** [TAN-teh-mownt] Adjective.
Equivalent in effect, significance, or value.

- The President's request to his staffers was **tantamount** to a command.
- Some say that leaving a dog home alone is **tantamount** to cruelty.

*Synonym:* equivalent, equal, identical, same, alike, indistinguishable
*Antonym:* diverse, different, opposite

Further Information
- Originated from the Anglo-French words *tant amunter* meaning "to amount to as much."
- Tantamount may originate from the Latin *tantus*, meaning "so" and *amonter* meaning "amount to."
- **Paramount**, a related word, means "the top, the highest, the primary."


**temerity:** [teh-MER-eh-tee] Noun.
Being confident and foolishly unafraid of danger.

- She had the **temerity** to call her teacher a liar.
- The realtor had the **temerity** to tell us that our house wasn't worth much.

*Synonym:* audacity, nerve, impudence, effrontery, cheek, presumption
*Antonym:* caution, cowardice, hesitation

Further Information
- Originated from the Latin word *temere* meaning "blindly, recklessly."
- Temerity also derives from the Old High German word *dinstar* for "dark."
- Related words include **temerarious** (adj.).


**tenable:** [TEH-neh-bel] Adjective.
Capable of being defended, held or maintained.

- The man's appointment to the position is **tenable** for a period of five years.
- This assumption is not **tenable** to the argument you are trying to make.

*Synonym:* defensible, reasonable, sound, stable, strong, firm
*Antonym:* unsustainable, untenable

Further Information
- Originated from the Old French word *tenir* meaning "to hold."
- Related words include **tenability** (n.) and **tenably** (adv.).

# REVIEW EXERCISE 38

*Match the word with its synonym.*

____ 1.  supine
____ 2.  supplicate
____ 3.  surfeit
____ 4.  surmise
____ 5.  surreptitious
____ 6.  swarthy
____ 7.  synchronous
____ 8.  taciturn
____ 9.  tangential
____ 10. tantamount
____ 11. temerity
____ 12. tenable

a.  concurrent
b.  recumbent
c.  surplus
d.  dark
e.  equivalent
f.  audacity
g.  guess
h.  extraneous
i.  stealthy
j.  reasonable
k.  beg
l.  silent

*Fill in the blanks with the most appropriate word from list above.* *(Word form may need changing.)*

1.  Even the _____characters are fleshed out well in this novel.

2.  She lay _____in her chair on the beach, enjoying the sun's rays.

3.  The policeman had the _____ to ask me if I had been drinking.

4.  I _____ you to tell me where you hid the flashlight.

5.  The swimmers practiced their _____ movements for the competition.

6.  We have a _____ of food from our garden so we will give some away.

7.  The natives in the story were described as _____fellows.

8.  She is _____in class, only speaking when called on by the teacher.

9.  If asked, I would _____ that the medicine will start to help you soon.

10. Not believing my story is _____ to calling me a liar.

11. She sneaked a_____ glance at her watch during class.

12. The theory that the earth is flat is no longer_____.

# WORD SET 39

**tenuous**: [TEN-yoo-us] Adjective.
Weak, having little strength or substance.
Not thick or dense.

- The police could only make a **tenuous** connection between the two crimes.
- She has a **tenuous** grasp of reality ever since her mental breakdown.

*Synonym:* flimsy, thin, fine, slight, slim, insignificant
*Antonym:* substantial, stable, thick
<u>Further Information</u>
- Originated from the Latin word *tenuis* meaning "slight or thin."
- Related words include **tenuously** (adv.) and **tenuousness** (n.).
- **Tenuous** implies "something that has been stretched thin and is in danger of breaking."


**terra**: [TER-eh] Noun.
Light-colored highland areas on the surface of a planet.

- A town in West Virginia, **Terra** Alta means "high land."
- When she traveled to Europe for the first time, it was **terra** incognita to her.

*Synonym:* earth, ground, world, globe, land, soil
*Antonym:* water, ocean, sea
<u>Further Information</u>
- Originated from the Latin word *terra* meaning "earth."
- The plural of **terra** is **terrae**.
- **Terra** has inspired other earth-related terms, including **terra firma**, or "firm land," **terra cotta**, a color which translates to "cooked earth," and **terra incognita**, or "unknown land."


**timorous**: [TIH-meh-res] Adjective.
Fearful, timid.

- She is a **timorous** creature, afraid of her own shadow.
- The **timorous** rabbit ran as soon as she heard the human's footsteps.

*Synonym:* timid, shy, fearful, diffident, apprehensive, bashful
*Antonym:* bold, brave, courageous
<u>Further Information</u>
- Originated from the Latin word *timor* meaning "fear."
- Related words include **timid** (adj.), **timorously** (adv.), **timidity** (n.) and **timorousness** (n.).
- **Timorous** appeared in English as an adjective before **timid** did.

**tirade:** [TI-rayd] Noun.
A long, angry speech.

- The man launched into a **tirade** at the airport ticket counter when his plane was delayed.
- The politician launched a **tirade** directed against his opponent at the debate.

*Synonym:* diatribe, rant, lecture, harangue, sermon, invective
*Antonym*: harmony, calm, praise

Further Information
- Originated from the Italian word *tirata* meaning "to volley, draw or shoot."
- **Tirade** was directly derived from the French word *tirade* meaning "long speech."


**toady:** [TO-dee] Noun/Verb.
A person who flatters another in hopes of gaining favors. (n.)
To flatter another in hopes of gaining favors. (v.)

- I will not **toady** to him just to save my job. (v.)
- He felt like a **toady** who was just hanging on to gain the favors of his friend. (n.)

*Synonym:* sycophant, flatterer, bootlicker, truckle, lackey, fawner
*Antonym:* disrespect

Further Information
- Originated from the English word *toad-eater* meaning "fawning flatterer."
- The derivation of *toad-eater*: It was believed that a **toady** ate a toad believed to be poisonous in hopes of allowing his master to display skill in expelling the poison.
- Related words include **toadyism** (n.).


**tome**: [TOM] Noun.
A book.

- The **tome** on the leader seems realistic; but the government staffer claims it is pure fiction.
- I am currently reading the latest **tome** to top the best-seller list.

*Synonym*: volume, book, publication, work, novel, writing
*Antonym:* none

Further Information
- Originated from the Greek word *tomos* meaning "section of papyrus."
- A **tome** may also be "a longer section or volume of a written work."

**torpid:** [TOHR-ped] Adjective.
Sluggish, having lost motion or energy.

- She still felt **torpid** after a long nap.
- The medicine my mother gave me made me feel **torpid** and sleepy.

*Synonym:* sluggish, inactive, lethargic, inert, dull, listless
*Antonym:* active, flirty, lively

Further Information
- Originated from the Latin word *torpere* meaning "to be sluggish or numb."
- Related words include **torpidity** (n.).
- In zoology, **torpid** means "a dormant hibernating animal."

**torrid:** [TOHR-ed] Adjective.
Giving off intense heat.
Passionate, ardent.

- You'll feel better if you get out of that **torrid** sun and under a shade tree.
- The **torrid** criticism against the politician was surprising to his supporters.

*Synonym:* burning, fiery, sweltering, hot, scorching, sultry
*Antonym:* frigid, arctic, cold

Further Information
- Originated from the Latin word *torridus* meaning "dried with heat."
- Related words include **torridly** (adv.), **torridity** (n.) and **torridness** (n.).
- **Torrid** is an ancestor of the English word **toast.**

**tractable:** [TRAK-teh-bel] Adjective.
Easily controlled, handled, managed or led.

- The issues have proven to be more **tractable** than the group first expected.
- His assistant was quite **tractable** and eager to help in whatever way possible.

*Synonym*: compliant, flexible, yielding, pliant, amenable, submissive
*Antonym:* stubborn, intractable, disobedient

Further Information
- Originated from the Latin word *tractare* meaning "to handle."
- Related words include **tractability** (n.) and **tractably** (adv.).

**tremulous:** [TREM-yeh-les] Adjective.
Characterized by trembling or timidity.
Sensitive, easily shaken.

- My fingers were **tremulous** as I opened the college acceptance letter.
- We waited in **tremulous** anticipation for our favorite speaker to take the stage.

*Synonym:* trembling, quivering, shaky, frightened, quaking, wavering
*Antonym:* brave, stable, steady

Further Information
- Originated from the Latin word *tremulus* meaning "shaking."
- Related words include **tremble** (n. or v.), **tremulously** (adv.) and **tremulousness** (n.).
- **Tremulous** and **timorous** are close in meaning. **Tremulous** is characterized by actual "trembling, quivering or shaking" while **timorous** is "timid or fearful."

**trenchant:** [TREN-chent] Adjective.
Sharp, effective and articulate.

- The father's criticism of his son was **trenchant** and surprising.
- The politician's speech was a **trenchant** attack against the resistance.

*Synonym:* incisive, sharp, caustic, keen, biting, sarcastic
*Antonym:* weak, ineffective

Further Information
- Originated from the Old French word *trenchant* meaning "sharp or cutting."
- Related words include **trenchantly** (adv.), **trenchancy** (n.), **trench** (n. or v.) and **retrench** (v.).
- An archaic meaning of **trenchant** is "physical sharpness" such as "a **trenchant** sword."

**truculent:** [TREH-kye-lent] Adjective.
Defiantly aggressive or hostile.

- The boy became **truculent** when confronted and started arguing with the principal.
- I admit, I might have sounded needlessly **truculent** when I argued with you yesterday.

*Synonym:* aggressive, fierce, belligerent, ferocious, savage, combative
*Antonym:* charitable, peaceful, kind

Further Information
- Originated from the Latin word *truculentus* meaning "savage."
- Related words include **truculently** (adv.), **truculence** (n.) and **truculency** (n.).
- An archaic meaning of **truculent** is "savage, fierce."

# REVIEW EXERCISE 39

**Match the word with its synonym.**

| | | | | |
|---|---|---|---|---|
| ___ | 1. | tenuous | a. | sharp |
| ___ | 2. | terra | b. | hot |
| ___ | 3. | timorous | c. | earth |
| ___ | 4. | tirade | d. | book |
| ___ | 5. | toady | e. | timid |
| ___ | 6. | tome | f. | rant |
| ___ | 7. | torpid | g. | trembling |
| ___ | 8. | torrid | h. | flatterer |
| ___ | 9. | tractable | i. | thin |
| ___ | 10. | tremulous | j. | compliant |
| ___ | 11. | trenchant | k. | sluggish |
| ___ | 12. | truculent | l. | aggressive |

**Fill in the blanks with the most appropriate word from list above.** *(Word form may need changing.)*

1. I was _____ as I took the stage to read my lines.

2. Grab that big _____ from the bookshelf—it should be an encyclopedia.

3. Sometimes I feel like I have a _____ hold on sanity.

4. He likes to lead _____ followers who are easily swayed.

5. The pottery was a beautiful _____ cotta shade.

6. "Who is at the door?" she asked in a _____ voice.

7. He passed the summer in a mostly _____ state, doing very little.

8. She refused to _____ to the teacher just to get a good grade.

9. He won't make a good leader because he's too temperamental and _____.

10. I was quite hot while sitting outside in the _____ sun.

11. I launched into a _____ about how unfairly I had been treated.

12. His _____ criticism of her cooking made her cry.

# WORD SET 40

**turpitude**: [TER-peh-tyud] Noun.
Possessing an evil quality or behaving evilly.

- Some equate acts of moral **turpitude** with violations of the law.
- The politician was considered unfit for office due to moral **turpitude**.

*Synonym:* depravity, baseness, corruption, evildoing, vice, degradation
*Antonym:* humbleness, humility

## Further Information
- Originated from the Latin word *turpitudo,* meaning "vile, base."
- **Turpitude** is often used in the legal phrase **moral turpitude**, to denote "behavior that violates accepted standards."

**tyro**: [TI-ro] Noun.
A beginner or novice.

- He is a **tyro** at playwriting, which is evident to all who went to see his first performance.
- I am a **tyro** in German as I just started learning the language this year.

*Synonym:* novice, beginner, learner, neophyte, amateur, apprentice
*Antonym:* expert

## Further Information
- Originated from the Latin word *tiro* meaning "young soldier."
- Related words include **tyronic** (adj.).
- **Tyro** may also be spelled **tiro**.
- The plural of **tyro** may be spelled **tyros** or **tiros**.

**ubiquitous**: [yuh-BIH-kweh-tes] Adjective.
Seeming to be everywhere at the same time, widespread.

- It seems that sugar is **ubiquitous** in our diets in modern times.
- Coffee shops are **ubiquitous** in this city; you can find one on every corner.

*Synonym:* omnipresent, universal, prevalent, everywhere, common, pervasive
*Antonym:* rare, absent, scarce

## Further Information
- Originated from the Latin word *ubique* meaning "everywhere."
- Related words include **ubiquity** (n.) and **ubiquitously** (adv.).
- **Ubiquitous** didn't appear in written English until 1830, although **ubiquity** was seen in the 16th century.

**umbrage:** [UM-brij] Noun.
A feeling of offense or resentment at a slight or insult.

- She takes **umbrage** against anyone who criticizes her work.
- The policeman took **umbrage** at even the slightest suggestion of disrespect.

*Synonym:* pique, offense, rage, resentment, anger, displeasure
*Antonym:* like, pleasure, happiness

Further Information
- Originated from the Latin word *umbra* meaning "shade."
- *Umbra* also gave us the English word **umbrella**, meaning "a sunshade or parasol."
- An archaic meaning of **umbrage** is "shadow or shade," or "trees that give shade."

**unctuous:** [UNK-ches] Adjective.
Characteristic of someone who speaks in a friendly manner but is not sincere.
Oily and fatty.
Abundant in organic materials.

- The **unctuous** clergyman who spoke at our aunt's funeral didn't even know her and was obviously insincere.
- The pharmaceutical preparation that the dermatologist prescribed to him was **unctuous**.
- The soil in which we planted our garden was **unctuous**, enabling plants to grow faster.

*Synonym:* oily, insincere, smarmy, hypocritical, smooth, obsequious, slick
*Antonym:* genuine, naive, sincere

Further Information
- Originated from the Latin word *unctum* meaning "ointment."
- Related words include **unctuosity** (n.), **unctuously** (adv.) and **unctuousness** (n.).

**untenable:** [un-TEN-uh-bel] Adjective.
Cannot be defended or occupied.

- Your theory is **untenable** and must therefore be rejected by serious scientists.
- Conditions within the city are **untenable** in many areas, with violence and drugs abundant.

*Synonym:* indefensible, invalid, unsound, unsustainable, unfounded, illogical
*Antonym:* reasonable, arguable, tenable

Further Information
- Originated from the Latin *tenere* meaning "to hold."
- Related words include **untenability** (adv.).
- **Untenable** suggests "a position or idea that is so implausible that holding onto it is inexcusable."

**unveiling:** [un-VAY-leng] Noun/Verb.
A formal removal of a covering or public revealing of a plan. (n.)
Uncovering or making public. (v.)

- We were at the **unveiling** of the new city community center. (n.)
- He **unveiled** his plans to transform the old bowling alley into a new youth center. (v.)

*Synonym:* disclosure, introduction, debut, uncovering, exposure, revelation
*Antonym:* veiling

Further Information
- Originated from the French word *veil* meaning "a head covering."
- Related words include **unveil** (v.) and **unveiled** (v.).


**upbraid:** [UP-brayd] Verb.
To severely criticize.

- The teacher **upbraided** the student when she found him smoking behind the school.
- I was tired of being **upbraided** for my mistakes.

*Synonym:* reproach, scold, berate, rebuke, castigate, reprove
*Antonym:* praise, extol, approve

Further Information
- Originated from the Old English word *upbredan* meaning "to bring forward as grounds for censure."
- Related words include **upbraiding** (n.).
- **Upbraid** as a noun has the archaic meaning of "the act of **upbraiding** or criticizing."


**urbane:** [ur-BAYN] Adjective.
Polite, polished and sophisticated in manner.

- Her suitor was charming and **urbane**.
- Some of the more mature jokes in that cartoon appeal to **urbane** adults.

*Synonym:* suave, refined, polished, smooth, sophisticated, polite
*Antonym:* uncouth, naive, rude

Further Information
- Originated from the Latin word *urbs* meaning "city."
- Related words include **urbanely** (adv.).
- At one time, **urbane** and **urban** were interchangeable, both meaning "relating to a city."

**utilitarian:** [yu-tih-leh-TAR-ee-en] Noun/Adjective.
A person who believes in utilitarianism, that is, the idea of usefulness over other values. (n.)
Designed for or upholding usefulness over other values. (adj.)

- His home is very **utilitarian** in style, with no aesthetic qualities or decorations. (adj.)
- She describes herself as a **utilitarian**, concerned more with practicality than beauty. (n.)

*Synonym:* useful, realist, functional, practical, pragmatic, advantageous
*Antonym:* unnecessary, impractical, useless

Further Information
- **Utilitarian** was coined by philosopher Jeremy Bentham in 1781 from the word *utility* and the suffix *-arian*, to mean "one who advocates usefulness over all else."
- Related words include **utilitarianism** (n.), **utility** (n.) and **utilitarianly** (adv.).


**vacillate:** [VAH-seh-layt] Verb.
To waver in feeling, mind or will.
To physically sway or be unsteady.

- Her parents tend to **vacillate**, unable to decide, when she asks them if she can go out.
- He **vacillated** as he stood on the stage, appearing as if he was about to faint.

*Synonym:* waver, fluctuate, oscillate, hesitate, alternate, vary
*Antonym:* decide, stay, persist

Further Information
- Originated from the Latin word *vacillatus* meaning "to be unsteady."
- Related words include **vacillatingly** (adv.) and **vacillator** (n.).
- To **vacillate** implies "to consistently hesitate due to the inability to make a firm decision."


**vapid:** [VAH-ped] Adjective.
Lacking interest, flavor or spirit, dull.

- She made a **vapid** comment about the film.
- He did the same thing every year and found life **vapid.**

*Synonym:* bland, flat, insipid, dull, tedious, uninteresting
*Antonym:* lively, active

Further Information
- Originated from the Latin word *vapidus* meaning "of wine having lost freshness, flat."
- Related words include **vapidly** (adv.) and **vapidness** (n.).
- **Vapid** originally referred to "wine or liquor that had gone flat."

# REVIEW EXERCISE 40

*Match the word with its synonym.*

___  1.  turpitude
___  2.  tyro
___  3.  ubiquitous
___  4.  umbrage
___  5.  unctuous
___  6.  untenable
___  7.  unveiling
___  8.  upbraid
___  9.  urbane
___  10. utilitarian
___  11. vacillate
___  12. vapid

a.  useful
b.  waver
c.  insincere
d.  invalid
e.  reproach
f.  depravity
g.  bland
h.  prevalent
i.  introduction
j.  novice
k.  offense
l.  refined

*Fill in the blanks with the most appropriate word from list above.* (*Word form may need changing.*)

1.  I can't decide; I keep _____ from one possibility to another.

2.  Unwilling to seem _____, he wanted to tell her his true feelings.

3.  The _____, witty young woman bewitched him.

4.  Cell phones are _____ and everyone seems to have one.

5.  The _____ of her art at the gallery made the onlookers sigh in awe.

6.  What he did could be considered an act of moral _____.

7.  Many of his ideas are _____ and seem easy to put into practice.

8.  She took _____ because she wasn't invited to the party.

9.  The leader did not want to give him too much responsibility since he is a_____.

10. Why would you _____ me for such a little mistake?

11. We knew the situation was becoming _____ and we needed to leave soon.

12. He quickly became tired of her _____ chatter.

**vehement**: [VEE-eh-ment] Adjective.
Powerful, emotional or deeply felt.

- Despite **vehement** opposition from her family, she quit school to become a rock musician.
- He made a **vehement** attack on the government's position.

*Synonym:* violent, fierce, intense, ardent, passionate, fervid
*Antonym:* apathetic, calm, indifferent

Further Information
- Originated from the Latin word *vehement* meaning "violent, impetuous."
- Related words include **vehemently** (adv.) and **vehemence** (n.).
- If one does something **vehemently**, they do so with emotion and force.


**veneer**: [veh-NEER] Noun/Verb.
A thin layer on the surface, a decorative facing. (n.)
A superficial show or facade. (n.)
To overlay a surface with a thin layer. (v.)
To conceal or hide with a facade. (v.)

- The stone **veneer** on that house is quite aesthetically pleasing. (n.)
- She put on a **veneer** of friendliness with her teacher, trying to win her favor. (n.)
- He **veneered** the furniture before selling it, as added protection for the wood. (v.)
- She **veneered** her true feeling with a smile, hiding the fact that she was upset. (v.)

*Synonym:* cover, gloss, coating, overlay, mask, facade
*Antonym:* reality

Further Information
- Originated from the French word *fournir* meaning "to furnish."
- Related words include **veneerer** (n.).
- In dentistry, **veneers** are "layers of material placed over a tooth."


**venerate**: [VEH-neh-rayt] Verb.
To regard with respect or honor.

- He is our country's most **venerated** novelist.
- She always **venerates** the president of her country, whomever he or she may be at the time.

*Synonym:* revere, worship, respect, adore, esteem, admire
*Antonym:* despise, scorn, dishonor

Further Information
- Originated from the Latin word *venerari* meaning "to pay homage."
- Related words include **venerator** (n.) and **venerated** (v.).

**veracity:** [veh-RAH-seh-tee] Noun.
Truthfulness, accuracy.

- The woman's **veracity** has never been in question, as we have always known her to be an honest person.
- Have you checked the **veracity** of their allegations against him?

*Synonym:* truth, verity, authenticity, honesty, accuracy, reality
*Antonym:* deceitfulness, dishonesty, mendacity

Further Information
- Originated from the Latin word *verax* meaning "truthful."
- Related words include **verity** (n.), **verify** (v.), **veraciousness** (n.) and **verisimilitude** (n.).
- **Veracity** has also been the name of many novels, albums and a software company.

**verbose:** [ver-BOS] Adjective.
Using more words than necessary.

- The lawyer's writing is often difficult, unclear and **verbose** to read.
- She was a **verbose** traveling companion, which is why I was not able to sleep on the bus.

*Synonym:* wordy, prolix, talkative, loquacious, garrulous, windy
*Antonym:* brief, concise, succinct

Further Information
- Originated from the Latin word *verbum* meaning "word."
- Related words include **verbosity** (n.), **verbosely** (adv.) and **verboseness** (n.).
- **Verbosity** suggests "dullness from being too wordy."

**verve:** [VERV] Noun.
Great enthusiasm and energy.

- He delivered his speech with wittiness and **verve**, keeping his audience engaged.
- Critics said that her performance was dull, boring and lacked **verve**.

*Synonym:* energy, spirit, enthusiasm, animation, zest, vitality
*Antonym:* laziness, lethargy, dullness

Further Information
- Originated from the Latin *verba* meaning "words."
- An archaic meaning of **verve** is "a special talent or ability."
- **Verve** may also refer to a variety of proper nouns, including a rock band, an album, a computer operating system and an Indian magazine.

**vestige:** [VEH-stij] Noun.
A trace or visible sign left by something.
The smallest possible amount of something.

- Is there even a **vestige** of truth in the witness's accusations against him?
- Not a **vestige** of the building remains after its implosion.

*Synonym:* trace, remnant, relic, hint, suggestion, sign
*Antonym: none*

Further Information
- Originated from the Latin word *vestigum* meaning "footprint."
- Related words include **vestigial** (adj.) and **vestigially** (adv.).
- The medical definition of **vestige** is "a body part that is small, underdeveloped and usually nonfunctioning, in comparison to another more fully developed part in an earlier generation or stage of development."

**vexatious:** [vek-SAY-shes] Adjective.
Causing distress, trouble or disorder.

- The allegations she made against him were **vexatious** and of no substance.
- We are tired of receiving **vexatious** calls from telemarketers at dinnertime.

*Synonym:* irritating, annoying, troublesome, irksome, pesky, bothersome
*Antonym:* comfortable, convenient, helpful

Further Information
- Originated from the Old French word *vexacion* meaning "abuse or harassment."
- Related words include **vexatiously** (adv.) and **vexatiousness** (n.).
- The legal definition of **vexatious** is "a legal action or proceeding begun without sufficient grounds, intended to annoy or harass the defendant."

**vicissitudes:** [veh-SIS-seh-tyuds] Noun.
Things that occur by chance, changes, variations.

- Despite the **vicissitudes** of his past life, he has always come through them victorious.
- Because he is used to life's **vicissitudes**, he does not give up easily.

*Synonym*: variations, differences, variances, shifts, fluctuations, changes
*Antonym:* stabilities

Further Information
- Originated from the Latin word *vicissitudo* meaning "change."
- The legal definition of **vicissitudes** is "circumstances."

**virtuoso**: [ver-chew-O-so] Noun/Adjective.
A person who excels at something very skillfully. (n.)
Having the ability of a person skilled in the arts or sciences. (adj.)

- He is a piano **virtuoso** with remarkable skills and talent. (n.)
- She gave a **virtuoso** display of dance at the performance. (adj.)

*Synonym:* master, expert, ace, whiz, maven, genius
*Antonym:* amateur, rookie, unskilled

Further Information
- Originated from the Latin word *virtus* meaning "excellence."
- Related words include **virtuosic** (adj.).
- The plural of **virtuoso** is **virtuosos** or **virtuosi**.


**viscous**: [VIH-skes] Adjective.
Thick or sticky, not flowing freely and easily.

- The doctor gave her blood thinner medication to try to change her blood's **viscosity**.
- The **viscous** lava from the volcano flowed slowly down the hill towards the village.

*Synonym:* thick, glutinous, sticky, gummy, gluey, fibrous
*Antonym:* thin, runny, watery

Further Information
- Originated from the Latin word *viscum* meaning "birdlime."
- Related words include **viscosity** (n.), **viscously** (adv.) and **viscousness** (n.).
- The technical definition of **viscous** is "having a high resistance to flow."


**vitriolic**: [vit-tree-OHL-ik] Adjective.
Severely scathing, caustic, harsh and angry in words.

- The protesters launched a **vitriolic** attack on the visiting foreign leader.
- She is the most **vitriolic** animal rights advocate I have ever seen.

*Synonym:* acid, caustic, bitter, acrimonious, acerbic, cutting
*Antonym:* pleasant, bland

Further Information
- Originated from the Latin word *vitreolus* meaning "glassy."
- Related words include **vitriol** (n.).
- In chemistry, **vitriolic** means "a highly corrosive chemical or substance."

# REVIEW EXERCISE 41

*Match the word with its synonym.*

____ 1.  vehement         a.  caustic
____ 2.  veneer           b.  truth
____ 3.  venerate         c.  trace
____ 4.  veracity         d.  variances
____ 5.  verbose          e.  facade
____ 6.  verve            f.  energy
____ 7.  vestige          g.  thick
____ 8.  vexatious        h.  fierce
____ 9.  vicissitudes     i.  revere
____ 10. virtuoso         j.  wordy
____ 11. viscous          k.  annoying
____ 12. vitriolic        l.  master

*Fill in the blanks with the most appropriate word from list above.* *(Word form may need changing.)*

1.  The fluid becomes _____ as it cools.

2.  She showed _____ and delight during her musical performance.

3.  I would never question your_____ as I've always known you to be honest.

4.  The _____ of your past cannot keep you from moving forward.

5.  Your _____ criticism of the child's drawing made her burst into tears.

6.  No _____ of the medieval fort remain at the archaeological site.

7.  Don't hide behind a happy _____when, in reality, you are quite sorrowful.

8.  She was pleasant to my face but _____behind my back.

9.  He is the most _____poet of our times, having won many awards.

10. The spy was a _____ enigma to intelligence officers trying to understand him.

11. You are too _____ in your essay, and it is therefore incomprehensible.

12. He is a musical _____ and bound to be a successful musician someday.

# WORD SET 42

**vituperate**: [vi-TOO-per-ayt] Verb.
To verbally criticize severely with harsh language, to berate.

- When he is drunk, he tends to **vituperate** everyone, especially his wife.
- The coach **vituperated** his team with abusive talk so often that he received a stern warning from the school principal.

*Synonym:* revile, scold, vilify, rail, abuse, upbraid
*Antonym:* compliment, praise, acclaim

Further Information
- Originated from the Latin words *vitium* and *parare,* meaning "fault" and "to prepare."
- Related words include **vituperator** (n.) and **vituperative** (adj.).
- **Vituperate** implies "making a violent verbal criticism against someone or something."


**vivacious**: [veh-VAY-shes] Adjective.
Full of energy, happiness and liveliness.

- The **vivacious** woman is also attractive and intelligent, adding to her charm.
- He has a **vivacious** disposition and is always ready for a good time.

*Synonym:* lively, spirited, cheerful, sprightly, active, animated
*Antonym:* dull, lifeless, spiritless

Further Information
- Originated from the Latin word *vivax* meaning "long-lived" or "high-spirited."
- Related words include **vivaciously** (adv.), **vivaciousness** (n.) and **vivacity** (n.).
- Other words descended from *vivax* include **convivial, vivid, vigorous, victual**, and **survive.**


**volition**: [vo-LIH-shen] Noun.
The ability to choose or the act of making a choice.

- We left the party entirely of our own **volition**, not because you told us to go.
- Is everything we think and everything we do a product of our **volition**?

*Synonym:* choice, will, desire, preference, wish, discretion
*Antonym:* force, destiny, karma

Further Information
- Originated from the Latin word *velle* meaning "to wish."
- Related words include **volitional** (adj.) and **volitionally** (adv.).
- In philosophy, **volition** means "an act of will characterized by the physical movement it causes."

**voluble:** [VOL-yeh-bel] Adjective.
Talking rapidly and energetically.

- He is very **voluble** on subjects about which he is passionate.
- The foreign leader's **voluble** praise of the neighboring government surprised its citizens.

*Synonym:* chatty, garrulous, loquacious, fluent, talkative, wordy
*Antonym:* quiet, silent, taciturn

Further Information
- Originated from the Greek word *eilyein* meaning "to roll or wrap."
- Related words include **volubility** (n.) and **volubly** (adv.).
- In botany, **voluble** means "twisting or twining."


**voracious:** [veh-RAY-shes] Adjective.
Having a large appetite, quite eager.

- He is a **voracious** reader who starts a new book as soon as the old one is finished.
- Her **voracious** appetite will cause her to gain weight if she doesn't exercise.

*Synonym:* greedy, ravenous, insatiable, gluttonous, rapacious, hoggish
*Antonym:* satisfied, balanced, quenched

Further Information
- Originated from the Latin word *vorare* meaning "to devour."
- Related words include **voraciously** (adv.) and **voraciousness** (n.).
- Other words derived from *vorare* include **herbivorous, carnivorous** and **omnivorous**.


**whet:** [WEHT] Verb/Noun.
To make sharper or more acute. (v.)
Something that sharpens or makes more acute. (n.)

- Those delicious odors are **whetting** our appetites for dinner. (v.)
- The appetizer was merely a **whet** readying him for the main course. (n.)

*Synonym:* sharpen, grind, quicken, arouse, kindle, hone
*Antonym:* blunt, dull

Further Information
- Originated from the Old High German word *wezzen* meaning "to sharpen."
- Related words include **whetter** (n.) and **whetting** (v.).
- In engineering, **whet** means "to sharpen through grinding or friction."

**wily:** [WI-lee] Adjective.
Crafty and cunning.

- The fox was described as a **wily** creature, as he stealthily pursued his prey.
- Her **wily** scheme to take over the company did not pan out as she had planned.

*Synonym:* cunning, crafty, foxy, sly, artful, shrewd
*Antonym:* naive, childlike, ingenuous

Further Information
- Originated from the Old Norse word *vel* meaning "trick."
- Related words include **wiliness** (n.) and **wilily** (adv.).
- **Wily** implies "using deception and skill in maneuvering someone or something."


**wistful:** [WIST-fel] Adjective.
Full of yearning and/or sadness, especially about something that made one happy in the past.

- The old lady was **wistful** as she described her youth.
- Some describe him as antisocial, but I think he is just **wistful** and quiet.

*Synonym:* melancholy, nostalgic, pensive, sad, longing, yearning
*Antonym:* satisfied, glad, pleased

Further Information
- **Wistful** came from a blend of the English word *wishful* and the obsolete English word *wistly* meaning "intently."
- Related words include **wistfully** (adv.) and **wistfulness** (n.).
- It is believed what **wistful** was once spelled **whistful**.


**yen:** [YEN] Noun/Verb.
The monetary unit of Japan. (n.)
A strong desire or inclination. (n.)
To have a strong desire for. (v.)

- We changed our dollars into **yen** when we arrived in Japan. (n.)
- I have a **yen** for some of my grandmother's famous cheesecake. (n.)
- He **yenned** for his wife's homemade stew when all he had at home was canned soup. (v.)

*Synonym:* hankering, lust, yearning, desire, hunger, craving
*Antonym:* dislike, contempt

Further Information
- From the Chinese word *yan* meaning "wish" (v.) or "round" (n.).
- Related words include **yenning** (v.) and **yenned** (v.).

**yoke**: [YOK] Noun/Verb.
Something that connects, subjugates, binds or joins. (n.)
To join or bind together. (v.)

- He was still under the **yoke** of drug addiction, despite efforts to get clean and sober. (n.)
- The farmer **yoked** his team of oxen together before plowing the field. (v.)

*Synonym:* burden, bondage, oppression, link, join, attach
*Antonym:* unyoke, disconnect, disjoin

Further Information
- Originated from the Old English word *geoc*, meaning "yoke."
- **Yoke** has a variety of specialized meanings. In electronics, **yoke** is "a series of two/more magnetic recording heads fastened together to play/record more than one track at a time." In nautical terms, **yoke** is "a crossbar on the rudder of a ship to which steering cables are joined."


**zealous**: [ZEL-us] Adjective.
Characterized by strong, energetic support for something or someone.

- His **zealous** support of the candidate helped her to get elected to office.
- The policeman's **zealous** enforcement of the law is sometimes questioned by onlookers.

*Synonym:* eager, enthusiastic, ardent, passionate, fervent, keen
*Antonym:* apathetic, uninterested, unenthusiastic

Further Information
- Originated from the Latin word *zelus* meaning "jealousy."
- Related words include **zeal** (n.), **zealously** (adv.) and **zealousness** (n.).
- In 16th-17th century English, **zealous** was a synonym for **jealous**.


**zephyr**: [ZEH-fer] Noun.
A gentle breeze.
A lightweight fabric or garment.

- The **zephyr** from the ocean helped cool us off on a hot day.
- A **zephyr** is a lightweight garment that competitors wear in rowing.

*Synonym:* breeze, puff, wind, air, gust, draft
*Antonym:* storm

Further Information
- Originated from the Greek word *Zephyrus* meaning "god of the west wind."
- William Shakespeare might have been the first Englishman to use the word **zephyr** in writing in 1611 in his play *Cymbeline:* "they are as gentle as **zephyrs** blowing below the violet."

# REVIEW EXERCISE 42

*Match the word with its synonym.*

___ 1.   vituperate
___ 2.   vivacious
___ 3.   volition
___ 4.   voluble
___ 5.   voracious
___ 6.   whet
___ 7.   wily
___ 8.   wistful
___ 9.   yen
___ 10.  yoke
___ 11.  zealous
___ 12.  zephyr

a.  insatiable
b.  breeze
c.  crafty
d.  yearning
e.  lively
f.  choice
g.  scold
h.  eager
i.  chatty
j.  sharpen
k.  nostalgic
l.  burden

*Fill in the blanks with the most appropriate word from list above.* *(Word form may need changing.)*

1.   The bad habit is like a great _____ sitting on my shoulders.

2.   The little boy was so tired that he went to bed of his own _____.

3.   He is _____ when he thinks back on his relationship with her.

4.   I knew she was _____ me in her own language by her facial expressions.

5.   The _____ businessman thought he could cheat customers easily.

6.   She is a _____ moviegoer, seeing a new movie every week.

7.   Her _____ was one reason she won the beauty pageant.

8.   The frosty _____ blew across our Alaskan porch this morning.

9.   When asked, I became very _____ and told the entire truth.

10.  I have a _____ to travel around the world to every continent.

11.  Did that appetizer _____ your appetite for dinner?

12.  If you hadn't been overly _____ she might have gone out with you.

# Review Exercises Solutions

## Review Exercise 1

### Matching

1. f
2. i
3. e
4. j
5. d
6. k
7. c
8. h
9. b
10. L
11. a
12. g

### Fill in the Blanks

1. abstemious
2. adulterate
3. Achilles
4. aggrandizing
5. adumbrated
6. abject
7. acumen
8. accosted
9. abjured
10. abrogate
11. alacrity
12. abnegation

## Review Exercise 2

### Matching

1. k
2. j
3. e
4. i
5. d
6. L
7. h
8. c
9. a
10. g
11. b
12. f

### Fill in the Blanks

1. alias
2. alleviate
3. ameliorate
4. apocryphal
5. alluded
6. anachronistic
7. antithesis
8. altruism
9. antediluvian
10. amorphous
11. annex
12. anathema

## Review Exercise 3

### Matching

1. c
2. g
3. a
4. L
5. e
6. d
7. k
8. j
9. i
10. f
11. b
12. h

### Fill in the Blanks

1. avaricious
2. artifice
3. archetypal
4. arcane
5. ascetic
6. artifact
7. attenuate
8. ardent
9. austerity
10. aspersion
11. approbation
12. assiduous

## Review Exercise 4

### Matching

1. e
2. g
3. d
4. j
5. h
6. L
7. f
8. a
9. k
10. b
11. i
12. c

### Fill in the Blanks

1. benevolent
2. bulwark
3. blandishment
4. beguile
5. bedlam
6. besmirch
7. bogus
8. balk
9. burgeon
10. boor
11. bigot
12. brittle

## Review Exercise 5

### Matching

1. k
2. c
3. i
4. g
5. d
6. j
7. L
8. e
9. f
10. b
11. h
12. a

### Fill in the Blanks

1. cache
2. cant
3. castigate
4. capitulate
5. capricious
6. buttress
7. cacophony
8. callow
9. cajole
10. carp
11. calumny
12. candor

## Review Exercise 6

### Matching

1. f
2. d
3. a
4. b
5. c
6. k
7. j
8. L
9. i
10. h
11. g
12. e

### Fill in the Blanks

1. celerity
2. chauvinism
3. chimerical
4. circumvent
5. catalyst
6. circumlocution
7. cogent
8. commodious
9. compunction
10. cognizant
11. comely
12. chagrin

## Review Exercise 7

### Matching
1. k
2. g
3. f
4. d
5. j
6. L
7. b
8. h
9. e
10. i
11. a
12. c

### Fill in the Blanks
1. condone
2. conduit
3. connived
4. consternation
5. concomitant
6. concoction
7. construed
8. conflagration
9. constituent
10. conjecture
11. connoisseur
12. congruity

## Review Exercise 8

### Matching
1. g
2. e
3. i
4. d
5. j
6. c
7. h
8. k
9. b
10. L
11. a
12. f

### Fill in the Blanks
1. copious
2. cupidity
3. contravened
4. consummate
5. coterie
6. crescendo
7. conundrum
8. contrite
9. coup
10. countenance
11. corpulence
12. culpable

## Review Exercise 9

### Matching
1. g
2. e
3. h
4. d
5. i
6. c
7. L
8. b
9. k
10. j
11. a
12. f

### Fill in the Blanks
1. decrepit
2. demagogue
3. demurs
4. desultory
5. dexterity
6. derided
7. deleterious
8. decadence
9. delirious
10. denigrating
11. deluge
12. defunct

## Review Exercise 10

### Matching

1. h
2. g
3. f
4. j
5. c
6. b
7. k
8. i
9. d
10. a
11. L
12. e

### Fill in the Blanks

1. diatribe
2. dour
3. duplicity
4. ebullient
5. domicile
6. eclectic
7. disparate
8. duress
9. diaphanous
10. dilettante
11. drudgery
12. didactic

## Review Exercise 11

### Matching

1. i
2. e
3. j
4. b
5. d
6. g
7. k
8. c
9. h
10. a
11. L
12. f

### Fill in the Blanks

1. egalitarian
2. elicit
3. empirical
4. emollient
5. embezzlement
6. effigy
7. elucidate
8. elegy
9. edict
10. emaciated
11. egregious
12. edifice

## Review Exercise 12

### Matching

1. f
2. d
3. g
4. i
5. c
6. e
7. k
8. b
9. j
10. a
11. L
12. h

### Fill in the Blanks

1. encumbrance
2. enigma
3. entourage
4. erudite
5. emulate
6. eschew
7. epitome
8. ennui
9. ephemeral
10. enunciation
11. enhanced
12. enervate

## Review Exercise 13

### Matching

1. f
2. c
3. j
4. d
5. k
6. e
7. g
8. b
9. i
10. a
11. L
12. h

### Fill in the Blanks

1. espoused
2. euphemism
3. exculpate
4. evanescent
5. excruciating
6. esoteric
7. expatiate
8. eulogy
9. exacting
10. exasperated
11. exhaustive
12. estimable

## Review Exercise 14

### Matching

1. g
2. f
3. j
4. c
5. i
6. d
7. k
8. a
9. L
10. b
11. e
12. h

### Fill in the Blanks

1. exulted
2. extolled
3. expunged
4. facetious
5. explicit
6. expiate
7. expurgated
8. exponent
9. expedient
10. expatriate
11. extant
12. extraneous

## Review Exercise 15

### Matching

1. d
2. c
3. g
4. j
5. k
6. b
7. h
8. L
9. e
10. i
11. a
12. f

### Fill in the Blanks

1. fetter
2. figurative
3. fatuous
4. fathom
5. facile
6. facilitated
7. fanciful
8. fidelity
9. felicitous
10. feasible
11. finesse
12. fiat

## Review Exercise 16

### Matching
1. g
2. e
3. f
4. d
5. j
6. h
7. k
8. b
9. i
10. a
11. L
12. c

### Fill in the Blanks
1. fortuitous
2. forbearance
3. fractious
4. fleeting
5. flagrant
6. foible
7. forfeit
8. foreshadowed
9. flag
10. foment
11. fortify
12. fray

## Review Exercise 17

### Matching
1. e
2. g
3. j
4. d
5. i
6. f
7. b
8. k
9. h
10. c
11. L
12. a

### Fill in the Blanks
1. germane
2. glib
3. garrulous
4. frugal
5. gauche
6. gamut
7. furtive
8. fringe
9. goosebumps
10. gainsaid
11. gawky
12. gist

## Review Exercise 18

### Matching
1. c
2. h
3. j
4. e
5. k
6. f
7. d
8. i
9. a
10. L
11. b
12. g

### Fill in the Blanks
1. hegemony
2. haven
3. harbinger
4. grandiloquent
5. gourmand
6. gradation
7. heterogeneous
8. gratuitous
9. happy-go-lucky
10. hedonist
11. hardy
12. hearken

## Review Exercise 19

**Matching**
1. i
2. f
3. e
4. j
5. h
6. g
7. c
8. L
9. a
10. b
11. k
12. d

**Fill in the Blanks**
1. hierarchy
2. hyperbole
3. idyllic
4. ilk
5. ignominious
6. idiosyncrasies
7. hodgepodge
8. iconoclast
9. heterogenous
10. homogenous
11. homogeneous
12. histrionics

## Review Exercise 20

**Matching**
1. g
2. i
3. f
4. j
5. c
6. k
7. b
8. L
9. d
10. h
11. a
12. e

**Fill in the Blanks**
1. imputed
2. incendiary
3. impaired
4. imminent
5. incontrovertible
6. incongruous
7. impresario
8. importuned
9. inchoate
10. inane
11. impeachment
12. illiberality

## Review Exercise 21

**Matching**
1. g
2. h
3. f
4. e
5. i
6. b
7. k
8. c
9. j
10. a
11. L
12. d

**Fill in the Blanks**
1. inimical
2. inexorable
3. indolent
4. inebriated
5. ingenuous
6. infraction
7. incumbent
8. incorrigible
9. indoctrinate
10. injunction
11. inert
12. ingrained

**Review Exercise 22**

**Matching**
1. h
2. f
3. g
4. j
5. c
6. i
7. b
8. k
9. d
10. L
11. a
12. e

**Fill in the Blanks**
1. inveterate
2. internecine
3. intransigent
4. instigate
5. interlocutor
6. intractable
7. inordinate
8. insidious
9. insouciant
10. invigorate
11. intimation
12. invectives

**Review Exercise 23**

**Matching**
1. h
2. e
3. i
4. j
5. b
6. c
7. k
8. d
9. f
10. L
11. a
12. g

**Fill in the Blanks**
1. knell
2. juxtapose
3. irreverence
4. inviolable
5. lacerations
6. irascible
7. irresolute
8. jettisoned
9. itinerant
10. laconic
11. kindle
12. labyrinth

**Review Exercise 24**

**Matching**
1. f
2. i
3. g
4. e
5. c
6. j
7. b
8. a
9. h
10. d
11. L
12. k

**Fill in the Blanks**
1. largesse
2. lauded
3. levy
4. libertarian
5. latent
6. libertine
7. linchpin
8. liability
9. lampoon
10. levity
11. languor
12. lassitude

## Review Exercise 25

### Matching
1. f
2. g
3. i
4. e
5. j
6. c
7. h
8. b
9. L
10. a
11. k
12. d

### Fill in the Blanks
1. mercurial
2. masticate
3. lithe
4. loquacious
5. metamorphosis
6. maverick
7. maudlin
8. lucid
9. maelstrom
10. malleable
11. mendacious
12. modicum

## Review Exercise 26

### Matching
1. g
2. j
3. c
4. d
5. e
6. k
7. b
8. h
9. a
10. i
11. L
12. f

### Fill in the Blanks
1. notoriety
2. nadir
3. neophyte
4. morass
5. mores
6. obdurate
7. multifarious
8. moribund
9. nascent
10. munificent
11. nefarious
12. nepotism

## Review Exercise 27

### Matching
1. e
2. d
3. j
4. c
5. k
6. h
7. b
8. g
9. L
10. a
11. i
12. f

### Fill in the Blanks
1. ostentatious
2. opprobrium
3. occult
4. obfuscated
5. palliate
6. obsequious
7. obstreperous
8. opaque
9. onerous
10. obviated
11. orthodox
12. ostracized

# Review Exercise 28

## Matching
1. g
2. h
3. i
4. e
5. d
6. j
7. c
8. L
9. b
10. f
11. k
12. a

## Fill in the Blanks
1. pecuniary
2. pathological
3. parable
4. panacea
5. paradigm
6. paucity
7. pandemonium
8. paradox
9. pariah
10. parsimonious
11. patent
12. paragon

# Review Exercise 29

## Matching
1. h
2. f
3. j
4. g
5. c
6. k
7. i
8. d
9. L
10. b
11. a
12. e

## Fill in the Blanks
1. perspicacious
2. perused
3. pejorative
4. penchant
5. perfidious
6. perfunctory
7. philanthropic
8. penurious
9. peregrinations
10. pert
11. pernicious
12. perturbed

# Review Exercise 30

## Matching
1. h
2. g
3. f
4. i
5. e
6. j
7. b
8. k
9. c
10. d
11. L
12. a

## Fill in the Blanks
1. ponderous
2. plethora
3. plaudits
4. phlegmatic
5. pithy
6. placate
7. platitudes
8. posthumous
9. placid
10. plenitude
11. polarization
12. portent

## Review Exercise 31

### Matching

1. g
2. i
3. e
4. h
5. j
6. d
7. L
8. c
9. a
10. b
11. k
12. f

### Fill in the Blanks

1. precipitate
2. premonition
3. preponderance
4. predisposition
5. prevaricate
6. precocious
7. predilection
8. presage
9. prelude
10. preclude
11. pristine
12. potentate

## Review Exercise 32

### Matching

1. e
2. b
3. f
4. i
5. j
6. h
7. k
8. c
9. L
10. a
11. d
12. g

### Fill in the Blanks

1. prosaic
2. profuse
3. probity
4. prodigious
5. privation
6. proscribed
7. probation
8. progeny
9. proclivity
10. promulgated
11. proliferated
12. propitious

## Review Exercise 33

### Matching

1. i
2. c
3. j
4. d
5. b
6. k
7. g
8. e
9. f
10. a
11. L
12. h

### Fill in the Blanks

1. recalcitrant
2. rabid
3. quixotic
4. recanted
5. puerile
6. pugnacious
7. punctilious
8. quandary
9. recondite
10. quibble
11. quotidian
12. raiment

## Review Exercise 34

### Matching
1. f
2. c
3. h
4. j
5. e
6. b
7. k
8. i
9. a
10. g
11. L
12. d

### Fill in the Blanks
1. restive
2. repudiated
3. rescind
4. redolent
5. remiss
6. repose
7. redoubtable
8. repertoire
9. relegate
10. reprobate
11. reticent
12. requisition

## Review Exercise 35

### Matching
1. d
2. h
3. i
4. e
5. b
6. k
7. c
8. L
9. a
10. g
11. f
12. j

### Fill in the Blanks
1. scathing
2. salubrious
3. saturated
4. ruminate
5. sanguine
6. rue
7. sanctimonious
8. rustic
9. schism
10. satiated
11. sacrosanct
12. savor

## Review Exercise 36

### Matching
1. d
2. c
3. f
4. j
5. g
6. e
7. k
8. b
9. i
10. a
11. L
12. h

### Fill in the Blanks
1. solicitous
2. sinecure
3. soluble
4. scurrilous
5. secular
6. sentient
7. sedulousness
8. soporific
9. skepticism
10. shibboleths
11. serendipity
12. slovenly

## Review Exercise 37

### Matching
1. e
2. d
3. g
4. h
5. b
6. j
7. L
8. i
9. a
10. f
11. k
12. c

### Fill in the Blanks
1. spectrum
2. stymie
3. stolid
4. supercilious
5. sportive
6. specious
7. succinct
8. spartan
9. stoical
10. subterfuge
11. strident
12. spate

## Review Exercise 38

### Matching
1. b
2. k
3. c
4. g
5. i
6. d
7. a
8. L
9. h
10. e
11. f
12. j

### Fill in the Blanks
1. tangential
2. supine
3. temerity
4. supplicate
5. synchronous
6. surfeit
7. swarthy
8. taciturn
9. surmise
10. tantamount
11. surreptitious
12. tenable

## Review Exercise 39

### Matching
1. i
2. c
3. e
4. f
5. h
6. d
7. k
8. b
9. j
10. g
11. a
12. L

### Fill in the Blanks
1. tremulous
2. tome
3. tenuous
4. tractable
5. terra
6. timorous
7. torpid
8. toady
9. truculent
10. torrid
11. tirade
12. trenchant

# Review Exercise 40

## Matching
1. f
2. j
3. h
4. k
5. c
6. d
7. i
8. e
9. L
10. a
11. b
12. g

## Fill in the Blanks
1. vacillating
2. unctuous
3. urbane
4. ubiquitous
5. unveiling
6. turpitude
7. utilitarian
8. umbrage
9. tyro
10. upbraid
11. untenable
12. vapid

# Review Exercise 41

## Matching
1. h
2. e
3. i
4. b
5. j
6. f
7. c
8. k
9. d
10. L
11. g
12. a

## Fill in the Blanks
1. viscous
2. verve
3. veracity
4. vicissitudes
5. vehement
6. vestiges
7. veneer
8. vitriolic
9. venerated
10. vexatious
11. verbose
12. virtuoso

# Review Exercise 42

## Matching
1. g
2. e
3. f
4. i
5. a
6. j
7. c
8. k
9. d
10. L
11. h
12. b

## Fill in the Blanks
1. yoke
2. volition
3. wistful
4. vituperating
5. wily
6. voracious
7. vivaciousness
8. zephyr
9. voluble
10. yen
11. whet
12. zealous

## List of Words

abject
abjure
abnegation
abrogate
abstemious
accost
Achilles
acumen
adulterate
adumbrate
aggrandize
alacrity
alias
alleviate
allude
altruistic
ameliorate
amorphous
anachronistic
anathema
annex
antediluvian
antithesis
apocryphal
approbation
arcane
archetypal
ardent
artifact
artifice
ascetic
aspersion
assiduous
attenuate
austerity
avaricious
balk
bedlam
beguile

benevolent
besmirch
bigot
blandishment
bogus
boor
brittle
bulwark
burgeon
buttress
cache
cacophony
cajole
callow
calumny
candor
cant
capitulate
capricious
carp
castigate
catalyst
celerity
chagrin
chauvinism
chimerical
circumlocution
circumvent
cogent
cognizant
comely
commodious
compunction
concoction
concomitant
condone
conduit
conflagration
congruity

conjecture
connive
connoisseur
consternation
constituent
construe
consummate
contravene
contrite
conundrum
copious
corpulence
coterie
countenance
coup
crescendo
culpable
cupidity
decadence
decrepit
defunct
deleterious
delirious
deluge
demagogue
demur
denigrate
deride
desultory
dexterity
diaphanous
diatribe
didactic
dilettante
disparate
domicile
dour
drudgery
duplicity

duress
ebullient
eclectic
edict
edifice
effigy
egalitarian
egregious
elegy
elicit
elucidate
emaciated
embezzlement
emollient
empirical
emulate
encumbrance
enervate
enhance
enigma
ennui
entourage
enunciate
ephemeral
epitome
erudite
eschew
esoteric
espouse
estimable
eulogy
euphemism
evanescence
exacting
exasperate
excruciating
exculpate
exhaustive
expatiate

## Word List

expatriate
expedient
expiate
explicit
exponent
expunge
expurgate
extant
extol
extraneous
exult
facetious
facile
facilitate
fanciful
fathom
fatuous
feasible
felicitous
fetter
fiat
fidelity
figurative
finesse
flag
flagrant
fleeting
foible
foment
forbearance
foreshadow
forfeit
fortify
fortuitous
fractious
fray
fringe
frugal
furtive

gainsay
gamut
garrulous
gauche
gawky
germane
gist
glib
goosebumps
gourmand
gradation
grandiloquent
gratuitous
happy-go-lucky
harbinger
hardy
haven
hearken
hedonist
hegemony
heterogeneous
heterogenous
hierarchy
histrionics
hodgepodge
homogeneous
homogenous
hyperbole
iconoclast
idiosyncrasy
idyllic
ignominious
ilk
illiberality
imminent
impair
impeach
importune
impresario

impute
inane
incendiary
inchoate
incongruous
incontrovertible
incorrigibility
incumbent
indoctrinate
indolent
inebriated
inert
inexorable
infraction
ingenuous
ingrained
inimical
injunction
inordinate
insidious
insouciant
instigate
interlocutor
internecine
intimation
intractable
intransigent
invective
inveterate
invigorate
inviolable
irascible
irresolute
irreverence
itinerant
jettison
juxtapose
kindle
knell

labyrinth
laceration
laconic
lampoon
languor
largesse
lassitude
latent
laud
levity
levy
liability
libertarian
libertine
linchpin
lithe
loquacious
lucid
maelstrom
malleable
masticate
maudlin
maverick
mendacious
mercurial
metamorphosis
modicum
morass
mores
moribund
multifarious
munificent
nadir
nascent
nefarious
neophyte
nepotism
notoriety
obdurate

## Word List

obfuscate
obsequious
obstreperous
obviate
occult
onerous
opaque
opprobrium
orthodox
ostentatious
ostracism
palliate
panacea
pandemonium
parable
paradigm
paradox
paragon
pariah
parsimonious
patent
pathological
paucity
pecuniary
pejorative
penchant
penurious
peregrination
perfidious
perfunctory
pernicious
perspicacious
pert
perturbed
peruse
philanthropic
phlegmatic
pithy
placate

placid
platitude
plaudit
plenitude
plethora
polarized
ponderous
portent
posthumous
potentate
precipitate
preclude
precocious
predilection
predisposition
prelude
premonition
preponderance
presage
prevaricate
pristine
privation
probation
probity
proclivity
prodigious
profuse
progeny
proliferate
promulgate
propitious
prosaic
proscribe
puerile
pugnacious
punctilious
quandary
quibble
quixotic

quotidian
rabid
raiment
recalcitrant
recant
recondite
redolent
redoubtable
relegate
remiss
repertoire
repose
reprobate
repudiate
requisition
rescind
restive
reticent
rue
ruminate
rustic
sacrosanct
salubrious
sanctimonious
sanguine
satiate
saturate
savor
scathing
schism
scurrilous
secular
sedulous
sentient
serendipity
shibboleth
sinecure
skepticism
slovenly

solicitous
soluble
soporific
spartan
spate
specious
spectrum
sportive
stoical
stolid
strident
stymie
subterfuge
succinct
supercilious
supine
supplicate
surfeit
surmise
surreptitious
swarthy
synchronous
taciturn
tangential
tantamount
temerity
tenable
tenuous
terra
timorous
tirade
toady
tome
torpid
torrid
tractable
tremulous
trenchant
truculent

## Word List

turpitude
tyro
ubiquitous
umbrage
unctuous
untenable
unveiling
upbraid
urbane
utilitarian
vacillate
vapid
vehement
veneer
venerate
veracity
verbose
verve
vestige
vexatious
vicissitudes
virtuoso
viscous
vitriolic
vituperate
vivacious
volition
voluble
voracious
whet
wily
wistful
yen
yoke
zealous
zephyr

## Further Resources

We hope you enjoyed this book and benefited from it.

We are in process of compiling a list of Further Resources that you may find useful.

Kindly contact us via email so we can share the latest information with you.

You may also report any 'errata' in this book to us via email.

Our email address is:

Jayjohna960@gmail.com

Made in the USA
Monee, IL
01 November 2019